Promises to Keep

ORGANIZATION OF AMERICAN HISTORIANS BICENTENNIAL ESSAYS ON THE BILL OF RIGHTS

General Editor

Kermit L. Hall

Promises to Keep

African-Americans and the Constitutional Order, 1776 to the Present

Donald G. Nieman

Other Volumes are in Preparation

Promises to Keep

*African-Americans
and the Constitutional Order,
1776 to the Present*

DONALD G. NIEMAN

New York   Oxford
OXFORD UNIVERSITY PRESS
1991

Oxford University Press

Oxford   New York   Toronto
Delhi   Bombay   Calcutta   Madras   Karachi
Petaling Jaya   Singapore   Hong Kong   Tokyo
Nairobi   Dar es Salaam   Cape Town
Melbourne   Auckland

and associated companies in
Berlin   Ibadan

Copyright © 1991 by Oxford University Press, Inc.

Published by Oxford University Press, Inc.,

198 Madison Avenue, New York, New York 10016-4314

Oxford is a registered trademark of Oxford University Press

Library of Congress Cataloging-in-Publication Data

Nieman, Donald G.
Promises to keep : African Americans and the constitutional order,
1776 to the Present / Donald G. Nieman.
p. cm.—(Organization of American Historians
bicentennial essays on the Bill of Rights)
Includes bibliographical references and index.
ISBN-13 978-0-19-505561-0
ISBN 0–19–505560–8.
ISBN 0–19–505561–6 (pbk)
1. Afro-Americans—Civil rights.
2. Civil rights movements—United States—History.
3. Civil rights—United States—History.
I. Title. II. Series.
E185.61.N5   1991   323.1′196073—dc20   90–43711

9 8

Printed in the United States of America

Editor's Preface

This book is part of the Organization of American Historians' Bicentennial Essays on the Bill of Rights, a series that has resulted from the fruitful collaboration of the OAH's Committee on the Bicentennial of the Constitution and Oxford University Press. The committee concluded in 1986 that one of the most appropriate ways in which historians could commemorate the then forthcoming bicentennial of the Bill of Rights was to foster better teaching about it in undergraduate classrooms. Too often, the committee decided, students could have learned more about the history of liberty in America if they would only have had basic texts analyzing the evolution of the most important provisions of the Bill of Rights. There are, of course, many fine specialized studies of the first ten amendments to the Constitution, but these works invariably concentrate on a particular Supreme Court case and technical legal developments. What the committee wanted, and what Nancy Lane at Oxford University Press vigorously supported, were books that would explore in brief compass the main themes in the evolution of civil liberties and civil rights as they have been revealed through the Bill of Rights. The books in this series, therefore, bridge a significant gap in the literature of the history of liberty by offering synthetic examinations rooted in the best and most recent literature in history, political science, and law. Their authors have, as well, framed these nontechnical studies within the contours of American history. The authors have taken as their goal making the history of rights and liberties resonate with developments in the nation's social, cultural, and political history.

Kermit Hall

. . . When the architects of our republic wrote the Declaration of Independence and the Constitution, they were signing a promissory note to which every American was to fall heir. This note was a promise that all men would be guaranteed the unalienable rights of life, liberty, and the pursuit of happiness.

It is obvious today that America has defaulted on this promissory note so far as her citizens of color are concerned. Instead of honoring this obligation, America has given the Negro people a bad check; a check which has come back marked "insufficient funds." But we refuse to believe that the bank of justice is bankrupt. . . . So we have come to cash this check—which will give us the riches of freedom and the security of justice. . . .

Martin Luther King, Jr.,
"I Have A Dream,"   August 28, 1963.

In the state of nature, men are in fact born equal; but they cannot remain so. Society deprives them of equality, and they only become equal again because of the laws.

Charles de Secondat, baron de Montesquieu,
The Spirit of the Laws (1748)

Preface

Since the seventeenth century, race has been a dominant and dynamic force in virtually all aspects of American life. Consequently, its vital role in shaping the American constitutional order bears close examination. During the Revolutionary era, as they forged their constitutional system, Americans fiercely debated the place of slavery in a republican society which espoused the "self evident" truth that "all men are created equal" and "are endowed by their Creator with certain unalienable rights," including the right to "Life, Liberty, and the pursuit of Happiness." Debate over slavery not only figured prominently at the Constitutional Convention in 1787, but played a crucial role in the evolution of constitutional doctrine during the next six decades. Fundamental matters—the scope of national power, the nature of the federal system, the meaning of citizenship, the rights of United States citizens—were affected by the debate over slavery and racial subordination. Ultimately, slavery proved to be the nemesis of the Union, shattering the constitutional order and plunging the nation into a long and bloody civil war.

The destruction of slavery did not, however, end the pivotal role of race in the American constitutional order. In attempting to root out slavery and its vestiges, Reconstruction-era Republicans adopted the Thirteenth, Fourteenth, and Fifteenth Amendments and the nation's first civil rights legislation. In the process, they created a new Constitution, extending to blacks full rights of citizenship, establishing for the first time a constitutional guarantee of equality, and empowering the national government to protect the fundamental rights of its citizens. Although by 1900 the rich promise of Reconstruction had been destroyed by pinched, formalistic judicial interpretation and congressional neglect, the Reconstruction Amendments nevertheless remained a major force in twentieth-century constitutionalism. Beginning in the 1920s and 1930s, black plaintiffs, challenging the repressive southern criminal justice system, prodded the Supreme Court to take a broader view of the Fourteenth Amendment's due process clause and the Bill of Rights. Meanwhile, the attack on segregation and disfranchisement—begun in the early years of the twentieth century and successfully advanced in the decades following World War II—reinvigorated and gave substance to the Fourteenth Amendment's promise of equality. In the process, modern American constitutionalism was again transformed.

African-Americans have been important players in this process, not merely as the subject of debate among whites but as agents of change. From the earliest days of the Republic, black leaders embraced principles of equality and constitutional rights, using them to attack slavery and racial subordination. They were well aware of the American paradox: that the land of the free was the home of the slave; that, in practice, equality meant equality among propertied white men; and that constitutional liberty extended only to whites. Yet black leaders understood that the general language of the Constitution made it a malleable document whose meaning was subject to redefinition through political and legal processes, that the polity was, in a sense, an ongoing constitutional convention. Appealing to the principles embodied in the Declaration of Independence and the Constitution, black Americans and their white allies forged an equalitarian constitutionalism and skillfully used it to reshape the Constitution itself and American society. From the antebellum conventions of northern free blacks to the constitutional conventions and state legislatures of the Reconstruction South to the National Association for the Advancement of Colored People's monumental campaign against segregation, black leaders effectively wielded republican principles to extend justice to all Americans, regardless of race.

Equalitarian political and constitutional principles have not been limited to the ranks of the black elite—to such prominent men and women as Frederick Douglass, Ida Wells-Barnett, Charles Hamilton Houston, Thurgood Marshall, and Martin Luther King, Jr. They have been embraced by the black masses, who have seen in them an affirmation of their dignity and a tool to free themselves from arbitrary white control. During Reconstruction, former slaves imbibed equalitarian constitutional ideas from black veterans, northern teachers, the press, and the Union Leagues and boldly invoked them to assert their rights. Although the promise of Reconstruction was cut short, the demand for equality among the black rank and file was not stilled. During the twentieth century it again came to life in the boycotts of segregated streetcars that swept southern cities between 1900 and 1906; the massive support generated by A. Philip Randolph's March on Washington Movement in the early 1940s; the willingness of Oliver Brown, a black railroad worker, to challenge segregated schools in Topeka, Kansas in 1951; and countless other individual and collective acts of protest against discrimination.

To be sure, blacks have not acted alone in their quest for freedom and equality. Since the late eighteenth century, white men and women have played a prominent role in the struggle. From the abolitionists and the Radical Republicans to the founders of the National Association for the Advancement of Colored People and the leaders of the Congress of Industrial Organizations, some whites have been willing to take a stand for equality. Indeed, given blacks' minority status and their historical denial of access to political power, most black leaders have realized the importance of white support and have worked to build interracial coalitions. Nevertheless, African-Americans have been at the center of the struggle and have played a major role in transforming the Constitution from a document primarily concerned with property rights and federal relations into a charter of equality. Together with their white allies, blacks have used the constitutional process to push a nation built on slavery and racial subordination closer to its self-proclaimed equalitarian ideals. In the words of Langston Hughes, they "let America be America again / The land that never has been yet" ("Let America Be America Again").

What follows is a brief history of the relationship between African-Americans and the nation's constitutional order. In telling this story, I have attempted to show how law, society, and politics interact. Emphasizing the malleability of the United States Constitution, I have stressed the powerful role of politics, ideology, and social forces in producing constitutional change. I have attempted to show, too, that legal principles and institutions have played an equally important role in shaping social relations and politics. Attempting to treat such a broad topic in a brief compass inevitably requires cursory treatment of many issues, persons, and episodes that deserve—indeed, cry out for—fuller coverage. Yet I hope that this brief survey of constitutional law and race in America will reveal the broad contours of constitutional change, highlight the pivotal role that race has played in American law, call attention to the important contributions of African-Americans to the constitutional order, demonstrate the vital role of the Constitution and law in the lives of black and white Americans, and offer a historical perspective on the contemporary debate over law and race, a debate that too often takes places in a historical vacuum.

Indeed, I hope that this book serves as a reminder that the nation's promise of equality has, historically, far outrun its performance. For most of the nation's history, law has served as a tool of white supremacy, marking blacks as inferior, rendering them politically powerless, and denying them justice and access to the society's resources and opportunities. Constitutional principles—states' rights, dual citizenship, separate but equal—have all too frequently served to legitimize racial oppression. In the recent past, much of the legal structure of racial subordination has been dismantled, and Congress and the courts have shown themselves willing to give substance to the promise of equality. Consequently, too many Americans now seem to believe that we have wiped the slate clean and have actually achieved equality. Indeed, during the past decade there has been a growing attack—led by the Reagan administration and recently joined by the new conservative majority on the Supreme Court—on many of the efforts to achieve equality that were undertaken in the 1960s and 1970s. Contrary to voices on the right, however, we have by no means escaped the effects of our history. We still live in a highly segregated society in which access to opportunity is defined in terms of race. Only by viewing the accomplishments of the recent past as a beginning rather than an end, can we hope to keep the long-deferred promise of equality.

Clemson, S.C.   D. G. N.
April 1990

Acknowledgments

I owe a special debt of gratitude to fellow scholars in legal history, African-American history, and the history of race relations. They have produced a body of scholarship that is extraordinary, both in volume and quality; without it, this book would not have been possible. Because of an editorial decision to keep notes to a minimum, I have cited in the endnotes only material that I have quoted or mentioned in the text. Consequently, the notes do not fully reflect my intellectual debts. In the bibliographical essay, however, I have acknowledged those works on which I relied and offer readers an introduction to a rich literature that has illuminated the troubling issue of race in United States history.

Librarians and archivists have been unfailingly generous with their time and expertise. The interlibrary loan staffs of the Cooper Library at Clemson University and Kansas State University's Farrell Library promptly and efficiently tracked down hard-to-locate materials. Ronald Brown graciously made available to me the rich collections of the Law Library at the New York University School of Law. Archivists and librarians at the New York Public Library's Schomburg Center for Research in Black Culture, Howard University's Moorland-Spingarn Research Center, and Emory University's Robert W. Woodruff Library went above and beyond the call of duty to locate manuscripts, pamphlets, newspapers, and illustrations.

The staff at Oxford has been unfailingly courteous and helpful. Nancy Lane, David Roll, Steve Bedney, and Kurt Hettner moved the project along with great professionalism and efficiency. Sharon Lahaye carefully copyedited the manuscript, saving me from numerous stylistic and substantive errors.

Dean Robert Waller of the College of Liberal Arts at Clemson came to my rescue at the last minute, graciously providing funds to cover the cost of illustrations and permissions. A timely grant from the Faculty Development Fund at Kansas State University helped defray the costs of research. In addition to institutional financial assistance, I have been fortunate in having three department chairpersons—John McCulloh and Marion Gray at Kansas State and David Nicholas at Clemson—who have created professional and colleagial atmospheres that have sustained my work. I am deeply grateful for their ongoing interest and support. Sean McMahon, my graduate assistant at Clemson, did an excellent job of verifying quotations and citations, saving me from countless errors.

Many friends and colleagues have read portions of the manuscript, offering praise when they thought I did things well, calling me to task when I made errors of fact and judgment, offering helpful suggestions, and providing enthusiastic encouragement. Ruth Bogin, Mary Gallagher, Rebecca Gruver, Elizabeth Nuxoll, Elaine Pescue, and Catherine Silverman read the first two chapters in an early form and offered searching criticism and helpful suggestions. Members of the Clemson University History Department Seminar provided comments and suggestions that improved the final chapter. Albert Hamscher, Burton Kaufman, John McCulloh, and George Dent Wilcoxon never seemed to tire of listening to my troubles and triumphs; as always, these friends offered support, encouragement, and sage advice. My friend and colleague Carol Bleser, who was deeply involved in completing her own book, was always willing to listen, offering encouragement and advice as I struggled to finish the manuscript and helping me deal with a myriad of problems as the book moved into production. Jubilee was always there during the long hours of writing and made me laugh.

LaWanda Cox, whose own work has provided a model of historical scholarship, offered a penetrating critique of the first two chapters of the manuscript. From the time I began to work on this book, she has listened to my ideas, made timely suggestions, and offered encouragement. Indeed, her faith in the project sustained me. Over the years, her friendship, as well as her example, have meant a great deal to Linda and me.

Michal Belknap, Harold Hyman, Kent Newmeyer, and Bill Wiecek, members of the editorial board of the OAH Bicentennial Essays on the Constitution, took time from their busy schedules to read the manuscript and offer welcome advice. I am especially grateful to Michal Belknap, who devoted an extraordinary amount of time to the task, offering especially thoughtful comments that significantly improved the entire manuscript. I cannot thank Kermit Hall, the series editor, enough. He continually offered sound advice on matters large and small, knew when to offer encouragement and when to give me a gentle prod, and efficiently moved the book into production. His good humor, professionalism, academic citizenship, and ability to get things done constantly amaze me.

My greatest debt is to Linda Nieman. Busy with a career, preparation for her doctoral qualifying exams, and work on her dissertation, she always found time for me and my work. She has listened endlessly to my ideas about civil rights and the law, offered gentle but nonetheless incisive criticism, and shared with me her considerable knowledge of African-American culture. She has also read two drafts of the manuscript, repeatedly helped me out of dead ends, and offered innumerable suggestions that have improved the book's style and clarity. Linda not only made completion of the book possible; she also made it worthwhile.

Contents

For Linda

Promises to Keep

1

With Liberty for Some: The Old Constitution and the Rights of Blacks, 1776–1846

Like thousands of other African-Americans, Jupiter Nicholson tasted the fruit of freedom that ripened during the age of the American Revolution. Born into slavery in North Carolina, Nicholson, his wife, and his parents were freed by their owners sometime in the 1780s. Taking advantage of his liberty, Nicholson went to work as a sailor, trying to scrape together enough money to buy a farm and acquire the economic independence that would give substance to his freedom. He soon found, however, that freedom's fruit had a bitter aftertaste. As a growing number of slave-owners—prompted by a combination of religious zeal and revolutionary principle—freed their slaves, many prominent North Carolinians feared that slavery was being undermined from within. In response, the legislature reiterated its restrictions on manumission: slaves could be freed only as a reward for meritorious service and all manumissions must be approved by a county court. Moreover, it authorized citizens to seize blacks who had been freed illegally and to sell them into slavery. Attracted by the prospect of a quick dollar, many white men began to seize illegally freed blacks, quickly turning the dream of freedom into a nightmare for Nicholson and other free blacks. Coming ashore one day about two years after he had been freed, Nicholson was set upon by armed whites who chased him with dogs. Although he eluded the slavecatchers and fled with his wife to Portsmouth, Virginia, his parents and his brother were not so fortunate, falling into the hands of whites who returned them to bondage.

Nicholson and his wife found refuge in Portsmouth, where they established a home and lived in relative safety as free persons of color, for four years. Yet they could not escape the reign of terror unleashed by the North Carolina legislature; any day slavecatchers from North Carolina might cross the Virginia border, track them down, and carry them back to slavery. Seeking greater security, they left Virginia in the early 1790s and settled in Philadelphia, which had a reputation among blacks as a "city of refuge."[1] A bustling seaport situated in a state that had adopted a program of gradual emancipation during the preceding decade, Philadelphia offered blacks a livelihood and the pure air of freedom. Yet even in Philadelphia, black emigres found security elusive. In 1793—about the time Nicholson and his wife arrived there—the United States Congress bowed to the demands of southerners and passed the Fugitive Slave Act. The law authorized slaveowners to seize runaway slaves who had fled to free soil and take them before federal or state judges, who were to issue warrants authorizing them to return fugitives to bondage. Because it did not afford alleged fugitives an opportunity to prove that they were free, the act made free blacks like Jupiter Nicholson vulnerable, even in a haven of freedom like Philadelphia. Indeed, this vulnerability was underscored in late 1796, when a North Carolina slavecatcher came to Philadelphia and arrested a black man who had been illegally freed by his owner, was subsequently captured and returned to slavery, and then regained his freedom and fled to the North.

Alarmed by the arrest, Nicholson and three other blacks who had sought refuge in Philadelphia immediately turned to Absalom Jones. As a founder of the city's Free Africa Society and its African Church, Jones had helped to forge a sense of identity and community among Philadelphia blacks and was an obvious source of assistance. He undoubtedly alerted members of the society and the church, warning them to be on the lookout for slavecatchers and to be ready to hide neighbors who were in danger. Jones also used the occasion as an opportunity to call Congress's attention to the evils of the Fugitive Slave Act. In the first petition to Congress by African-Americans, Jones described the terror of men and women threatened with reenslavement after having once had their "human right to freedom . . . restored" and called on lawmakers to honor the nation's commitment to liberty and natural rights. "May we not be allowed to consider this stretch of power, morally and politically, a

Governmental defect, . . ." he asked, "and . . . is not some remedy for an evil of such magnitude highly worthy of the deep inquiry and unfeigned zeal of the supreme Legislative body of a free and enlightened people?"[2]

Jones's eloquent appeal to revolutionary principles failed to move the members of the House of Representatives. Although George Thatcher of Massachusetts moved to instruct the committee on commerce to study the matter and suggest amendments to the Fugitive Slave Act, southerners adamantly resisted any action that might weaken the law. William L. Smith of South Carolina led the offensive against Thatcher's motion, arguing that the petitioners were "not entitled to the attention of this House" and demanding that their petition be dismissed.[3] In the face of southern opposition, northern congressmen broke ranks and Thatcher's motion went down to defeat, 50–33.

Congress's action was symptomatic of the retreat from the equalitarian possibilities of the American Revolution which was already well underway. Revolutionary principles had fueled a potent attack on slavery and racial subordination during the 1770s and 1780s. Yet slavery and racism were deeply rooted in the new Republic, proving to be more than a match for revolutionary principles. By the late 1780s the practical exigencies of nation building led to a compromise of revolutionary principle that soon transformed the American constitutional-legal order into a bulwark of slavery and white supremacy. As a result, the chains of bondage were tightened on slaves in the plantation South, and free blacks like Jupiter Nicholson lived, even in the North, under the shadow of slavery in a land of liberty.

Revolutionary Ideals and Political Realities

The dream of freedom, security, and opportunity, which Jupiter Nicholson found so elusive, had its genesis in the momentous changes that transpired during the age of the American Revolution. In the heat of revolution, Americans forged doctrines of liberty and equality that quickly became an integral part of American political culture and sparked widespread criticism of slavery. The intellectual currents of the Enlightenment deeply influenced the attitudes and assumptions of educated Americans as well as Europeans during the second half of the eighteenth century. Enlightenment thinkers asserted that in the mythical state of nature—before the formation of society and government—all individuals were born free and equal and had enormous capacity for improvement. They believed that human beings were malleable and contended that differences among individuals and cultures were the result of environment and circumstance. This helped them explain the gap between human capacity for improvement and the reality of an imperfect world. The evil and misery experienced by humanity was not a result of defects in human nature but a product of superstition, bigotry, and flawed social and political institutions inherited from the past. Reason and institutional reform, however, could remove these barriers to progress and secure human happiness. For European intellectuals and many of the Americans whom they influenced, slavery was a perfect example of an inherited institution that upset the natural order and stifled progress: it denied the natural equality of all persons, produced incalculable suffering, and denied slaves the opportunity for mental and moral improvement. Once removed from the debasing effects of slavery, they maintained, blacks had the potential to become the equals of whites.

Powerful religious currents also encouraged antislavery sentiment. During the Revolutionary Era the Quakers and the two most rapidly growing denominations in America, the Baptists and Methodists, subjected slavery to withering criticism. These groups emphasized the importance of humility, the equality of all persons in the eyes of God, and the imperative for Christians to treat others in the spirit of Christian love. This led them to criticize slavery as an embodiment of hierarchy and coercion that flew in the face of Christ's great commandment: that Christians should love their neighbors. Because they believed that slavery was a sin, they often attacked it with a sense of urgency, pressing members of their congregations to free their slaves and organizing antislavery societies.

Ideas unleashed by the Revolution interacted with these beliefs to strengthen antislavery sentiment. Between 1763 and 1776, patriot leaders charged that Parliament repeatedly denied the colonists rights guaranteed by the British Constitution. Parliamentary legislation, they argued, limited their right to jury trial and peaceable assembly, eroded constitutional restrictions on a standing army, and, most importantly, deprived them of liberty and property without their consent. These acts were ominous because they suggested that Parliament was under no restraints in dealing with the colonists and could govern them arbitrarily.

Without rights, subject to arbitrary power, merely enjoying such privileges as their parliamentary masters chose to give them, Americans repeatedly asserted, they were reduced to slavery. Parliament's program was clearly "a system formed to enslave America," the Continental Congress declared in 1774. A year later, in the Declaration of the Causes and Necessity of Taking Up Arms, Congress asserted that Americans were "resolved to die freemen rather than to live Slaves."[4]

Patriots did not refer to the chattel slavery that blacks suffered, but, instead, invoked a political concept that was ubiquitous in eighteenth-century polemical writing on both sides of the Atlantic. As the historian John Phillip Reid has noted, "To warn against slavery was the way Britons raised questions about constitutionality."[5] Nevertheless, many Americans realized that as long as they held half a million blacks in bondage their defense of liberty rang hollow and argued that fidelity to revolutionary principles demanded abolition. Combined with Enlightenment notions of the natural equality of all persons and evangelical warnings that British tyranny was divine punishment for the sin of slavery, the rhetoric of rights and liberty convinced many Americans to join the attack. A Virginia conference of Methodists, acting in the wake of the Revolution to bar slaveholders from communion, suggested this melding of secular and religious ideas when it noted that slavery was "contrary to the Golden Law of God . . . and the inalienable Rights of Mankind, as well as every Principle of the Revolution. . . ."[6]

Revolutionary thought contained an equalitarian emphasis that reinforced antislavery arguments. As Americans rejected monarchy in 1776, they embraced republicanism, a set of ideas with far-reaching implications. Republican government, according to American writers, was more than government purged of monarchy and resting on popular will. Its survival required a virtuous people willing to sacrifice for the common good. Virtue, they claimed, could only exist in a society that did not suffer great extremes of wealth. The lure of opulence would make the very rich self-indulgent and reluctant to sacrifice, while the misery of the poor would provide pliable material for self-serving demagogues. Although republicanism did not lead to leveling programs designed to redistribute wealth, it did suggest that some degree of material equality was necessary for the survival of republican government. Republicanism also demanded that government promote the common good and refuse to serve the special interests of the privileged few, a principle asserted in the revolutionary state constitutions. Hostility to privilege carried with it the implication that all men—few extended the principle to women—were entitled to equal rights.

During the decades following the Revolution, ideals of liberty and equality came squarely into conflict with the realities of slavery and racial subordination, systems supported by powerful economic interests and entrenched social mores. When the Revolution began, slavery existed in all of the American colonies. Slaves were most numerous in the South, where they were substantial minorities (thirty to forty-two percent) in Virginia, North Carolina, and Maryland and a majority (sixty percent) in South Carolina. Slave agricultural laborers and craftsmen were essential to the plantation economies of these states. Even in the North, where they ranged from less than two percent of the population in Massachusetts to more than ten percent in New York, slaves played an important economic role because of the general shortage of labor. Moreover, white attitudes toward blacks, which had taken root during the previous century, reinforced slavery and the system of racial hierarchy which it created. The vast majority of blacks were slaves who occupied a degraded and subordinate position, and most whites viewed them as ignorant, shiftless, and lazy. Such attitudes legitimized existing social arrangements and provided ready arguments against emancipation: once freed from white control, blacks would become paupers and criminals and threaten social stability.

Although they faced formidable obstacles, antislavery advocates made great strides toward implementing the truths proclaimed self-evident by the Declaration of Independence. They achieved their greatest success in the North where there were few slaveholders and blacks were not numerous. Vermont, with a slave population of fifty, quickly abolished slavery in its 1777 Constitution. In Massachusetts, the Supreme Court of Judicature used the equalitarian language of the state's 1780 constitution ("all men are born free and equal") to undermine the institution in the early 1780s. Northern opposition to abolition was not always so completely or quickly overcome, however. Most northern states passed post-nati abolition laws that stipulated that slaves born prior to enactment of the legislation would remain in slavery while those born thereafter would be freed when they reached adulthood. Pennsylvania (1780), Connecticut (1784), and Rhode Island (1784) quickly passed post-nati bills, but New York (1799) and New Jersey (1804) acted only after twenty years of pressure from well-organized antislavery groups. The hard-earned victory over slavery in the North was significant because it transformed slavery from a national to a sectional institution.

Southerners also subjected slavery to criticism. Baptists, Methodists, and Quakers, groups which drew members primarily from nonslaveholders, led the way. Although slaveholders refrained from calling for abolition, some acknowledged that slavery violated the ideals of the Revolution, supported legislation permitting individual owners to free their slaves, and manumitted some of all of their own slaves. In Virginia, where private manumission was widespread, the free black population grew from 2,000 in 1782 to 20,000 in 1800. Nevertheless, the private acts of well-intentioned slaveholders did not imperil the institution; 345,000 Virginia blacks remained in bondage in 1800. Indeed, slavery was the social and economic foundation of the planter class, the most influential group in Virginia and the rest of the South, and it was economically important to tens of thousands of farmers who owned one or two slaves. Moreover, because blacks constituted between thirty and sixty percent of the population of the southern states, even nonslaveholders—conditioned by racism to believe that blacks were incapable of freedom—equated abolition with social chaos. As a result, no southern legislature seriously considered even a gradual emancipation law during the late eighteenth century.

Antislavery reformers also encountered formidable obstacles to their effort to guarantee the rights of free blacks. Most whites viewed free blacks as pariahs, generally excluding them from their churches, theaters, and inns and relegating them to unskilled, low-paying jobs. In the South, antiblack feeling prompted lawmakers to consign free blacks to an inferior legal status; throughout the region they were prohibited from testifying against whites or having sexual relations with them. In addition, most southern states barred blacks from voting and serving in the militia, and South Carolina and Georgia explicitly denied them citizenship.

Although they experienced social and economic discrimination, northern free blacks escaped widespread legal discrimination during the late eighteenth century. They were routinely excluded from the militia, and a 1788 Massachusetts law (which was not enforced) barred them from entering the state. Throughout the North, however, free blacks enjoyed the same right to vote and testify as whites, were eligible for citizenship on the same terms as whites, and generally had the same legal rights and obligations as whites. In 1785, when the New York legislature passed a bill denying free blacks the right to vote and to testify against whites and prohibiting interracial marriages, the state's Council of Revision vetoed it. According to the council, the measure created "an aristocracy of the most dangerous and malignant kind, rendering power permanent and hereditary in the hands of those persons who deduce their origin through white ancestors only."[7] Thus revolutionary principles did occasionally prevail over racial prejudice and class interest.

The Constitutional Convention, however, was not one of those occasions. The delegates who met in Philadelphia during the summer of 1787 believed that the weakness of the existing national government had created an economic and political crisis that threatened America's republican experiment. Most agreed that the Articles of Confederation was the root of the problem. A new Constitution creating a strong national government was imperative in order to achieve economic recovery, promote prosperity, cope with threats from abroad, reestablish the public credit, and restrain the states from interfering with property rights. Although many delegates expressed reservations about slavery and a few passionately denounced it, there was little likelihood that the convention would take meaningful antislavery action. Constitutional reform and continued union were impossible without the support of southerners, and southern delegates were unwilling to accept constitutional provisions that threatened the economic well-being of the South and the existence of its powerful planter class. Consequently, the price of constitutional reform was northern concessions on the slavery issue.

Southerners won a significant victory in debates on representation in Congress. Although they failed to have slaves counted fully for purposes of determining representation, southern delegates did win acceptance of a provision that apportioned representatives among the states "according to their respective Numbers, which shall be determined by adding the whole Number of free Persons . . . and . . . three fifths of all other Persons."[8] Because these "other persons" were slaves, northerners objected to the three-fifths clause, charging that it allowed southerners to use property to increase their clout in the national government. Southerners, however, insisted on the extra political security that the three-fifths clause conferred. North Carolina's William Davie, for example, explained that he "was sure that N. Carola. would never confederate on any terms that did not rate them [slaves] at least 3/5. If the Eastern [i.e., northern] States meant . . . to exclude them altogether the business was at an end."[9] In the end, northern delegates accepted the three-fifths clause as the price of a strengthened national government that they deemed vital to their interests.

Inclusion of the three-fifths clause rested solely on considerations of sectional power and had nothing to do with whether slaves—who could not vote—would be represented in the national government or whether they were considered persons in the eyes of the law. The South's share of population and therefore seats in the House of Representatives increased from forty-one percent when only free persons were counted to more than forty-six percent under the three-fifths formula. This increased the region's strength in the House and also in presidential politics because a state's presidential electors were equal to the number of its senators and representatives. Consequently, it became an important tool that southerners would use during the next seventy years to bend national policy to their will and make the Constitution a proslavery document.

The convention also bowed to the South on the infamous slave trade. In early August, after the convention had been in session for more than two months, delegates considered a controversial proposal denying Congress authority to enact "prohibitions on ye Importations of such inhabitants or people as the sevl. States think proper to admit" or "duties by way of such prohibition."[10] Representatives from South Carolina and Georgia, eager to protect the flow of slaves from Africa, were the principal supporters of this measure. A number of northern delegates, however, objected because it protected the most brutal aspects of slavery: tearing Africans away from their homeland; crowding them into the hot, foul holds of ships where they suffered unspeakably and many died; and selling them like cattle at auctions in America. Gouverneur Morris, the voluble Pennsylvania delegate, charged that it protected "the inhabitant of Georgia and S.C. who goes to the Coast of Africa, and in defiance of the most sacred laws of humanity tears away his fellow creatures from their dearest connections & damns them to the most cruel bondages."[11] These northerners were joined by delegates from Maryland and Virginia who not only regarded the slave trade as immoral, but represented states that had a surplus of slaves and stood to benefit from the higher prices that would result from closing the African trade.

Although debate became acrimonious, delegates accepted a compromise. New Englanders agreed to support an obliquely worded provision prohibiting congressional interference with the slave trade for twenty years: "The Migration or Importation of such Persons as any of the States now existing shall think proper to admit, shall not be prohibited by the

Congress'' prior to 1808.[12] In return, the South Carolinians supported deletion of a provision requiring two-thirds majorities for Congress to pass commercial regulations. The New Englanders thus abandoned their scruples against the slave trade in order to win a concession vital to northern commercial interests. Connecticut's Oliver Ellsworth captured the spirit of pragmatism that paved the way for the compromise: ''let every State import what it pleases. The morality or wisdom of slavery are considerations belonging to the States themselves—What enriches a part enriches the whole, and the States are the best judges of their particular interest.''[13]

On the heels of the slave trade compromise, the convention quickly agreed to another southern demand. Slaveholding delegates in the convention knew that their slaves, far from being docile, frequently ran away, and they sought a constitutional remedy. Pierce Butler and Charles Cotesworth Pinckney of South Carolina moved adoption of a clause requiring ''fugitive slaves and servants to be delivered up like criminals.''[14] The following day, delegates adopted the Constitution's fugitive slave clause with little debate. As finally approved, it was an indirect and obscurely worded guarantee: ''No Person held to Service or Labour in one State, under the Laws thereof, escaping to another, shall, in consequence of any Law or Regulation therein, be discharged from such Service or Labour, but shall be delivered up on Claim of the Party to whom such Service or Labour may be due.''[15]

Delegates conferred perhaps the greatest Constitutional protection on slavery when they granted Congress enumerated powers rather than giving it plenary legislative authority. They did not intend to limit Congress to exercise of those powers expressly listed in the Constitution. Indeed, the framers gave it authority ''to make all laws which shall be necessary and proper'' for carrying out any of the enumerated powers. This broadened national authority and gave Congress considerable flexibility without threatening slavery. The nature of Congress's enumerated powers precluded it from outlawing slavery or from interfering with its day-to-day operation in any state that chose to make it lawful. The framers, concerned more with union than with liberty, thus made freedom a matter of local option.

When the final gavel fell at Philadelphia, delegates had created a framework of government that tacitly recognized slavery, offered protection to it, and, most important, strengthened the hand of its advocates in the national government. Yet it would be wrong to view the Constitution of 1787 as uniformly and consistently proslavery; the framers created an open-ended document that, while favorable to slavery in many respects, contained a reservoir of antislavery potential. Because many of the framers believed, with James Madison, that it would be "wrong to admit in the Constitution the idea that there could be property in men,"[16] they refrained from including the words "slave" or "slavery" and thus refused to give explicit recognition to the institution. Moreover, the Constitution did not require the national government to promote slavery or, as southerners would subsequently argue, refrain from any action hostile to it. For example, the slave trade clause prohibited Congress from interfering with the importation of slaves into the original states until 1808. This suggested that after that date Congress could use its power to regulate commerce (a power denied it in the Articles) to end the trade. Indeed, it did so at the earliest possible moment. Moreover, the fugitive slave clause did not require or explicitly authorize Congress to help slaveowners recapture runaways. The wording of the clause and its placement in Article IV, Section 2 (which deals with interstate relations) suggested merely that states ought not prevent slaveowners from reclaiming fugitives.

Several other features of the Constitution mitigated the concessions to slaveholders. Because Americans had begun by the late eighteenth century to migrate to the Trans-Appalachian West, the future of slavery depended on whether it moved with the settlers. The Northwest Ordinance of 1787, passed by the Confederation Congress as the Constitutional Convention met, prohibited slavery in the territories north of the Ohio River. This, coupled with the postrevolutionary emancipation acts of the northern state legislatures, was an important stride toward making slavery a local—a peculiar—institution rather than the national institution it had been in 1776. The Constitution gave Congress authority to carry out the spirit of the Northwest Ordinance and further circumscribe slavery. It empowered Congress "to make all needful Rules and Regulations respecting the Territories," thus conferring authority to exclude slavery from the western territories, thereby containing it in the southeast. Moreover, the Bill of Rights, the ten amendments which became part of the Constitution in 1791, proclaimed a host of fundamental liberties—freedom of speech, the right to jury trial, protection against unreasonable search and seizure, the guarantee of due process of law— which were hostile to the arbitrary power essential to maintain slavery.

This is not to suggest—as abolitionists and Republicans would do later—that the framers were closet abolitionists who created a thoroughly antislavery Constitution. They made important concessions to slavery that proslavery advocates later effectively exploited. Nevertheless, the antislavery sensibilities of many delegates placed limits on how far they would go to protect slavery. Northern delegates made concessions to slaveholders' demands, but they did not seek to create a document that would promote slavery. Moreover, the framers did not carve the Constitution in stone. They wrote it in general language that was susceptible to a variety of interpretations. And they created a document that was inherently political because it defined governmental authority. Of necessity, such a document would evolve as rival political forces mustered their strength to shape the general language of the Constitution to their ends, whether proslavery or antislavery.

Toward a Proslavery Constitution

Between ratification of the Constitution and the Mexican War (1846–1848), the American political system worked against realization of the Constitution's antislavery potential. As they had at the Philadelphia Convention, southern political leaders doggedly insisted that the national government show solicitude for slavery and challenged measures that threatened the institution. Although northern politicians sometimes resisted these demands, more often they backed down or broke ranks in the face of southern initiatives. Confronted with southern assertiveness, many northern leaders believed that preservation of the Union required them to make concessions to southerners on an issue so vital to their interests. Moreover, the growth of a two-party system served to mute criticism of slavery within the national government. Between 1795 and 1815, as Federalists and Republicans vied for power, and, again, from 1832 until 1854, as Democrats and Whigs dominated the political scene, both major parties sought support in the North and the South. Consequently, party leaders generally avoided action with respect to slavery that would alienate southerners and splinter their party organizations.

The antebellum party system strengthened the South's hand in another way. The Republican party of Jefferson and Madison, which came to power in 1800 and remained dominant into the 1820s, attracted crucial support in the North, but drew most of its strength from the South, guaranteeing southerners a powerful influence over national policy. In the aftermath of the War of 1812, the demise of the Federalist opposition encouraged factionalism in Republican ranks and quickly led to a breakdown of party unity. This was a blow to southerners, undermining the bisectional political alliance that had served to protect slavery. Indeed, in 1819, when Missouri sought admission to the Union as a slave state, northerners in the House of Representatives closed ranks in an effort to block the spread of slavery. The Missouri crisis precipitated bitter sectional conflict, arrayed northern politicians against slavery, and resulted in legislation (the Missouri Compromise of 1820) excluding slavery from the northern portion of the vast Louisiana Purchase Territory. Nevertheless, southern leaders quickly recovered. In the late 1820s and early 1830s, supporters of Andrew Jackson—most notably New York's Martin Van Buren—forged a powerful new coalition, the Democratic party. Resting on a strong southern base, it also attracted considerable support in the North and the rapidly growing Midwest. Despite competition from a formidable Whig opposition, it became the dominant force in antebellum politics, controlling the White House for all but eight years between 1829 and 1861. Because southerners played a prominent role in party councils, Democratic hegemony. guaranteed a national policy favorable to slavery.

Northern politicians were able to make concessions to southerners because of the attitudes of their constituents. A small minority of northerners worked actively against slavery, but the majority was not deeply concerned about the institution. Some were proslavery, others tolerated slavery, and still others opposed slavery in the abstract but placed antislavery low on their list of priorities. A variety of factors were responsible for this state of affairs. Many settlers in Ohio, Indiana, Illinois, and Iowa had been born in the South, and they and their descendents were generally sympathetic with southern mores. Apart from southern immigrants, racism was strong throughout the North and led many to have little sympathy with enslaved blacks. In fact, many northerners feared that emancipation in the South would lead to a northward migration of members of a despised race. Still other northerners believed that acceptance of slavery was the cornerstone of the Union and were willing to make concessions to the South on slavery in order to preserve national unity.

The national government began its support for slavery shortly after George Washington assumed the presidency in 1789. Presidents and Congresses allowed slavery to take root in the Old Southwest (the area south of the Ohio River stretching from the Appalachian Mountains to the Mississippi River). In 1789, Congress accepted North Carolina's cession of its western lands to the United States, even though the grant stipulated that "no regulation made or to be made shall tend to emancipate slaves."[17] Lawmakers organized territories in the region without reference to slavery, fully aware that immigrants from the older southern states would establish slavery, and subsequently admitted these territories to the Union as slave states. In 1801, shortly after the government moved to Washington, D.C., Congress decreed that the laws of Virginia and Maryland, which recognized slavery, should remain in force in the District of Columbia. The nation's capital thus became a slave city, replete with a slave market where human beings were bought and sold, and city officials, acting under congressional authority, enforced laws supporting the institution.

Federal officials also worked to insulate slavery from attack. During the 1830s radical abolitionists in the North subjected slavery and slaveholders to withering criticism in hundreds of pamphlets and thousands of petitions to Congress. Southerners were offended by this criticism and feared that it would incite slave insurrection. Although Congress refused to enact legislation excluding abolitionist pamphlets from the mail, it did not object when President Andrew Jackson's postmaster general authorized local postmasters to destroy antislavery tracts. Though a violation of the postal laws and the First Amendment's guarantee of freedom of the press, postal officials continued to enforce the policy until the Civil War. Faced with abolitionist petitions, Congress also acted with flagrant disrespect for the Constitution. In 1836, the House of Representatives adopted a resolution, popularly known as the "gag rule," that prohibited members from reading or even discussing petitions concerning slavery. Although the rule abridged the right "to petition the Government for a redress of grievances" which was guaranteed by the First Amendment, the rule remained in force until 1844.

Congress also bolstered slavery by helping slaveowners secure the return of runaway slaves. In 1793, after little debate, Congress passed "An Act respecting fugitives from justice, and persons escaping from the service of their masters." The first part of the law implemented the constitutional provision requiring states to extradite fugitives from justice. Without providing any federal enforcement machinery, it simply admonished state officials to return fugitives from justice when requested to do so by the governor of another state. The fugitive slave clause, like the extradition clause, was a directive to the states and did not expressly authorize congressional action. At the insistence of southerners, however, the second part of the 1793 act went beyond admonishing state officals to fulfill their obligation to return runaway slaves. It authorized slaveholders (or their agents) to seize runaways and take them before a United States district judge or any state justice of the peace. After presenting evidence of ownership—either an oral statement or a written affadavit made before a justice of the peace in the owner's home state—the claimant was to be given a warrant authorizing him or her to take the fugitive back to slavery. Alleged fugitives were denied due process of law: they had no right to testify, to command witnesses to appear, or to counsel. By establishing this procedure, Congress not only commanded state and federal officials to aid in the return of runaways but stipulated that they employ the assumptions and procedures of slave state law in doing so. Northern state law presumed all persons to be free and required slaveowners to establish their claims beyond a reasonable doubt. Under the Fugitive Slave Act, however, blacks were presumed to be slaves, and claimants had to provide only minimal evidence that they owned the alleged fugitive. Thus to protect slaveowners Congress gave extraterritorial application to southern state law.

Because of the summary procedure it authorized, the act threatened free blacks as well as runaway slaves. Free blacks who were kidnapped or mistaken for fugitive slaves were denied the procedural means necessary to establish their freedom. This undoubtedly violated the Fifth Amendment's guarantee that no person shall "be deprived of life, liberty, or property without due process of law." As commonly understood by contemporaries, due process obligated the government to follow traditional common law procedures when it deprived persons of life, liberty, or property. Because the Fugitive Slave Act allowed blacks to be denied liberty through *ex parte* testimony (the testimony of only one party to the case) and without the right to counsel or to trial by jury, it violated the common understanding of due process.

Despite criticism of the procedure employed by the law, during the five decades following its enactment the northern states generally cooperated with slaveowners who sought the return of runaways. Nevertheless, many northern legislatures took action to protect free blacks. Some merely passed statutes imposing fines and imprisonment on persons convicted of kidnapping free blacks with the intention of selling them into slavery. Several legislatures went further, however, stipulating that state

judicial officers who heard fugitive slave cases must afford blacks greater
procedural protection than required under the Fugitive Slave Act. An
1826 Pennsylvania law, for example, insisted that slaveowners could
only take runaways out of the state if they obtained a certificate of
rendition from a state or federal judge, thus denying them the right to
return fugitives without judicial intervention. The law also provided that
in hearings before justices of the peace, slaveowners and other interested
parties could not testify and that alleged fugitives were to be given
sufficient time to obtain evidence that they were free. Thus Pennsylvania
attempted to balance its obligation under the fugitive slave clause with its
interest in protecting free black citizens from kidnapping or being
condemned to slavery in a kangaroo-court proceeding.

A complicated series of events brought questions concerning the
meaning of the fugitive slave clause and the constitutionality of the
Pennsylvania statute before the United States Supreme Court in 1842.
Margaret Morgan was the daughter of Maryland slaves who had been
permitted by their owner to live as free persons. Like her parents, she was
not claimed by her owner, married a free black man, and in 1832 moved
to Pennsylvania, where at least one of her daughters was born. When
Morgan's owner died in 1837, his niece and heiress hired Edward Prigg
to go to Pennsylvania and claim Morgan and her children as fugitive
slaves. Although Pennsylvania law recognized as free persons all children born in the state, Maryland law provided that slave status passed
through the mother, thus making Margaret Morgan and all of her children
slaves. Prigg obtained a warrant for the arrest of Morgan and her
children, but the justice of the peace before whom they were brought
refused to hear the case. Prigg then took matters into his own hands,
seizing his prey and carrying them across the Maryland line to slavery.

Subsequently, Prigg was convicted of kidnapping by a Pennsylvania
court, and the state supreme court upheld his conviction. In the 1842
case, *Prigg* v. *Pennsylvania*, he appealed to the United States Supreme
Court, contending that the Pennsylvania law under which he was convicted violated the Constitution's fugitive slave clause and the Fugitive
Slave Act of 1793. Justice Joseph Story, the distinguished Massachusetts
jurist, wrote the opinion for the Court. Although Story personally
disliked slavery, he feared that northern impediments to the return of
fugitives would produce sectional animosity that might ultimately destroy the Union. Therefore, as the historian Paul Finkelman has shown,
he offered a strongly proslavery interpretation of the fugitive slave

clause, sacrificing black rights to the interest of sectional harmony and national unity.[18]

The decision upheld the constitutionality of the Fugitive Slave Act. Even though the fugitive slave clause did not expressly authorize congressional action, Story argued that it recognized the right of slaveowners to recover runaways and therefore implicitly empowered Congress to adopt legislation to enforce the right. He also struck down the Pennsylvania law under which Prigg had been convicted, asserting that the fugitive slave clause gave Congress exclusive authority to regulate the return of fugitive slaves (even though it did not give Congress express, much less exclusive, authority to legislate). Therefore, he reasoned, any state legislation on the subject was unconstitutional. Three of the nine justices disagreed on this point, arguing that state legislatures could or must pass laws to help slaveholders regain their property; however, even these justices agreed that the procedure mandated by the 1826 Pennsylvania law created barriers to the return of fugitives and was therefore unconstitutional. Despite this disagreement, the Court clearly suggested that the summary procedure authorized by the 1793 Fugitive Slave Act was constitutional and that state legislation which sought to add procedural safeguards to allow blacks to prove their freedom was unacceptable. When blacks were involved, even when it was possible that they could be free, the Court did not consider it necessary to require Congress to honor the procedural guarantees of the Bill of Rights or to permit state legislatures to compensate for Congress's omission.

A final aspect of the opinion, which went unchallenged, bears mention. Story held that the fugitive slave clause recognized a property right that extended throughout the Union. Therefore, he reasoned, slaveowners and their agents had the right to enter free states, seize fugitives, and carry them back to the South without obtaining judicial authorization. The definition of personal status contained in the law of the southern states thus had extraterritorial force in the free states, regardless of the policy of those states. Moreover, Story's interpretation left free blacks at the mercy of those who had the audacity to claim them as slaves and the power to seize them and carry them out of the state. Any legislation enacted by the states that established mandatory procedures which gave alleged fugitives the opportunity to prove their freedom and protect themselves from enslavement was impermissible.

Ironically, *Prigg* offered blacks some hope. Story's opinion asserted that since justices of the peace were state officers, Congress could not compel them to enforce the Fugitive Slave Act. States might accept Congress's invitation to have their officials execute the law, but they were not required to do so. Many northern states responded by ordering state functionaries—sheriffs and jailers as well as justices of the peace—to refuse to arrest, hold, and return fugitives. Since there were few federal district judges to enforce the act (generally only two in each state) this aspect of the ruling made it difficult for slaveholders to obtain official assistance in securing runaways. Despite this bright spot, the *Prigg* decision gave explicit constitutional sanction to slavery, eroded the rights of free blacks, and made their liberty precarious. Moreover, the benefit that blacks received from *Prigg* was short-lived; in 1850, Congress gave in to southern demands, passed an even harsher fugitive law, and provided a small army of federal officials to enforce it.

Although fugitive slave legislation posed a special threat, other congressional measures eroded the rights of free blacks. In 1790, when Congress established regulations for immigrants to become naturalized citizens, it excluded blacks. Two years later it limited service in the militia (one of the responsibilities of citizenship in a republic) to whites, and in 1810 denied blacks the right to carry the mail. In 1820 lawmakers authorized white citizens of the District of Columbia to establish a municipal government and to create a legal code for slaves and free blacks. In 1848, when Congress created the Oregon Territory, and again in 1850, when it established the New Mexico Territory, it denied blacks the right to claim federal land there.

Because the national government exercised limited functions during the nineteenth century, state and local governments were far more significant in determining the rights that blacks enjoyed. Moreover, in defining these rights, states operated virtually without restraint by the national government. The Constitution contained no guarantee of equal rights (except to states, which were guaranteed equal representation in the Senate) and few provisions protecting individual rights from infringement by state and local governments. It forbade states to enact ex post facto laws, bills of attainder, and laws impairing the obligation of contracts, but these restrictions offered slender protection to blacks. The Bill of Rights contained a long list of fundamental rights such as freedom of speech, press, and religion; the right to counsel and jury trial; and protection from self-incrimination and unreasonable search and seizure. In *Barron* v. *Baltimore* (1833), however, the United States Supreme Court ruled that the Bill of Rights had been added to the Constitution to assuage fears of a powerful national government and served as a restriction on the national government but not on the states.[19] Although state constitutions generally contained provisions similar to those in the national Bill of Rights, state legislatures and courts determined the scope and applicability of such guarantees.

The privileges and immunities clause of Article IV, section 2 ("the Citizens of Each State shall be entitled to all Privileges and Immunities of Citizens in the Several States") held out the possibility of national protection of individual rights. During the early nineteenth century, however, politicians, judges, and constitutional commentators disagreed over what the clause meant, and the United States Supreme Court did not resolve the dispute. Some, including James Kent of New York, one of the nation's most influential judges and legal writers, believed that it did not create a body of fundamental rights that were protected against violation by the states. Rather, Kent contended, it merely guaranteed that a citizen of one state who entered a second state was entitled to whatever rights that state accorded its own citizens. In Kent's words, the clause "means only that citizens of other states shall have equal rights with our own citizens."[20] This reading of the clause neither shielded free blacks from denial of basic rights by the state in which they resided, nor protected them if they ventured into states that imposed discriminatory laws on their own black citizens.

Other judges and legal commentators argued that the clause was designed to protect the fundamental rights of United States citizens. United States Supreme Court Justice Bushrod Washington gave the most thorough statement of this position in his opinion in *Corfield* v. *Coryell* (1823), a case he decided while sitting as a United States circuit court judge. Equating the rights guaranteed by the privileges and immunities clause with natural rights, he argued that they included those rights which "are, in their nature, fundamental; which belong, of right, to the citizens of all free governments. . . ." Noting that these were "more tedious than difficult to enumerate," Washington explained that they included "Protection by the government; the enjoyment of life and liberty, with the right to acquire and possess property of every kind, and to pursue and obtain happiness and safety; subject nevertheless to such restraints as the government may justly prescribe for the general good of the whole." Because these rights were fundamental and existed throughout the nation, presumably citizens were entitled to enjoy them at home as well as in other states.[21]

Even when judges and legislators accepted this approach, it did not offer blacks unassailable protection. Washington himself noted that the fundamental rights he sketched were "subject . . . to such restraints as the government may justly prescribe for the general good of the whole." This had important implications in light of the expansion of state police power during the 1830s and 1840s. Most judges and legal experts agreed that the Constitution divided power into federal and state spheres, and that the police power—the authority to promote the public health, safety, and welfare—lay within the state sphere. Thus states might justify special restrictions on free blacks on the grounds that they were necessary to prevent slave insurrection or to control individuals who were incapable of exercising responsibly rights enjoyed by whites.

A more fundamental problem stood in the way of using the privileges and immunities clause to protect blacks from discriminatory state action: there was no consensus that free blacks were citizens entitled to constitutional rights. The Constitution did not define national citizenship. Some legal writers pointed out that under traditional legal norms birth conferred citizenship and contended that all free persons born in this country were United States citizens. Others argued that state citizenship was controlling and that all state citizens were citizens of the United States. The fact that the Constitution conferred important rights on state citizens seemed to support this view. For example, Article III provided that federal judicial authority extended to cases "between Citizens of different States," suggesting a federal right (to bring suit in federal court) that rested on one's status as a state citizen. Similarly, the privileges and immunities clause, read literally, conferred rights on persons who were state citizens. Because most free blacks were born in the United States and many were state citizens, either of these definitions entitled a significant number of free blacks to United States citizenship.

Most white southerners, however, denied that free blacks were United States citizens. They feared that as citizens, free blacks would be entitled by the privileges and immunities clause to travel freely throughout the South, something that they believed posed a clear threat to slavery. As Philip Barbour, who later served on the United States Supreme Court remarked in 1820, free blacks were "the most dangerous [class] to the community that can possibly be conceived. They are just enough elevated to have some sense of liberty, and yet not the capacity to estimate or enjoy all its rights . . . and being between two societies, above one and below the other, they are in a most dissatisfied state . . . firebrands to the other class of their own color.''[22] To protect themselves, southerners argued that the framers had not considered blacks eligible for citizenship and that, consequently, they were not entitled to any rights created by the federal Constitution (including the rights conferred by the privileges and immunities clause). In 1820, for example, Charles Pinckney, who had been a delegate to the Constitutional Convention, asserted, ''There did not then [1787] exist such a thing in the Union as a black or colored citizen, nor could I have conceived it possible such a thing could ever have existed in it. . . .''[23]

During most of the antebellum period, there was no authoritative resolution of the debate over black citizenship. In the winter of 1820–1821, Congress discussed the issue when Missouri sought approval of a state constitution that barred immigration by free blacks. Northern congressmen argued that this provision was unconstitutional because it denied free blacks rights (to enter any state in the Union and to enjoy the rights of citizenship there) protected by the privileges and immunities clause. Southerners responded that blacks were not U.S. citizens and therefore were not entitled to rights created by the Constitution. Congress failed to resolve the issue, ending the debate by adopting an ambiguous compromise. Shortly after the Missouri debate, Attorney General William Wirt, a southerner, issued an opinion that lent support to the southern position.[24] Nevertheless, it had no legal authority and left the question unresolved.

During the 1820s and again in the 1840s passage of state laws requiring incarceration of black sailors who entered southern ports renewed the debate. Because blacks who were citizens of northern states and who claimed to be United States citizens were affected, the laws raised the question of whether blacks were citizens who were protected by the privileges and immunities clause. As in the Missouri debates, however, there was no resolution of the question. In 1823, Justice William Johnson of the United States Supreme Court, while sitting as circuit judge for South Carolina, struck down the South Carolina law, and Attorney General William Wirt issued an official opinion declaring the law unconstitutional. However, both did so on the grounds that it interfered with Congress's power to regulate interstate and foreign commerce and violated the treaty rights of foreign shippers. Neither held that the law violated rights enjoyed by black American sailors as state or United States citizens under the Constitution's privileges and immunities clause.

In the early 1840s, when a congressional committee examined the constitutionality of the Negro seamen's laws, a majority of its members supported a resolution declaring that the laws violated the rights of free blacks; however, a minority report asserted that blacks were not United States citizens and therefore were not entitled to protection by the privileges and immunities clause. The full House of Representatives rejected the majority's resolution, implicitly endorsing the minority report. Dissatisfied by the House's action, the Massachusetts legislature dispatched lawyers to Charleston and New Orleans to file suits challenging the constitutionality of the laws. This tactic also failed to produce a ruling because angry mobs in both cities ran the Massachusetts emissaries out of town before they could begin litigation.

Slaves, Free Blacks, and the Law

Although the issue of black citizenship remained unresolved, one thing was clear. There were few Constitutional limitations on the manner in which states might treat persons residing within their borders and even fewer if they were black. States, in the North as well as in the South, used this discretion to enact laws denying blacks equal rights.

The slave codes of the southern states were, of course, the most egregious examples of this. They included statutes enacted by state legislatures and rules established by state courts as they interpreted and applied existing law to individual cases. Although this body of law varied among states and changed over time, there are enough similarities between states and sufficient continuity during the antebellum years to permit generalization. Southern law stipulated that a person born of a slave mother was the property of his or her mother's owner, who had an absolute legal right (in the words of the Louisiana code) to "sell him, dispose of his person, his industry, and his labor."[25] Regarded as things rather than persons, slaves did not enjoy a legal right to own property. In practice, some slaves were allowed to work for others during their spare time or to sell produce raised in their gardens, and many used the proceeds to acquire property; however, they had no legal title to this property and held it at the sufferance of their masters, not as a matter of legal right.

Slaves could not enter legally binding contracts and, because marriage was a civil contract, could not legally marry. Certainly, most slaves established long-term monogamous relationships, expected fidelity from their spouses, and established families and complex kinship networks. Because slave marriages were not recognized by the law, however, masters could separate husbands from wives and parents from children. "The relationship between slaves is essentially different from that of man and wife joined in lawful wedlock," noted the North Carolina Supreme Court, for "with slaves it may be dissolved . . . by the sale of one or both, depending upon the caprice or necessity of the owners."[26] Indeed, the sale of slaves—whether to obtain needed capital, to be rid of a recalcitrant slave, to complete the settlement of an estate, or to satisfy the judgment of a court against a slaveowner—was common. And sales frequently ended marriages and separated family members.

Southern law also stripped slaves of other personal rights. Concerned about the problem of runaways, legislatures required slaves to carry passes when they left their owners' plantations and established slave patrols whose members had authority to beat slaves found traveling without passes. In order to prevent slaves from reading abolitionist tracts and forging passes, statutes barred anyone from teaching a slave to read or write. Southern legislatures attempted to prevent slave insurrections by prohibiting slaves from possessing firearms or other weapons and by making it illegal for slaves to gather in groups of five or more outside the presence of a white person. To encourage deference from slaves, southern law made it a crime for a slave to strike a white person and authorized whites to chastise insolent slaves. According to a North Carolina judge, this could be "a look, the pointing of a finger, a refusal or neglect to step out of the way when a white person is seen to approach. . . . such acts violate the rules of propriety, and, if tolerated, would destroy that subordination, upon which our social system rests."[27]

In order to protect slaveowners' property and to bring the law into line with southerners' claim that theirs was a mild, paternalistic form of slavery, the slave codes afforded slaves protection against abuse by their owners and other whites. Statutes defined as murder the willful and malicious killing of a slave by an owner or other white person and provided that whites might be fined for undue cruelty to slaves even if it did not result in death. Thus the Louisiana code provided that an owner or overseer might be fined for punishing a slave with "unusual rigor . . . so as to maim or mutilate him."[28] As might be expected, such laws afforded slaves little protection. Masters and overseers had the right to whip or use other forms of "moderate correction" on slaves who disobeyed, worked poorly, stole, or ran away. And if a slave resisted, a master, overseer, or patrol member might employ sufficient force to quell the resistance, even if it led to the slave's death. Because whites had such broad authority to use force and juries were lily-white, whites rarely were indicted or convicted of murdering or abusing a slave.

Policy as well as prejudice led southern whites to subordinate free blacks as well as slaves. "If all blacks see all of their color slaves, it will seem to them a disposition of Providence, and they will be content," observed one Virginia legislator in 1806. "But if they see others like themselves free, and enjoying rights they are deprived of, they will repine."[29] Lawmakers throughout the South did their best to guarantee that free blacks enjoyed few rights. In the early years of the nineteenth century most southern states regarded free blacks as citizens, albeit citizens who did not enjoy all the rights of white persons, and several permitted free blacks to vote if they met existing property-holding requirements. By the 1820s and 1830s, however, the rapid growth of the free Negro population in the Upper South, combined with growing fear of slave insurrection and the insistence of proslavery writers that all blacks were naturally suited to slavery, led to a steady erosion of the rights of free blacks. As the century progressed, the few states that had permitted free blacks to vote disfranchised them, judges handed down decisions declaring that they were not citizens, and legislators enacted a remarkable array of restrictions on their freedom. Joseph Lumpkin of the Georgia Supreme Court perhaps best summarized the position of the South's 250,000 free blacks on the eve of the Civil War:

> "The *status* of the African in Georgia, whether bond or free, is such that he
> has no civil, social or political rights or capacity, whatever, except such as
> are bestowed upon him by statute; . . . the act of manumission confers
> no other right but . . . freedom from the dominion of the master, and
> the limited liberty of locomotion. . . ."[30]

As Lumpkin's statement suggests, the law frequently equated free blacks with slaves, in the process diminishing their status as free persons. In most states free blacks accused of noncapital crimes were tried by the informal panels of justices of the peace and citizens that meted out summary justice to slaves. When convicted, they were not only liable to imprisonment but, like slaves, might receive thirty-nine lashes at the public whipping post. The law also demanded that free blacks as well as slaves be submissive to whites. Mississippi and Florida provided that any black who "shall at any time use abusive and provoking language to, or raise his hand'' against a white person might be whipped. Other states authorized whites to chastise ''insolent'' free blacks. ''Free negroes . . . ought by law to be compelled to demean themselves as inferiors,'' noted John B. O'Neall of the South Carolina Supreme Court. ''I have always thought [this] and while on the circuit ruled that words of impertinence and insolence addressed by a free negro to a white man, would justify an assault and battery.''[31] In addition, every slave state except Delaware and Louisiana denied free blacks as well as slaves the right to testify in cases involving whites, making it difficult to prosecute whites who committed crimes against them.

Free blacks also suffered significant restrictions of their personal liberty. Because southern state law assumed that blacks were slaves, free blacks were required to carry papers proving their freedom and could be seized as fugitives if they were unable to produce them. They also had to register periodically with local authorities, thus subjecting themselves to questioning and scrutiny by whites. Southern state and local officials used laws prohibiting free blacks from meeting without white supervision to deter them from establishing independent churches, and several states went so far as to make it illegal for free blacks to learn to read and write. Highly subjective vagrancy laws provided that free blacks who lived in idleness or who lacked industrious habits could be bound to labor for whites. State laws and municipal ordinances prohibited free blacks from practicing numerous occupations.

Worst of all, the legal system left free blacks at the mercy of whites. Those who were suspected of criminal activity or impropriety, offended the sensibilities of whites, or aroused the jealousy or enmity of whites were likely to be victims of mob violence. ''Who does not know that when a free Negro . . . has rendered himself obnoxious to a neighborhood,'' noted a Virginian in 1832, ''how easy it is for a party to visit him one night, take him from his bed and his family, and apply to him the gentle admonition of a severe flagellation, to induce him to go away.''[32] Indeed, blacks could be induced to go away because there was little chance that white sheriffs and lily-white juries would afford them redress against their assailants. Moreover, given the complex web of laws that entwined them and the fact that many of these regulations gave considerable discretion to local officials, whites could snatch away the limited liberty that free blacks enjoyed. If they failed to register with local authorities at the prescribed time, lacked adequate documentation to prove their freedom, practiced a forbidden occupation, or appeared to local whites to be indolent, they could be dragged to the whipping post, hired out to white farmers, or (in some states) sold into slavery.

Between 1800 and the mid 1840s, blacks who lived north of slavery also witnessed a steady erosion of their rights. Most northern states banned racial intermarriage, and many either permitted or required school boards to establish segregated schools. Six northern states denied blacks an essential tool of self-protection by prohibiting them from testifying in cases in which a white person was a party. Ohio (1804), Indiana (1831), Illinois (1813), Iowa (1839), and Michigan (1827) attempted to prohibit blacks from entering their borders by enacting measures requiring black immigrants to post bonds guaranteeing their good behavior or by imposing fines or imprisonment on black immigrants.

Northern states also restricted blacks' political rights. In 1800 most permitted black men to vote, provided they met the property requirements that applied to white men; however, as states expanded whites' access to the ballot box by abolishing property requirements, they generally excluded blacks from the polls. With the exception of Maine, none of the states that entered the Union after 1800 permitted blacks to vote in general elections. Among the older states, New Jersey (1807), Connecticut (1818), and Pennsylvania (1838) stripped blacks of political rights as they established universal white manhood suffrage. By 1860, only Massachusetts, Maine, New Hampshire, Vermont, and Rhode Island allowed blacks to vote on the same terms as whites, and New York permitted black men to vote if they owned $250 worth of property, a requirement that did not apply to white men.

Still there were significant differences between the plight of northern and southern free blacks. Southern laws governing free blacks were much more restrictive and repressive than those on northern statute books, making southern free blacks little better than slaves without masters. Moreover, because it was absolutely unthinkable for them to demand equal rights and because they had no allies in the white community, the plight of southern free blacks could only worsen. In the North proponents of racial equality were not popular and were sometimes mobbed or even murdered. There was sufficient tolerance, however, that blacks could organize and protest against discrimination and find white allies to help them press their demands. Therefore, while the position of southern free blacks steadily deteriorated, northern free blacks would make important gains during the late 1840s and the 1850s.

That was in the future, however. In the mid-1840s, as the nation annexed Texas in 1845 and prepared for war with Mexico in 1846, it had moved far away from the antislavery and equalitarian promise of the Revolution. Delegates to the constitutional convention had made important concessions to slavery, and during the succeeding decades politicians and judges had used these to create a constitutional order that promoted slavery and permitted racial subordination. As a result, free blacks in the North as well as the South had seen their rights steadily erode. Slavery, which had appeared to be receding in the Revolution's aftermath, had marched triumphantly westward, establishing beachheads across the Mississippi River in Louisiana, Arkansas, Missouri, and Texas. And as the United States went to war with Mexico in 1846, many predicted that it would move to the Pacific. Yet not everyone was willing to concede that the Constitution was a proslavery document; northern blacks and white abolitionists were already busy creating an antislavery constitutionalism. The war with Mexico would prove to be a watershed, polarizing American politics along sectional lines, reviving a broad-based northern antislavery sentiment, and reestablishing the allure of the Revolution's commitment to the "rights of man" among northerners.

2

Law and Liberty, 1830–1860

On January 15, 1851, thirty-seven black delegates assembled in the Second Baptist Church of Columbus, Ohio, to open the annual Convention of the Colored Citizens of Ohio. Representing 26,000 black Ohioans, the delegation included artisans, barbers, teachers, and ministers. Although delegates discussed strategies for winning repeal of discriminatory state laws and for building a united, self-conscious black commmunity, they were especially concerned about the Fugitive Slave Act of 1850, which Congress had passed the previous fall to replace the venerable 1793 law. Like the old law, the 1850 statute allowed masters to reclaim runaway slaves merely on the basis of sworn testimony and denied alleged fugitives basic procedural rights that were essential to protect their freedom. The new law went further, however, creating a formidable enforcement apparatus; it authorized appointment of hundreds of U.S. commissioners to conduct hearings and to authorize the return of runaways, making it much easier for slaveowners to recover their human chattels. It also provided that commissioners would receive a ten-dollar fee if they ruled in favor of masters and only half that amount if they found in favor of an alleged fugitive, giving them an incentive to be especially solicitous of slaveowners' interests. Thus the law not only posed a serious threat to fugitive slaves but placed northern free blacks in danger of legally sanctioned kidnapping. Indeed, thousands of northern blacks—including some of the delegates' friends and neighbors—had fled to Canada in the wake of its passage, and as the convention met, delegates learned that a black man had been seized as a fugitive slave in southwest Ohio.

Emotions were therefore high as the delegates denounced the new law

30

and demanded its repeal. In leading the attack, John Mercer Langston—
who would later join the bar, establish the Law Department at Howard
University, and become president of that institution—invoked the Constitution. Citing its guarantee of trial by jury, due process of law, and
habeas corpus, he contended that the fugitive law was not only unjust but
flagrantly unconstitutional. "This enactment," Langston charged, "pos-
sesses neither the form nor the essence of true law . . . [and] is a
hideous deformity in the *garb* of law. It kills alike, the true spirit of the
Declaration of Independence, the Constitution, and the palladium of our
liberties."[1]

That Langston's speech invoked constitutional principles to attack
slavery and discrimination was hardly surprising. The Constitution was a
vital part of antebellum popular consciousness, and nineteenth-century
Americans—not just lawyers—commonly spoke in constitutional terms
when debating political and social issues. Indeed, Langston's constitutional analysis was quickly challenged by H. Ford Douglas, a nineteen-
year-old barber from Cleveland. Although he had escaped from a
Virginia plantation only four years earlier, Douglas was a formidable
opponent who was rapidly becoming one of the most forceful abolitionist
orators in the state. He argued that the Constitution protected slavery and
was an obstacle to black liberation:

> I hold, sir, that the Constitution of the United States is pro-slavery,
> considered so by those who framed it. . . . It is well known that . . .
> in the Convention that framed the Constitution, there was considerable
> discussion on the subject of slavery. South Carolina and Georgia refused to
> come into the Union [unless] the Convention would allow the continuation
> of the Slave Trade for twenty years . . . the Convention submitted to
> that guilty contract. . . . Here we see them engrafting on the Constitu-
> tion a clause legalizing and protecting one of the vilest systems of wrong
> ever invented by the cupidity and avarice of man. . . . That instrument
> also provides for the return of fugitive slaves. And, sir, . . . the "Fugi-
> tive Law" is in accordance with that stipulation;—a law unequaled in the
> worst days of Roman despotism, and unparalleled in the annals of heathen
> jurisprudence. . . .

Douglas concluded that blacks must reject such a document and refuse to
participate in a constitutional order that held millions of African-
Americans in chains. Consequently, he urged delegates to adopt a
resolution declaring that "no colored man can consistently vote under the
United States Constitution."[2]

Douglas's characterization of the Constitution did not meet a sympathetic response. William Howard Day charged that Douglas failed to distinguish between the Constitution and the interpretation given it by proslavery judges and politicians. The Constitution was a malleable document, he contended, and, correctly understood, it was a force for black liberty and equality. Day explained,

"Sir, coming up as I do, in the midst of three millions of men in chains, and five hundred thousand only half-free, I consider every instrument precious which guarantees to me liberty. I consider the Constitution the foundation of American liberties, and wrapping myself in the flag of the nation, I would plant myself upon that Constitution, and using the weapons they have given me, I would appeal to the American people for the rights thus guaranteed."[3]

In the end, Langston and Day easily prevailed, and Douglas's motion went down to defeat, 28–2.

The debate at Columbus suggested that northern blacks had kept the dream of freedom, citizenship, and equality alive. In the face of six decades of steady defeats, they continued to cling to the equalitarian principles of the Revolution. Indeed, between 1830 and 1860, northern free blacks and their white abolitionist allies skillfully used these principles to develop a powerful constitutional attack on slavery and racial subordination. Initially rejected as the work of a lunatic fringe, by the late 1840s and the 1850s important elements of their analysis gained wider currency as they were taken up by mainstream northern politicians, subjecting proslavery constitutionalism to its severest challenge and the Union to its supreme test.

Blacks, Abolitionists, and the Emergence of Antislavery Constitutionalism

Northern blacks took the lead in challenging proslavery constitutionalism. Beginning in 1830, northern black leaders organized a series of national conventions that met sporadically throughout the antebellum years. Given the state-centered nature of the pre-Civil War constitutional system, however, many of the problems confronting free blacks were local rather than national. Therefore, black leaders increasingly turned their efforts to state conventions; the first state convention met in New

York in 1837 and was followed by a proliferation of such local meetings during the 1840s and 1850s. These national and state conclaves—like the 1851 Columbus meeting—not only helped beleaguered free black communities develop the institutions and solidarity necessary to survive in an increasingly hostile world, they also served as the whetstone on which blacks honed their attack on slavery and racial discrimination to razor sharpness.

The genesis of the convention movement paralleled the emergence of a small but imaginative cadre of radical abolitionists. Rising to prominence in the North during the early 1830s, this diverse group, which included blacks and whites, women and men, denounced slavery in harsh, uncompromising terms. While they charged that slavery made a mockery of the republican principle of equality, the abolitionists rested their attack primarily on religious principles and passions. Slavery was a sin, they contended, because it "debased the physical, and defiled the moral workmanship of the great God" and ignored the Gospel's admonition to "love your neighbor as yourself." Claiming that "there is no such thing as holding on to sin with safety," abolitionists eschewed gradualism and called for immediate emancipation.[4] Abolitionists also recognized that racism violated Christian principles and, by asserting that blacks were different than and inferior to whites, provided the most powerful weapon in the proslavery arsenal. Consequently, they created a powerful argument for black equality.

Not content to wage a campaign of conversion, abolitionists were inexorably drawn to political action. Shortly after its inception in 1833, the immediatist American Anti-Slavery Society sponsored a massive petition campaign designed to prod Congress to abolish slavery in the nation's capital. Throughout the 1830s abolitionists also attempted to influence the political process by questioning candidates about their views on slavery and throwing their support to those who came closest to the antislavery standard. By the late 1830s, however, many were disenchanted with the effectiveness of this strategy and moved toward formation of a third party. Although some prominent leaders (most notably William Lloyd Garrison) opposed them, such antislavery radicals as Henry Stanton, Alvan Stewart, James Birney, Joshua Leavitt, William Goodell, and Gerrit Smith eagerly embraced independent political action, forming the Liberty Party in 1839.

The debate over political action led abolitionists into the realm of constitutional theory, as they, like other Americans, looked to the

Constitution for justification of their political agenda. Garrison and his supporters, eager to prevent northerners from smugly assuming that they had nothing to do with slavery, argued that the Constitution was a proslavery document. Exploiting James Madison's notes on the Constitutional Convention, which first appeared in 1840, Garrisonians gleefully debunked the framers' reputation as opponents of slavery. They charged that southern delegates had demanded protection for slavery and that northerners had cravenly abandoned their principles and acquiesced in provisions that protected, even promoted, slavery. According to Garrison, who dramatized his position by publicly burning a copy of the Constitution, the document was "a covenant with death, and an agreement with Hell."[5] Northerners should annul it and withdraw from the Union because it protected slavery and slaveholders.

Other abolitionists categorically rejected Garrison's analysis. Their position was most persuasively and eloquently articulated by the black abolitionist Frederick Douglass, a one-time ally of Garrison who rejected Garrisonian constitutional ideas in the late 1840s. Douglass argued that a close reading of the Constitution demonstrated that it did not expressly mention slavery, much less guarantee its existence. On the contrary, it contained colorblind libertarian provisions that were incompatible with slavery. He also brushed aside the contention that Madison's notes proved that the framers had acceded to southerners' demands for provisions that would protect and promote slavery. Douglass suggested that such an argument was preposterous: it "disregarded the plain and common sense reading of the instrument itself" and assumed that "the Constitution does not mean what it says and says what it does not mean." He also chided his opponents for confusing the Constitution with the way in which it had been interpreted by proslavery politicians and judges. "The Constitution is one thing, its adminstration is another," he noted, "and, in this instance, a very different and opposite thing." Finally, Douglass recognized that the Constitution, because it was written in general language, was an open-ended document capable of serving the cause of freedom and equality. "The Constitution, as well as the Declaration of Independence, and the sentiments of the founders of the Republic," he explained, "give us a platform broad enough, and strong enough, to support the most comprehensive plans for the freedom and elevation of all the people of this country, without regard to color, class, or clime."[6]

Rejection of the Garrisonian position led to an outpouring of abolitionist books and pamphlets that found in the Constitution a powerful weapon against slavery and discrimination. Although abolitionist constitutional theory did not win acceptance by the courts, Congress, or the president in the decades preceding the Civil War, it was not without effect. It gave birth to constitutional principles that would become influential during the 1860s, helping to transform the Constitution into a document that promoted equality, was a source of individual rights, and empowered the national government to protect those rights.

The dominant group in the Liberty party developed a moderate antislavery constitutionalism. Led by Salmon P. Chase, a future United States senator and chief justice of the United States, they attempted to deflect charges that they were irresponsible radicals whose policies would drive southerners to secession. Moderates conceded that in order to bring the South into the Union, the framers had agreed to deny the national government authority to interfere with slavery in states where it already existed. And they pledged to honor this limitation. Nevertheless, moderates argued that the framers had been hostile to slavery and had attempted to put it on the road to extinction. They insisted that the Declaration of Independence stated the fundamental values that the framers of the Constitution attempted to implement and argued that its powerful assertion of equality and natural rights clearly established the framers' antipathy to slavery. They reinforced this argument by reference to the Northwest Ordinance of 1787. In attempting to keep slavery from spreading into new territory, moderates claimed, the Confederation Congress, which included a number of delegates to the Philadelphia Convention, reasserted its hostility to slavery and its commitment to the Declaration of Independence.

Moderates also found specific provisions in the Constitution that were hostile to slavery. The clause recognizing congressional power to end the importation of slaves after 1808, they argued, was designed to restrict the growth of the hated institution. They contended that the commerce clause, by giving Congress plenary authority over interstate commerce, empowered it to prohibit the interstate slave trade. This would prevent slaveowners in Virginia and Maryland, where the soil was depleted and plantation agriculture was unprofitable, from shipping their slaves to the West and, instead, would encourage manumission. Moderates even read the fugitive slave clause to restrict federal support for the return of runaways, arguing that it did not permit federal action but was merely an admonition to the states. Constitutional provisions giving Congress full authority over the District of Columbia and the territories, antislavery moderates asserted, also enabled it to strike at slavery by abolishing it in the District and, following the example of the Northwest Ordinance, forbidding it to enter the territories.

The most innovative aspect of the moderate position was its use of the Fifth Amendment's due process clause. Traditionally, lawyers understood due process to guarantee persons accused of crimes certain procedural rights such as the right to be informed of the charges against them, the right to counsel, the right to trial by jury, and protection against self-incrimination. Abolitionists, however, gave the clause a substantive interpretation, suggesting that there were certain fundamental rights—such as liberty of movement, freedom to pursue the occupation of one's choosing, and the absolute right of self-ownership—that government could not abridge. Consequently, they argued that slavery was an obvious violation of the due process clause and that the federal government could not tolerate it anywhere within its jurisdiction, whether in the District of Columbia or the territories.

Moderates asserted that the framers had intended to make slavery a local institution, confined to the southeastern states, where it would gradually wither and die. This farsighted policy, they contended, had been subverted by proslavery domination of the national government which had resulted in federal action to protect slavery and, worst of all, to promote its expansion. Moderates thus called for a return to the original principles of the founders: the federal government must divorce itself from slavery, abolishing it in the District of Columbia and the territories, repealing the Fugitive Slave Act, and prohibiting the transit of slaves in interstate commerce. Because moderate abolitionists, like most other Americans, believed that slavery had to expand to remain economically viable, they assumed that this would put slavery on the road to extinction, as the founders had intended.

A number of radical abolitionist legal theorists, most notably Alvan Stewart, William Goodell, Lysander Spooner, and Joel Tiffany, took this argument further. Radicals argued that all persons possessed certain natural rights, including freedom, personal security, and a right to the fruits of their labor, and that government existed to guarantee these rights. Although this led them to the radical conclusion that Congress had an obligation to extirpate slavery, they drew on a tradition of natural rights that had deep roots not only in popular political culture but in Constitutional theory. Indeed, United States Supreme Court Justices

Samuel Chase, John Marshall, and Joseph Story had suggested that statutes that violated principles of natural law lacked legitimacy. In using the Declaration of Independence as the authority to attack slavery, radicals also appealed to deeply rooted values that had broad popular appeal. They argued that the Declaration contained the principles on which the nation had been founded and asserted that the framers had intended to implement these principles when they drafted the Constitution. To accept the Constitution as a substitute for the Declaration, they insisted, "would be to accept the shell, and throw the kernel away."[7] They contended, therefore, that principles of natural rights and equality suffused the Constitution, empowering—indeed, requiring—Congress to abolish slavery throughout the nation.

Radicals also found warrant for emancipation in the text of the Constitution. They argued that the Fifth Amendment's due process clause applied not only to the federal government but to the states and prohibited them from enforcing the laws that maintained slavery. Although the Supreme Court had held that the Bill of Rights restricted only the federal government, the radical position was not chimerical. As agitators for constitutional change, they could hope to convince the Court to reverse itself, as it had done on more than one occasion. Indeed, unlike the First Amendment which explicitly restricts Congress, the wording of the Fifth Amendment ("No person shall be . . . deprived. . . .") could be easily construed to apply to state governments, giving the Court an opening to reverse itself. Radicals also exploited the guarantee clause (Article IV, section 4) which provided that "the United States shall guarantee to each State in this Union a Republican form of Government." Because slavery created a privileged caste and stripped blacks of the most fundamental rights, they argued, no state that tolerated slavery could be truly republican. Radicals therefore concluded that Congress could only fulfill its obligation under the guarantee clause by abolishing slavery in any state that maintained it.

Abolitionists also devoted considerable attention to the plight of free blacks. Black abolitionists were especially sensitive to this issue because they understood the social consequences of discrimination. They realized that discriminatory law was not merely an effect of racism, but that it marked blacks as inferiors and thus deepened the racism that constrained black economic opportunity. "The colored people of this State are, from the non-possession of the right of suffrage, the proscribed class," representatives of New York's black community explained. "This proscription is the fountain Marah, from whence proceed those bitter waters that run through all the various ramifications of society, connecting themselves with all our relations. . . ." Black leaders also understood that only by asserting their right to equal treatment could blacks achieve self-respect. As Michigan blacks noted in demanding political rights, "the enjoyment of those rights in a free country, is a stimulant to enterprise, a means of influence, and a source of respect; they send life, vigor and energy through the entire heart of a people. . . ."[8]

Black abolitionists, together with their white allies, built their case for equal rights on the foundation of black citizenship. They argued that native-born free blacks were citizens of the state where they resided and of the United States. They pointed out that European, English, and American authorities agreed that "the strongest claim to citizenship is birthplace" and that "in whatever country or place you may be born, you are in the first and highest sense a citizen." "The claims are . . . founded in the fact that they [blacks] are citizens by birth and blood," noted Hosea Easton, a black minister, in 1837. "Complexion has never been made the legal test of citizenship in any age in the world. It has been established generally by birth and blood. . . ."[9] Because the framers did not explicitly define citizenship, abolitionists contended, they must be presumed to have accepted this common understanding. The most potent argument on behalf of black citizenship, however, grew out of the historical memory of the black community. Black abolitionists reminded Americans that in 1787 free blacks had been citizens with access to the ballot box in many states and that they had shouldered the responsibilities of citizens, serving with distinction in the Revolution and the War of 1812. "We are Americans. We were born in no foreign clime," explained the report of the 1840 New York State Convention of Colored People. "We have not been brought up under the influence of other strange, aristocratic, and uncongenial political relations. In this respect, we profess to be American and republican."[10]

Abolitionists argued that if they were to be true to the principles of republicanism and the ideas expressed in the Declaration of Independence, states must grant all citizens equal rights, regardless of race. "That Declaration, and that Constitution . . . may be considered as more fully developing the ideas of American republicanism, than any other documents," delegates to the 1840 New York Convention of Colored Men asserted in a petition calling for an end to discriminatory voting requirements. "In these, individuals are regarded distinctly and respectively—each and every one as men, fully capacitated by the Creator for government and progressive advancement. . . .'' Members of the Liberty party agreed. The party's 1844 platform urged ''the friends of Liberty in all those free States where any inequality of rights and privileges exists on account of color, to employ their utmost energies to remove all such remnants and effects of the slave system.''[11]

Many abolitionists went beyond this, urging that the national government had authority to protect individual rights against infringement by the states. Radical constitutional theorists, most notably Joel Tiffany and Lysander Spooner, argued that the national government, by its very nature, had the authority, indeed, the obligation to protect the fundamental rights of its citizens. Such rights included ''full and ample protection. . . of . . . personal security, personal liberty, and private property, . . . protection against the oppression of individuals, communities and nations, foreign nations and domestic states: against lawless violence exercised under the forms of governmental authority.''[12] Moreover, Tiffany and Spooner insisted that the Constitution and Bill of Rights were designed to protect these fundamental rights from encroachment by national and state governments and private individuals.

In the antebellum federal system, as we have seen, states were free to define the rights of individuals with only minimal interference or supervision by the national government. Consequently, Tiffany's and Spooner's argument was truly radical. While it would enter political discourse and become influential in the 1860s, it had limited utility in the antebellum years. Not only did it go against the assumptions of most Americans, who saw local autonomy as essential to democracy and necessary to the continued existence of a nation as large and diverse as the United States. But with the federal courts, Congress, and the presidency in the hands of those sympathetic to slavery, it made little sense to press for federal action against state discrimination. Nevertheless, other aspects of the abolitionist argument, especially the notion that black citizenship, the Declaration of Independence, and the principles of republicanism made it impermissible to make distinctions in state law based on race, proved more serviceable. Consequently, black leaders and their white allies employed these ideas to challenge discrimination by state and local governments.

Consider two examples. During the early nineteenth century the Boston School Committee established a separate elementary school for black children and excluded blacks from the city's other elementary schools. During the 1840s, after a campaign of sit-ins and political action that compelled the state's railroads to end segregation, Boston blacks trained their sights on segregated schools. When in 1849 the committee rejected petitions calling for admission of blacks to the white schools, Benjamin Roberts, a black activist whose six-year-old daughter Sarah had been denied admission to the school closest to her home, challenged school segregation in the Massachusetts courts.

Robert Morris, a black lawyer, and Charles Sumner, a white abolitionist who would go on to a distinguished career in the United States Senate, represented Roberts. Building their case on the Declaration of Independence and the Massachusetts Constitution's assertion that "All men are created free and equal," they rejected the Boston School Committee's contention that it provided blacks with an equal, but separate, education. Morris and Sumner argued that segregation recognized distinctions among citizens on the basis of birth and therefore violated the principle of equality. "The equality declared by our fathers . . . was *Equality before the Law*," they explained. "Its object was to efface all political or civil distinctions, and to abolish all institutions founded upon *birth*." Morris and Sumner also charged that segregation hurt blacks by marking them as a proscribed class and teaching white children to despise them. "Nursed in this sentiment of Caste . . . they [whites] are unable to eradicate it from their natures . . . and . . . continue to embody and perpetuate it in their institutions."[13] The Massachusetts Supreme Judicial Court rejected these arguments, holding that as long as blacks enjoyed access to schools that provided an education equivalent to that provided to whites, the Constitution's guarantee of equality was met. Undaunted by their failure in court, blacks turned their attention to the legislature, which recognized their claim to substantive equality by outlawing segregation in the state's schools in 1855.

Blacks in New York City also challenged segregation. Manhattan's numerous street railroads, operated by private companies under charters from the city, offered thoroughly segregated service. Black customers might ride outside on the platforms of the cars reserved for whites or wait for one of the few cars set aside for the exclusive use of blacks. Shortly after the street railroads began their operations in the early 1850s, blacks engaged in direct action to challenge segregation, entering whites-only cars, refusing to leave, and, usually, being assaulted and thrown into the streets by drivers and conductors. In 1854, Elizabeth Jennings sued the Third Avenue Railroad after being forcibly expelled from a whites-only car, and a jury awarded her $225 in damages. Black leaders used Jennings's victory to encourage black assertiveness. "Don't let them [railroad officials] frighten you with words," one urged, "the law is right, and so is public sentiment."[14]

Most of the companies, however, continued to practice segregation. In 1855, Reverend James Pennington, a black Presbyterian minister, was thrown out of a whites-only car on the Sixth Avenue Railroad. Seeking another legal victory that would seal the fate of segregation, Pennington sued the company. He argued that, as a citizen, he was entitled to service without distinction or discrimination from a company that was chartered to serve the public. As the suit dragged on, Pennington and other black leaders encouraged continued resistance to segregation by forming the Legal Rights Association, an organization designed "to raise means to protect persons who are assaulted while standing up for their rights." The association did not win a ruling against segregation, however. When Pennington's case went to trial, the judge informed the jury that the companies might make reasonable rules and regulations to govern passengers. In deciding whether rules prescribing segregated service were reasonable, he added, jurors must consider "the probable effect upon the capital, business and interests of companies admitting blacks into their cars indiscriminately with whites." Not surprisingly, the jury decided against Pennington. Despite this setback, the city's blacks continued to enter whites-only cars, convincing some, but not all, of the companies to abandon segregation.[15] Thus in New York, as in Boston, equalitarian ideas served as a rallying point for blacks, encouraging them to assert their rights and challenge the caste system.

Antislavery Constitutionalism Enters the Political Mainstream

The political crisis of the late 1840s and 1850s broadened the appeal of abolitionist constitutional ideas, giving them currency outside the ranks of northern blacks and white abolitionists. The annexation of Texas in 1845 and the Mexican War of 1846–1848 added the vast territories of the Southwest to the Republic. They also ignited a bitter debate over slavery and whether it should be permitted in the newly acquired territories. While Congress patched over the territorial question in the Compromise of 1850, a part of the compromise, the draconian Fugitive Slave Act of

1850, brought the grim reality of slavery to northern attention as slaveowners stepped up efforts to capture runaways, and blacks and abolitionists resisted. While this perceptibly increased northern antislavery sentiment, it was the Kansas-Nebraska Act of 1854 that irreversibly damaged sectional harmony. By accepting southern demands for repeal of the Missouri Compromise's exclusion of slavery from the two territories, Congress appeared to many northerners to be in the grip of proslavery forces intent on expanding slavery and, concomitantly, southern political power. Northerners flocked to the Republican party, which emerged in the uproar over the Kansas-Nebraska Act, calling for an end to southern domination of the national government, denouncing the social system of the slave South, and demanding containment of slavery.

The new party made the Kansas-Nebraska Act and the issue of slavery extension matters of vital importance to northerners. Republicans denounced the Kansas-Nebraska bill as yet another example of slaveholders' domination of the national government. Embracing the abolitionist interpretation of the Constitution as an antislavery document, they contended that the Kansas-Nebraska Act subverted the design of the framers and further eroded the principles of equality and natural rights on which the nation had been founded. They also argued that the expansion of slavery had serious social consequences for whites; slavery destroyed the work ethic by associating labor with a despised caste, discouraged whites from diligent toil, and thereby deprived individuals of the means of advancement. If slavery took root in the West, Republicans warned, it would diminish opportunities there for aspiring northerners and increase the strength of a decadent social system. Even though the party won virtually no support in the South, it spread triumphantly across the North and enjoyed substantial strength in Congress by 1855 and came remarkably close to winning the presidency in 1856.

Despite Republican denunciation of the South and slavery, it was not an abolitionist party and in fact sought to distance itself from the abolitionists. Republicans did promise to stop the spread of slavery, which they asserted would lead to the gradual death of slavery where it already existed; however, they were eager to dispel the charge that they were irresponsible fanatics who threatened the Union and repeatedly said that the national government had no authority to interfere with slavery in those states that sanctioned it. Moreover, Republicans, themselves by no means free of prejudice, realized the depth of northern racism and trimmed their position accordingly. In the face of taunts by Democrats denouncing them as proponents of Negro equality who condoned interracial marriage, most Republicans repeatedly proclaimed that they did not support black suffrage or social contacts between the races. In addition, many Republicans asserted that colonization was the best solution to the nation's racial problem and enthusiastically supported schemes to encourage free blacks to emigrate and establish colonies in the Caribbean, Central America, and Africa.

The party, nonetheless, took a position on black rights that reflected the influence of abolitionist constitutional ideas and was in advance of northern public opinion. Republicans agreed with non-Garrisonian abolitionists that the framers of the Constitution had attempted to prevent the spread of slavery and had hoped to set it on the path to extinction. Like moderate abolitionists, they asserted that the Fifth Amendment's due process clause guaranteed all persons freedom and natural rights and of its own force abolished slavery in all areas—such as the territories—under the exclusive control of the national government. Many Republicans also contended that native-born free blacks were state citizens and thus entitled to rights guaranteed by the United States Constitution. During the late 1850s Republican conventions in several states affirmed that free blacks were citizens, as did Republican-controlled legislatures in New Hampshire, New York, Vermont, and Ohio, and the Republican justices on the Maine Supreme Court.

Perhaps even more remarkable, given widespread northern racism, Republicans argued that the principles of the Declaration of Independence were the foundation of republican government and applied to all persons, regardless of race. Granted, they hedged their position, explaining that this did not entitle blacks to political rights or to social equality. What it did guarantee, they asserted, was equality of civil and natural rights. Thus while most Republicans did not believe that free blacks were entitled to the right to vote or to service in hotels and restaurants frequented by whites, they did insist that all free men should enjoy the same rights to freedom of movement, to own and control property, to testify in courts, and to the protection of the laws. Abraham Lincoln best articulated this position in his 1858 debates with Stephen Douglas. He admitted that he had "no purpose to introduce political and social equality between the white and the black races," but asserted that "there is no reason in the world why the negro is not entitled to all the natural rights enumerated in the Declaration of Independence. . . . I hold that he is as much entitled to these as the white man."[16] Indeed, Republicans worked to guarantee blacks' civil rights: in Ohio they blocked efforts by Democrats to pass legislation barring black immigration (the state's old antiimmigration laws had been repealed in 1849); in Indiana and Illinois they unsuccessfully supported repeal of laws excluding black immigration; in New Hampshire they repealed the law excluding blacks from the militia; and in Iowa they repealed the statute prohibiting blacks from testifying against whites.

Not only did mainstream Republicans offer cautious support for freedom and black rights, a powerful minority of genuine radicals pressed the party to claim higher ground. Salmon Chase, Joshua Giddings, and Charles Sumner were influential Republican radicals, and all three had played a role in developing abolitionist constitutional ideas. Their presence in party councils guaranteed a hearing for these ideas. Most radicals, for example, urged the party to support political as well as civil equality for blacks, and in several states—Iowa (1857), Wisconsin (1857), and New York (1860)—they had sufficient influence to persuade state legislatures to authorize referenda on black suffrage. Although black suffrage was rejected in all three states with many (and in Iowa most) Republicans voting against it, radicals' success in forcing the party to bring the issue before the electorate suggested that they were capable of moving the party.

The Climax of Proslavery Constitutionalism

Although Republicans offered a genuine challenge to proslavery constitutionalism, opponents of slavery were not optimistic as the 1850s drew to a close. A solidly proslavery administration controlled the presidency, and southerners in Congress pressed their demand for a federal code establishing and protecting slavery in the territories. Even more distressing, the Supreme Court, in its 1857 ruling in *Dred Scott* v. *Sandford*, offered a stinging rejection of antislavery constitutionalism and a resounding affirmation of the South's views on slavery in the territories and black citizenship.

Dred Scott began his long, tortuous road to the Supreme Court when he accompanied his owner, an Army surgeon named John Emerson, on a long tour of duty in Illinois and the Wisconsin Territory during the 1830s. In 1846, after he had returned to St. Louis and Dr. Emerson had died, Scott obtained the services of several local lawyers and sued Irene

Emerson, the doctor's wife, for his freedom. He argued that during his travels with Dr. Emerson, he had lived for two years in the free state of Illinois and for three years in Wisconsin Territory, where the Missouri Compromise of 1820 prohibited slavery. Since slavery was illegal in both places, Scott claimed, he had become a free man and was illegally held in bondage. The proceedings in state circuit court ended with a verdict for Scott, but Mrs. Emerson appealed. In 1852 the Missouri Supreme Court overturned the decision of the lower court, holding that under principles of comity[17] Missouri courts were not bound to enforce the law of another state or territory that was against its policies. In a departure from its earlier decisions, the court ruled that Missouri did not accept and would not give effect to the laws of states which freed slaves who were temporarily taken there by their owners. Whatever Scott's status had been in Illinois or Wisconsin, he was still a slave in Missouri.

Scott, however, refused to give up. In 1850, Irene Emerson had remarried and left Missouri, and her brother, John Sanford (the Supreme Court's reporter spelled his name incorrectly, making him San*d*ford in the title of the case), had gained control of Scott. Because Sanford was a citizen of New York (he frequently traveled to St. Louis on business), Scott was able to begin his freedom suit anew in federal court. Under Article III of the Constitution and the Judiciary Act of 1789, United States circuit courts had jurisdiction over cases between citizens of different states, and Scott claimed that this allowed him, as a citizen of Missouri suing a New Yorker, to have a hearing in the United States circuit court in St. Louis. Yet Scott fared no better in the new forum; the trial in federal court ended in 1854 with a jury verdict against him.

Scott appealed to the United States Supreme Court, but he had little reason to expect victory. Chief Justice Roger B. Taney and four of his colleagues were southerners, and two northern justices were Democrats sympathetic to the South and slavery. Moreover, Taney's opinion for the Court in *Strader* v. *Graham* (1851) boded ill for Scott. The chief justice had asserted that when slaves returned to a slave state after having traveled or resided in a free state, the courts of the slave state could decide whether they had become free or remained in bondage. Because Missouri's highest court had already ruled against Scott on this very point, the *Strader* precedent seemed to doom his chance for victory in the United States Supreme Court. There was little surprise, therefore, in early 1857 when the Court ruled against Scott by a 7–2 majority. Nonetheless, few observers could have predicted that the Court would issue such a sweeping proslavery polemic. But the chief justice and his southern brethren, embittered and threatened by the rising tide of northern antislavery sentiment, were determined to slay the twin dragons of abolitionist equalitarianism and Republican antiextensionism.

Each justice wrote an opinion, and historians have endlessly debated what (beyond the fact that Scott was still a slave) the Court actually decided. The chief justice's opinion, however, was authoritative. Not only did a majority authorize Taney to write "the opinion of the Court," but as Don Fehrenbacher notes in his Pulitzer Prize-winning study of the case, "Taney's opinion was accepted as the opinion of the Court by its critics as well as its defenders."[18] Taney held that the circuit court should have dismissed the case for want of jurisdiction. Because Scott was a Negro, he explained, he could not be a citizen, even if free, and therefore he had no right to sue in federal court on the basis of diversity of citizenship. He reinforced this position by arguing that Scott could not be a citizen because he was a slave. The Missouri Compromise, which Scott claimed had made him free, was unconstitutional because Congress lacked authority to exclude slavery from the territories.

Taney's holding that free blacks were not United States citizens was a shot at antislavery constitutionalism. The chief justice asserted that at the time of the Revolution and the Constitutional Convention, Americans regarded blacks as inferior beings who had "no rights which the white man was bound to respect."[19] Consequently, the framers of the Constitution had not regarded blacks as citizens of the United States. Because United States citizenship gave persons certain rights that were enforceable throughout the United States, Taney argued that no state could confer United States citizenship on blacks merely by making them state citizens. To do so would enable a single state to confer national citizenship on a group that the states had collectively excluded when the Constitution was adopted. Thus even if Scott was a citizen under Missouri law, he could not be a United States citizen entitled to rights (such as bringing suit in federal court on the basis of diversity of citizenship) created by the United States Constitution.

Taney's analysis not only rested on bad history, but on a careless reading of the Constitution. The Constitution did not define national citizenship and crucial provisions guaranteed rights, not to United States citizens, but to state citizens. The chief justice's poorly reasoned argument was, nevertheless, purposeful. By denying that free blacks were entitled to rights under the Constitution (including those conferred by the privileges and immunities clause) he enabled southern states to prevent the entry of free blacks from other states and thus to protect themselves from outside agitators bent on fomenting slave insurrections. Moreover, by excluding free blacks from citizenship, he reinforced the principles of white supremacy which undergirded the South's slave system.

The second part of Taney's ruling—that Scott's residence on free soil had not made him free—was equally polemical and unpersuasive. Here the question of Scott's freedom involved residence in a free state and in a territory where Congress had prohibited slavery. Taney realized that his agenda would be ill-served by first addressing himself to the effect of Scott's residence in Illinois. If he ruled (as he subsequently did) that it did not affect Scott's status once he returned to Missouri because Missouri law denied that temporary residence on free soil freed slaves, he would also dispose of the effect of Scott's residence in Wisconsin Territory. Consequently, Taney turned first to Scott's sojourn in Wisconsin Territory, arguing that residence there did not free Scott because Congress did not have the authority to exclude slavery from the territories. Therefore the prohibition on slavery contained in the Missouri Compromise, which Scott claimed made him free, was unconstitutional and of no effect. Only after he had disposed of Scott's claim to freedom on the basis of living in Wisconsin Territory did Taney turn to Scott's Illinois sojourn, ruling that it did not affect Scott's status once he returned to Missouri.

The chief justice's attack on the Missouri Compromise was as poorly argued as his polemic on citizenship. Despite the clear language of Article IV, section 3, authorizing Congress to "make all needful Rules and Regulations respecting the Territory and other property belonging to the United States," Taney flirted with the implausible argument that Congress did not have authority to govern the territories; however, he ultimately retreated from this position. While it would have denied Congress the power to prohibit slavery in the territories, it would also have taken away Congress's authority to enact a slave code for the territories, which was rapidly becoming a crucial southern demand.

This led Taney to focus on the rights of the residents of the territories. Turning abolitionist constitutionalism on its head, he suggested that the Fifth Amendment's due process clause prohibited Congress from excluding slavery from the territories because to do so would interfere with the property rights of slaveowners who migrated there, depriving them of their slave property. This remained a suggestion; however, as Professor Fehrenbacher notes, Taney did not explicitly declare the Missouri

Compromise unconstitutional on due process grounds. He also flirted with the notion, popularized by the great proslavery theorist John C. Calhoun, that the territories were the common property of the states, held in trust for them by the national government. Congress, Taney hinted, could not prejudice the rights of the southern states by preventing their citizens from migrating to the territories with their property. Yet he failed to develop this argument fully or use it to strike down the Compromise's ban on slavery. He also asserted that the Constitution "distinctly and expressly affirmed" the right to slave property and, in the fugitive slave clause, pledged the national government to protect it. While this assertion accurately stated the proslavery reading of the Constitution, it was (as we have seen) a distorted reading of the Constitution itself. Nevertheless, Taney contended that Congress did not have "greater power over slave property . . . than property of any other description" and that "the only power conferred is the power coupled with the duty of guarding and protecting the owner in his rights."[20] Yet he did not explicitly conclude from these assertions that Congress lacked authority to exclude slavery from the territories. Indeed, while Taney clearly declared the antislavery provision of the Missouri Compromise unconstitutional, he did not explain precisely his grounds for doing so.

Despite the manifest weaknesses of Taney's argument, it dealt a devastating, if temporary, blow to antislavery constitutionalism and the Republican party. In declaring that blacks, whether free or slave, were not citizens and were not entitled to constitutional rights, he undermined one of the strongest arguments for black rights. In asserting that Congress did not have the power to exclude slavery from the territories and hinting that it had an obligation to protect it there, he also repudiated important abolitionist constitutional ideas. According to Taney, the Constitution, far from being intended to promote freedom in all areas save the states in which it had already been established, demanded that slavery be allowed and perhaps promoted except in those states that explicitly excluded it. Turning the abolitionist argument on its head, Taney asserted that slavery was national and freedom local. The chief justice also repudiated the Republican program, saying, in effect, that the key element in the party's platform was unconstitutional.

Abolitionists and Republicans subjected Taney's opinion to withering criticism. Lincoln, for example, refused to accept the *Dred Scott* case as the final word on the subject, noting that the Supreme Court did not have exclusive authority to interpret the Constitution and that courts sometimes reversed themselves. Nevertheless, the Court's ruling, when coupled with memories of the annexation of Texas, the Fugitive Slave Act of 1850, and the Kansas-Nebraska Act, did little to encourage faith in the triumph of antislavery constitutionalism. Indeed, Lincoln and many Republicans predicted that the Court would soon hand down an opinion prohibiting the northern states from excluding slavery, thus completing the process of nationalizing the institution. Among northern blacks, the decision was the latest blow to the dream that one day they would enjoy true freedom and equality in their native land. Consequently, it gave impetus to the black emigration movement that already had the support of such prominent leaders as Henry Highland Garnet, Martin Delany, Robert Campbell, and H. Ford Douglas.

Despair was not uniform, however. Frederick Douglass argued that antislavery forces had "nothing to fear" from the *Dred Scott* decision. "The whole history of the antislavery movement," he explained, "is studded with proof that all measures devised and executed . . . to . . . diminish the antislavery agitation, have only served to increase, intensify, and embolden that agitation." Douglass argued that the true principles embodied in the Constitution would ultimately triumph and allay the possibility that "it might be necessary for my people to look for a home in some other country."[21] Of course, the events of the 1860s would at least partially vindicate Douglass's faith. Taney's proslavery Constitution would be swept away and a new Constitution, informed by the antislavery ideas that emerged in the dark days of the 1840s and 1850s would emerge. This new Constitution, the more perfect Union, however, would be forged, not solely through normal political and constitutional processes, but on the bloody fields of Antietam, Gettysburg, Cold Harbor, and Petersburg.

3

The National Commitment to
Civil Equality, 1861–1870

On August 21, 1872, seven years after the Civil War had ended, Mary Coger, a teacher from Quincy, Illinois, prepared to return home after visiting friends in Keokuk, Iowa. Although her complexion was fair, Coger had one black grandparent, making her a Negro in the eyes of race-conscious nineteenth-century American whites. When she went to the office of the North West Union Packet Company to purchase a ticket for passage aboard the Mississippi River steamer, *S.S. Merrill*, the agent detected her African ancestry and refused to sell her a first-class ticket. Following company policy, he offered her passage without a private sleeping berth or access to the dining room. Coger demanded first-class passage and initially refused to purchase a ticket when the agent refused. She finally relented, accepting a ticket entitling her to separate and unequal accommodations.

Aboard the steamer, Coger continued to encounter demeaning treatment. When she sent the ship's chambermaid to purchase a dinner ticket for her, she received a pass marked "colored girl," not "lady," the term of respect universally applied to middle-class white women, and was informed that she would be served in the pantry. Refusing to accept such treatment, she persuaded a white traveler to purchase a first-class dining ticket for her. When dinner was announced, she entered the cabin, took a seat at a table reserved for ladies traveling without male escort, and refused to move when a waiter ordered her to the pantry. The dining room abuzz over the confrontation, the captain appeared, demanded that Coger leave the ladies' table, and attempted to remove her. Coger resisted "so that considerable violence was necessary to drag her out of the cabin, and, in the struggle, the covering of the table was torn off and dishes broken, and the officer received a slight injury."[1]

Determined to challenge such degrading treatment, Mary Coger filed suit in state district court, seeking damages from the company for the assault on her by its employees. She alleged that the Iowa Constitution, which declared that "All men are, by nature, free and equal," entitled her to colorblind service on the *Merrill*, which had a common law obligation to serve the public. She also claimed that changes in federal law and the United States Constitution growing out of the abolition of slavery and the postwar effort to protect the rights of the former slaves reinforced this right. The Fourteenth Amendment, ratified in 1868, not only conferred national and state citizenship on blacks, but prohibited discrimination, stipulating that no state "shall deny . . . any person . . . equal protection of the laws." Moreover, Coger pointed out that Congress's Civil Rights Act of 1866 provided that all citizens were entitled to "the same right . . . to make and enforce contracts . . . as is enjoyed by white persons." Because a steamboat ticket was a contract, she contended, the company was obligated to offer her the same ticket and service that it offered white women.[2]

The state courts sustained Coger's position. In his charge to the jury, the trial court judge explained that, while the company might make reasonable rules and regulations, it could not make distinctions among passengers on the basis of race. When the jury returned a verdict for Coger, the company appealed to the Iowa Supreme Court, which upheld the lower court. Chief Justice Joseph M. Beck's opinion indicated that he was not free of racial stereotypes, noting that Coger's "spirited resistance . . . exhibited evidence of the Anglo-Saxon blood that flows in her veins." He nonetheless rejected the company's claim that it was free to practice racial segregation. Dismissing as irrelevant arguments concerning Coger's race, Beck paid tribute to the radical transformation brought about by emancipation and postwar constitutional change. "However pertinent to such a case the discussion may have been, not many years ago . . . the doctrines and authorities involved in the argument are obsolete, and have no longer existence or authority, anywhere within the jurisdiction of the federal constitution, and most certainly not in Iowa," Beck explained. Equality before the law, "the very foundation principle of our government," had been expressly extended to include blacks by the Fourteenth Amendment and the Civil

Rights Act of 1866. "If the negro must submit to different treatment, to accommodations inferior to those given to the white man, when transported by public carriers," Beck concluded, "he is deprived of the benefits of this very principle of equality."[3]

Although it had authority only within Iowa, Beck's opinion suggested how far the revolutionary upheaval of the Civil War and Reconstruction had moved the nation. Only a dozen years before, the United States Supreme Court's holding that blacks were not citizens had stood as the supreme law of the land, and Republican critics of slavery had been tentative in their support for black rights. Under the pressure of Civil War, however, Lincoln and the Republican leadership in Congress embraced emancipation as a war goal and recruited 180,000 black troops to help subdue the Confederacy. In the war's aftermath Republican leaders, determined to secure the fruits of victory, were pulled inexorably toward abolitionist constitutionalism. They not only removed the incubus of *Dred Scott* and admitted blacks to citizenship, but expanded federal responsibility for protecting individual rights from violation by states and individuals, thereby significantly altering the antebellum federal system. Furthermore, they moved beyond antebellum distinctions between civil (or legal) rights and political rights, extending to blacks the full rights of citizenship, including the right to vote. Well might Daniel Corbin, a South Carolina Republican, remark in 1871, "we have lived over a century in the last ten years."[4]

War, Emancipation, and Equal Rights

In the spring and summer of 1861, few predicted the revolutionary consequences of the Civil War for American constitutionalism and the rights of blacks. Lincoln and Republican leaders in Congress made it clear that they prosecuted the war in order to preserve the Union, not to extirpate slavery. Although hostile to slavery, they entered the war clinging to the time-honored notion that slavery was a local institution and that the national government lacked constitutional authority to interfere with it in any state that chose to sanction it. More to the point, expediency militated against antislavery action. Republicans needed support from their Democratic opponents if they were to unite the nation (or what remained of it) behind the war effort, and many northern Democrats were willing to support a war to preserve the Union but not an antislavery crusade. Then, too, four border slave states—Delaware, Maryland, Kentucky, and Missouri—remained in the Union despite pressure from secessionists. Embracing emancipation as a war aim might drive these states and their considerable resources into the Confederacy. In a message to Congress on July 4, 1861, Lincoln explained that his administration had "no purpose, directly or indirectly, to interfere with the institution of slavery in the States where it exists." Several weeks later Congress, with little dissent, passed a joint resolution declaring that the United States government had no intention of "overthrowing or interfering with the rights or established institutions" of the rebel states, but sought only "to defend and maintain the supremacy of the Constitution and to preserve the Union."[5]

Although impatient with such timidity, abolitionists rallied to support the war effort, perceiving that, for the first time in the nation's history, the exigencies of preserving the Union would promote black liberty. From the outset, northern blacks, abolitionists, and Republican radicals argued that the Union could be saved only by abolishing slavery. Because slavery had pushed the nation to war, restoration of the Union without abolition, they claimed, would prove illusory. "Slavery is the disease, and its abolition in every part of the land is essential to the future quiet and security of the country," argued Frederick Douglass in early 1861. They also pointed out that, as an integral part of the southern economy, slavery supported the rebellion. Slave laborers in southern fields and factories— not to mention the tens of thousands of blacks who built fortifications and roads for the Confederate army—provided crucial support to the rebellion and freed white men for combat service. A forthright policy of emancipation would not only weaken the Confederacy's ability to fight, but, coupled with an aggressive program of recruiting black troops, would strengthen Union forces. "[M]ore effective remedies ought now to be *thoroughly* tried, in the shape of warm lead and cold steel," a meeting of New York blacks urged, "duly administered by two hundred thousand black doctors."[6]

Prodded by abolitionists, Republican leaders soon began to reassess the government's policy with respect to slavery. Aware that victory would not be achieved quickly or easily and that slavery supported the Confederacy, Republicans began to find antislavery action more attractive. Expediency alone did not drive Republicans to act, however. Democrats like Horatio Seymour and George B. McClellan were no less committed to preserving the Union than Republicans, but their proslavery attitudes led them to balk at antislavery measures as a means to that end. Because Republicans had entered the war opposed to slavery on moral grounds, they were more inclined to equate antislavery action with military necessity. Indeed, the expediency of antislavery measures complemented Republican antislavery inclinations. By linking antislavery policies with preservation of the Union, Republicans were able to deflect the charge that they were fanatics willing to sacrifice white soldiers for black liberty. The military necessity argument also permitted Republicans to invoke the Constitution's war powers to attack slavery, helping them transcend concerns about the constitutionality of antislavery action. As LaWanda Cox has explained in her analysis of the Republican president, "Lincoln was alert to the expanding potential created by war. Military needs . . . did not force him upon an alien course but helped clear a path toward a long-desired but intractable objective."[7]

During the first half of 1862, Republicans invoked the concept of military necessity and the war powers to justify radical antislavery action. After abolishing slavery in the District of Columbia and the territories, areas clearly within Congress's jurisdiction, Republicans turned on slavery in the states, something that even moderate abolitionists had admitted to be unconstitutional fifteen months before. The war had changed things, Republicans argued. By giving Congress the power to declare war, to raise and make regulations for armies and navies, and to provide for calling out the militia to suppress insurrection, the Constitution conferred on it broad war powers that it might use to enact legislation, even antislavery legislation, necessary to prosecute the war. In July 1862, Congress invoked this power to pass a Confiscation Act that authorized seizure of property owned by persons who aided or abetted the rebellion.[8] With respect to human property, it stipulated that slaves owned by rebels "shall be forever free of their servitude" on entering Union lines, thus providing a legal claim to freedom for tens of thousands of slaves who had fled to Union forces by the summer of 1862.[9]

At the time Congress passed the Confiscation Act, Lincoln initiated sweeping action against slavery. On July 21, 1862, he informed members of his cabinet that, under his constitutional authority as commander-in-chief, he would issue a proclamation freeing all slaves in areas that were in rebellion against the United States. Heeding the advice of Secretary of State William H. Seward, who argued that recent Union military defeats would make the proclamation look like a desperate appeal for European support, Lincoln agreed to await a Union victory. On September 22, after

Union troops turned back a Confederate invasion of Maryland, he promptly issued a preliminary proclamation, promising that if the rebellion continued on January 1, he would free all slaves in states and parts of states under rebel control. On New Year's Day, 1863, as northern blacks and abolitionists crowded churches and public halls throughout the North in celebration, Lincoln proclaimed the Jubilee.

Many historians have characterized the Proclamation as an act of expediency or even a meaningless sham. Because it applied only to slaves within rebel lines and not to those in the border states or parts of the Confederacy occupied by Union troops on January 1, 1863, they argue that it actually freed no slaves. Critics have also claimed that the text appealed to military necessity, not moral principle, and had "all the moral grandeur of a bill of lading."[10] These charges distort the Proclamation by taking it out of its political and constitutional context. While Lincoln hoped to cripple the Confederacy, he equally welcomed the opportunity to act on antislavery principles he had espoused for years. He couched the document in terms of military necessity because his constitutional authority as commander-in-chief permitted him to free slaves as an act of war, but not to strike at slavery as a moral evil. This also helps explain why Lincoln did not free slaves within Union lines. To have done so could not have been justified as an act of war aimed at weakening the enemy, and it would have opened Lincoln to charges of usurpation and provided critics ammunition to attack the Proclamation's constitutionality. Moreover, Lincoln used the military necessity argument to assuage conservatives who supported the war effort but opposed black liberty. By tying emancipation to preservation of the Union, he created a broader base of popular support for black freedom, transforming the war into a struggle for liberty and Union. Finally, while the Proclamation freed no slaves at the moment it was promulgated, it brought freedom to hundreds of thousands of slaves in the ensuing months as Union troops pushed deeper into the Confederacy.

Because the Proclamation left many slaves—including most of those in the border states—in bondage and was almost certain to be challenged in the courts, Republicans employed the amendment process to make emancipation universal and irreversible. Senate Republicans mustered enough votes to pass an antislavery amendment in early 1864, but despite solid Republican support, the House fell several votes shy of the two-thirds majority necessary to pass it. On January 31, 1865, however, with Lincoln promising patronage to gain votes from the opposition, Congress passed an amendment prohibiting slavery and involuntary servitude in the United States and giving Congress authority to enforce the prohibition. Before the year was out, three-fourths of the state legislatures had given their assent, and the Thirteenth Amendment became part of the Constitution.

The amendment significantly altered the American constitutional order. Prior to its adoption, most judges, lawyers, and politicians had agreed that slavery was beyond the reach of the national government and that states possessed almost unlimited authority to define and protect individual rights. By banning slavery and giving Congress enforcement power, the new amendment expanded national power and limited the authority of the states, although the extent to which it did so depended on how slavery was defined. If it merely meant chattel slavery—ownership of one person by another—Congress's newly won authority was quite narrow. But if slavery included such vestiges of slavery as racially discriminatory laws and customs or denial of rights essential to freedom, the amendment gave Congress extensive authority.

Debating the amendment, supporters in Congress did not argue expressly that it went beyond elimination of chattel slavery. Perhaps they feared that articulating a broader interpretation of the amendment would alienate conservative Republicans and Democrats whose votes were needed for passage. Or perhaps with chattel slavery still alive, they simply focused on the most immediate problem. Congressional silence, however, did not necessitate a narrow reading of the amendment. During the Civil War, Republicans had developed what the historian Harold Hyman has described as "adequacy constitutionalism."[11] They did not view the Constitution negatively, as simply a list of restrictions on government, but as an instrument that empowered government to pursue certain broad objectives and gave it discretion to choose the means most suitable to achieve those ends. To Republicans, the Constitution was organic, a document capable of meeting new exigencies. Viewed through this prism, the Thirteenth Amendment offered Congress authority to root out slavery and all of its vestiges and to guarantee former slaves the rights essential to freedom.

Republicans' understanding of those rights sharpened considerably as the war progressed. During the 1850s Republicans had invoked the Declaration of Independence to criticize slavery, charging that it violated the principle of equality on which the Republic had been founded. As Union war aims expanded to include emancipation, and 180,000 black men shouldered the obligations of citizenship by serving in the Union Army, Republicans became more vigorous in their support for equality. Indeed, by 1865, the war to preserve the Union had become for most Republicans a war to create a more perfect Union, one that guaranteed the equality of all citizens.

Republicans' commitment to equality was reflected in policy as well as rhetoric. By 1865, California and Illinois Republicans had repealed all discriminatory state statutes except those denying blacks the ballot. In Massachusetts, Republicans pushed further, enacting a public accommodations law that prohibited racial discrimination by operators of inns, places of public amusement, common carriers, and public meeting places. Congressional Republicans likewise demonstrated a clear commitment to civil equality for blacks. In 1862 they repealed the ban on black mail carriers. Two years later, they permitted blacks to testify against whites in federal courts and granted black soldiers equal pay and benefits. Congressional Republicans underscored their growing commitment to equality when they created the Freedmen's Bureau, in March 1865. Aware of the myriad problems faced by newly emancipated blacks, Republicans saw the necessity of a federal agency to assist them in their transition from slavery to freedom. Carefully avoiding any suggestion that the former slaves were a separate class incapable of full freedom and subject to restraints not applicable to other free persons, they marked the bureau as a temporary agency, locating it in the War Department and limiting its existence to one year after the war. They also carefully pruned language giving the bureau authority to make special regulations for blacks and provided that the agency was to assist white refugees as well as emancipated slaves. As Representative Robert Schenck of Ohio explained, the law made "no discrimination according to color—a favorite phrase . . . in these days among us all."[12]

Reconstruction and National Protection for Civil Rights

Although the pace of constitutional change during the war years was dramatic, it accelerated during the years after Appomattox. Conflict between black and white southerners over the meaning of freedom was the driving force behind this change, spurring Republicans to translate their support for equality into bold measures that dramatically expanded national protection for individual rights. Although tens of thousands of

blacks had won their freedom during the war, most slaves first tasted
liberty in the weeks and months after Confederate forces surrendered and
Union troops occupied the Confederacy. Blacks viewed emancipation as
a providential act of deliverance, "the work of Almighty God," one
former slave later recalled. Indeed, it was such a pivotal event that
seventy years later, many elderly ex-slaves gave vivid accounts of the
day they learned that they were free, conveying the sense of joy and
excitement they had felt. "I won't never forget dat day," recalled Lydia
Jefferson in 1937. ". . . Yes suh, de freedom sun shine, and de black
times all gone." For men and women whose family life, work, religion,
and physical well-being had been subject to white control, emancipation
offered a new beginning free of white domination. "Glory, halleluyer,
dere ain't no marster and dere ain't no slave!," a black minister informed
a meeting of Florida blacks. "From now on my brudders an' my sisters,
old things have passed away an' all things is bekum new."[13]

Blacks had clear expectations of the new order. They placed a pre-
mium on freedom of movement, not only because it allowed them to
break the master–slave relationship by leaving their former owners, but
because it enabled them to search for husbands, wives, and children from
whom they had been separated forcibly as slaves. Indeed, black's greatest expectation of freedom was that it would permit them to reunite
families and protect them from interference by whites. In the predominantly agricultural society of the South, landownership was also a high
priority. Land would enable former slaves to become independent farmers and permit them to escape supervision by plantation owners and
overseers, affording heads of household greater control over their own
work and also removing wives and children from white authority.
Blacks' hopes for land were whetted as word spread across the South that
wartime legislation authorized confiscation of land owned by rebels and
distribution of it to former slaves.

There was also a nascent demand for equality among blacks. During
1865 southern blacks organized a number of state conventions that, like
the antebellum conventions of northern blacks, demanded that the nation
live up to the promise of the Declaration of Independence. These conventions reflected the views of the literate urban free men who dominated
them. Yet former slaves also became politically conscious, as black army
veterans, black teachers from the North, and agents dispatched by the
conventions spread the gospel of republicanism among them.

Black's aspirations clashed with southern whites' determination to maintain control over their former slaves. Planters and farmers feared that emancipation would destroy their operations unless they could impose on black workers restrictions that would enable them to maintain a cheap, tractable labor force. But whites' concerns rested on far more than economic considerations. Products of a deeply racist culture that viewed blacks as incapable of living in a civilized society without white guidance and control, they assumed that freed blacks would refuse to labor and would turn to crime, transforming southern society into a hell for whites. Fear of retribution by former slaves was also widespread among whites, sparking rumors of a bloody uprising that swept the white South like a wildfire during the last months of 1865.

Given the stakes, southern whites quickly mounted an informal campaign to minimize the consequences of emancipation. Although the threat of confiscation hung over them, whites nevertheless controlled the land. In a predominantly agricultural society, this conferred considerable economic leverage against blacks. Whites refused to rent land to blacks, fearing that to do so would encourage black independence. Instead, they used their control of the land to compel blacks to work as plantation laborers under white supervision. Planters frequently colluded to hold wages down and—in order to restrict blacks' movement—sometimes refused to hire those who could not produce references from their former owners. In many areas whites formed vigilante groups to shore up their control. Occasionally vigilantes beat or murdered those who attempted to leave their former owners and, more commonly, compelled blacks to work on terms favorable to planters. They also frequently visited blacks' cabins, seizing firearms and beating and driving away those perceived as encouraging black assertiveness—especially black veterans and teachers. Moreover, in day-to-day encounters between whites and blacks, white men frequently beat or even murdered blacks who were insufficiently deferential. As an Arkansas Freedmen's Bureau agent noted in informing his superiors of the appalling number of assaults on blacks, "in nine cases out of ten" whites attacked blacks simply because they "dared to refute a charge prejudicial to their character as false; and have been impudent enough to take a stand for their rights as men."[14]

Southern whites also used the power of the state to reassert control over blacks, a benefit made possible by President Andrew Johnson's program of Reconstruction. Johnson was a Unionist Democrat from Tennessee who had been selected as Lincoln's running mate in 1864 to strengthen the Republican ticket's appeal among Democrats. When he came to the

White House in April 1865 after Lincoln's murder, Johnson turned his attention to Reconstruction. A state's rights advocate who shared white southerners' views on race, Johnson quickly adopted policies that speedily restored self-government to southern whites and gave them authority to define the legal status of blacks. He freely offered amnesty and pardon to former rebels, thereby restoring their political rights. He also recognized the white Unionist governments Lincoln had established during the war in Louisiana, Arkansas, Tennessee, and Virginia and appointed provisional governors for the other seven rebel states. These men were to conduct elections (in which only whites could vote) for delegates to state constitutional conventions. After these conventions drafted new constitutions, the governors would hold another round of elections to choose state officials and members of Congress. When this process was complete, Johnson expected Congress to seat southern senators and representatives, completing the process of Reconstruction.

Johnson's program seriously threatened the newly won rights of the freedmen. By the summer of 1865, the Freedmen's Bureau—which was authorized to take possession of land seized under the confiscation laws and to lease it to the freedmen—held 800,000 acres of land taken from Confederate supporters during the war. But Johnson ruled that his pardons entitled the recipients to restoration of their property rights, and ordered bureau officials to surrender this land to owners who had received pardons. Furthermore, the president prevented further seizure of land by forbidding United States attorneys to institute new cases under the confiscation laws. These directives protected southern planters, dashed blacks' hopes of obtaining land, and reinforced whites' economic leverage against blacks.

As state legislatures elected under Johnson's program met during the winter of 1865–1866, they passed repressive measures known as *black codes*. Designed to reinforce white power, these laws attempted to guarantee whites a cheap and tractable labor force and to compel blacks to remain on plantations and farms where they would live and work under close supervision by whites. In some states, blacks who wished to live in towns and cities were required to obtain permits from local officials, and in all southern states blacks were subjected to harsh vagrancy laws. These measures authorized local officials to fine persons who were not gainfully employed. Those who could not pay the fines, which combined with court costs, typically totaled $100 or more (an amount far beyond the means of impoverished blacks), were sentenced to labor without compensation for as much as one year for anyone who would pay their fines. This not only subjected blacks to forced labor, but undermined their bargaining power as well. If blacks withheld their labor in an effort to force planters to offer better wages and working conditions, local officials could use threats of prosecution for vagrancy to break blacks' resistance and compel them to work on terms favorable to planters.

Other provisions of the black codes further extended white control over blacks. Apprenticeship laws authorized state judges to apprentice orphans and children whose parents failed to support them adequately, thereby making black families vulnerable to white interference. Judges used the discretionary authority conferred by these laws to order thousands of black children removed from their families and apprenticed to labor-starved white planters, ostensibly to learn agricultural and domestic service trades. The criminal law provisions of the codes undercut blacks' chances of securing justice. Although they did allow them to testify in cases in which at least one party was black, this was of little practical benefit because all-white juries—which were notoriously hostile to black witnesses, plaintiffs, and defendants—decided the cases. The black codes also enabled judges to impose harsher criminal punishments on blacks than on whites, virtually guaranteeing that black convicts would be executed more frequently and receive longer prison terms than whites found guilty of comparable crimes.

Republicans, firmly in control of both houses of Congress, were appalled by the results of Johnson's program. Clearly, southerners had demonstrrated that they were intent on preserving the essence of slavery even as they surrendered formal claims to ownership of blacks. Congressional acceptance of Johnson's program, Republicans believed, would permit white southerners to restore through politics what they had lost on the battlefield. In the eyes of Republicans and a majority of northerners this would deny the nation one of the most important fruits of victory and mean that 400,000 Union soldiers had died in vain. If Congress recognized the Johnson governments, senators and representatives from the South would join forces with northern Democrats, who were strident foes of black rights. Together they would not only threaten Republican hegemony, but would have sufficient power to block legislation necessary to ensure black liberty. Consequently, when Congress met in December 1865, Republican leaders quickly agreed that they would not seat representatives from the rebel states until Congress devised measures to protect black freedom.

Radicals, most notably Pennsylvania's Thaddeus Stevens, advocated new confiscation legislation to reverse the effect of Johnson's pardon policy and provide land to the freedmen. Former slaves, they argued, would remain vulnerable to control by whites as long as they remained propertyless laborers. The vast majority of Republicans, however, rejected confiscation, viewing legal equality, not grants of land, as the best means to protect black freedom. In part, this perspective was a legacy of the antislavery movement. Because slavery had rested on the systematic denial of rights to slaves and free blacks, its critics had attacked legal restrictions on blacks and had invoked Christian principles and the Declaration of Independence in arguing that blacks were entitled to equal rights. The fixation on equal rights that grew out of antislavery agitation was reinforced by the widespread appeal of what the historian Eric Foner has called the *free labor ideology*.[15] As products of a rapidly expanding, highly competitive capitalist economy that was dominated by small-scale producers, most nineteenth-century Americans believed that theirs was an open society in which individuals could advance by hard work and careful planning. Accepting this belief, Republican leaders assumed that if blacks were not restrained by artificial legal barriers and enjoyed the same rights as whites, they would rise according to their merits. Indeed, they argued that by giving blacks land, the government would discourage self-reliance, undercutting blacks' chances of success in a competitive society. Although these ideas were naive and ill-suited to the needs of impoverished former slaves, they were accepted as conventional wisdom by nineteenth-century Americans and exerted a powerful influence on Republican policy.

Republican leaders also rejected radicals' call for black suffrage. They realized that by extending the franchise to blacks, Congress would repudiate the presidentially reconstructed governments (which had been elected by white voters) and necessitate beginning the reconstruction process anew. This not only guaranteed conflict between Congress and the president, but risked alienating conservative Republican senators and representatives as well as many northern voters. Unwilling to accept the political risks inherent in supporting black suffrage, Republican leaders settled for a program that permitted presidentially reconstructed governments to stand but compelled them to grant blacks equality before the law.

Lyman Trumbull of the Senate Judiciary Committee introduced two pieces of legislation designed to provide national protection for the rights of blacks. The first offered temporary protection by extending the life and expanding the power of the Freedmen's Bureau. Trumbull argued that Congress's war powers "do not cease with the dispersion of the rebel armies," but "are to be continued and exercised until the civil authority of the Government can be established firmly."[16] With the war power still in force, he asserted that Congress could provide summary protection for black rights in the rebel states. Thus the bureau bill stipulated that blacks were entitled to equal rights in state law and authorized bureau officials to establish military tribunals to enforce these rights when state authorities failed to do so. Persons accused of enforcing discriminatory laws and regulations were subject to prosecution in bureau courts and fines of as much as $1,000 and imprisonment for up to one year. Moreover, bureau courts might try cases involving blacks—cases involving contract disputes, property rights, violations of criminal law, and the like—who were denied or unable to enforce their rights because of any "State or local law, ordinance, police, or other regulation, or custom or prejudice."[17]

Because the Freedmen's Bureau's judicial authority rested on the war power, it extended only to the rebel states and would cease there as soon as Congress restored those states. In order to provide long-term protection throughout the nation, Trumbull introduced the Civil Rights Act of 1866. Resting on the Thirteenth Amendment, which Republicans viewed as authorizing Congress to eradicate the vestiges of slavery, the Civil Rights Act declared that blacks were citizens and guaranteed them legal equality throughout the nation. Carefully excluding political rights, the bill provided that blacks "shall have the same right in every State . . . to make and enforce contracts, to sue, be parties, give evidence, to inherit, purchase, lease, hold, and convey real and personal property . . . as is enjoyed by white citizens. . . ." They were also entitled to "full and equal benefit of all laws and proceedings for the security of person and property" and liable to the same criminal laws as whites. Persons denied these rights might seek redress in the federal courts. Anyone acting "under color of any law, statute, ordinance, regulation, or custom" to deny a citizen's civil rights was subject to prosecution in federal court and, on conviction, a fine of $1,000 and imprisonment for one year. Persons who were "denied or cannot enforce" their rights in state courts might have their cases tried in federal courts, giving them impartial forums in which to obtain justice.[18]

The Freedmen's Bureau and civil rights legislation represented a radical departure in American constitutional history. By declaring that all persons born in the United States were citizens regardless of race, the Civil Rights Act ended decades of uncertainty over the definition of national citizenship and repudiated the Supreme Court's *Dred Scott* ruling. Both measures asserted broad national authority to define the rights essential to freedom and, if necessary, to protect them through federal courts, matters over which the states had enjoyed almost exclusive authority in the antebellum era. Thus they embraced ideas of colorblind citizenship and national protection of individual rights that only abolitionists had dared assert a few years earlier. Speaker of the House Schuyler Colfax, a Republican moderate, reflected this in his assessment of the Civil Rights Act. "Wasn't yesterday a glorious day," he inquired the day after the bill was enacted. "Our birthright being born on American soil means something now for everyone. . . ." Democrats made the point more directly, denouncing the bill as a revolutionary measure "designed to take away the essential rights of the States."[19]

Nevertheless, as the historian Michael Les Benedict has demonstrated, Republicans did not break completely with antebellum constitutionalism.[20] They valued the decentralized federal system because it permitted local self-government and obviated the need for a vast national bureaucracy. Therefore they wanted states, not the national government, to continue to exercise primary responsibility for defining individual rights. The bureau and civil rights bills compelled states to grant blacks the same legal rights they conferred on whites, but left them free to define these rights. The bills also left with state courts primary authority to protect civil rights; only if they failed to guarantee equal rights would national courts have authority to act.

As Trumbull pushed his bills through the legislative process, Congress's Joint Committee on Reconstruction hammered out a constitutional amendment designed to settle a variety of problems arising from the war. Although committee members were primarily concerned about political matters, they could not escape settling the issue of civil rights. A few Republicans, believing that the Thirteenth Amendment did not authorize the Civil Rights Act, demanded that the new amendment provide clear constitutional support for it. Others, aware that Democrats would repeal the act if they regained control of Congress, wanted to write civil rights guarantees into the Constitution, putting them beyond the reach of transient congressional majorities. Section 1 of the Fourteenth Amendment reflected these concerns. It declared that all persons born or naturalized in the United States were United States citizens and citizens of the state in which they resided. This offered a clear definition of United States citizenship and prevented states from excluding blacks from the benefits of state citizenship. Section 1 also established constitutional guarantees for individual rights reminiscent of those championed by abolitionist legal writers. It forbade states to "make or enforce any law which shall abridge the privileges and immunities of citizens of the United States," to "deprive any person of life, liberty, or property without due process of law," or to deny persons "equal protection of the laws." Section 5 of the amendment authorized Congress to enact "appropriate legislation" to enforce these guarantees.

The language of section 1 was sweeping and majestic, but what did it mean? What were the privileges and immunities of citizens of the United States? What guarantees did the due process clause encompass? When Congress debated the amendment, senators and representatives offered different interpretations and frequently demonstrated confusion about the amendment's implications. John A. Bingham of Ohio, the author of section 1, asserted that the privileges and immunities and due process clauses must be read broadly to "protect . . . the inborn rights of every person . . . whenever the same shall be . . . denied by the unconstitutional acts of any State."[21] But what precisely were these "inborn rights?" Senator Jacob Howard of Michigan, another member of the Joint Committee, was more specific, asserting that whatever these provisions meant, they clearly included the rights enumerated in the first eight amendments. Other influential Republicans, however, denied that the amendment reached as far as Bingham and Howard suggested, and most did not comment on the issue, leaving the precise meaning of these phrases shrouded in uncertainty.

The framers of the Fourteenth Amendment also created uncertainty by wording section 1 as a series of restrictions on the states. If state officials themselves did not deny persons the rights guaranteed by section 1, but were unable or unwilling to punish private citizens who assaulted, robbed, murdered, or discriminated against blacks, did the amendment authorize congressional action? If one read the amendment narrowly, it did not. It authorized Congress to provide remedies against state action, not against the acts of private citizens. A broader reading was not only possible, but truer to Republican principles. By failing to bring wrong-doers to justice, state officials as effectively denied persons equal protection as if they enforced blatantly discriminatory laws. Because the amendment authorized Congress to provide appropriate remedies when states denied persons equal protection, it might therefore be construed to authorize federal law enforcement officials and federal courts to provide the protection that state officials were unwilling or unable to offer. Indeed, such an interpretation was consistent with the determination that Republicans repeatedly expressed during 1866 to guarantee former slaves genuine freedom and legal equality, not merely their forms. Nevertheless, in debates on the Fourteenth Amendment Republicans did not define precisely the extent of congressional power to provide remedies against private (as opposed to state) action. Like the meaning of the privileges and immunities clause, therefore, it would be determined in the future by Congress and the courts.

Regardless of these uncertainties, Republican leaders believed that the Freedmen's Bureau and civil rights bills, along with the Fourteenth Amendment, constituted a program that would guarantee black freedom. Most assumed that if the southern states signaled their acceptance of the war's outcome by ratifying the amendment, Congress would complete restoration. (When Tennessee ratified in June 1866, Republicans voted to seat the state's senators and representatives.) Republican expectations, however, were quickly dashed. Before the Joint Committee completed work on the amendment, President Johnson announced his unqualified opposition to Congress's program, vetoing both the Freedmen's Bureau and civil rights bills. Both measures, he charged, gave preferential treatment to blacks and usurped powers that the Constitution reserved to the states. Republicans had sufficient strength to override the vetoes. In April they mustered the two-thirds majority necessary to enact the civil rights bill, and after an initial failure to override the Freedmen's Bureau veto, they passed an almost identical bill over Johnson's veto in July. Nevertheless, Johnson's opposition was not without effect. By encouraging southern politicians to reject the Fourteenth Amendment, he helped delay ratification (the amendment remained unratified until 1868), ensuring that the Republican program remained incomplete.

Despite conflict between the president and Congress, former slaves eagerly attempted to avail themselves of the remedies offered by recently enacted congressional legislation. Aware of the Civil Rights Act's guarantee of equality, they pressed federal officials to prosecute whites who discriminated against them. When the trustees of a Catholic church in Louisiana denied blacks the right to rent church pews, for example, black parishioners demanded that the trustees be tried for violation of the act. Under threat of prosecution the trustees relented and reserved one side of the sanctuary for blacks. Most frequently, blacks sought justice in informal hearings before local Freedmen's Bureau agents. "My office is so crowded . . . with freedmen coming to complain of not being settled with [by their employers] that . . . it takes four of us from 9 o'clock in the morning to 5 o'clock in the evening doing scarcely anything else but trying to adjust cases of cheating and stealing," noted a typical bureau agent in early 1867.[22]

Blacks' experience in seeking redress from federal officials had important consequences. As slaves, they had lived under the personal authority of their owners, whose arbitrary decisions had affected every aspect of their lives. Through contact with bureau agents and northern teachers, however, former slaves learned that law—a body of impersonal rules defining individual rights and obligations—existed as a restriction on arbitrary personal authority. Granted, these men and women, fearful that former slaves might confuse liberty with license, emphasized the obligations imposed as well as the rights conferred by the law. Nonetheless, they did stress that law was a restraint on personal will and was essential to ordered liberty. Although it was alien to their experience, former slaves quickly grasped the concept of law, finding in it a means of curbing arbitrary white authority. A group of Newberry, South Carolina blacks reflected this understanding when, in asking the Freedmen's Bureau to afford them protection from "a reign of terror" established by local whites, they complained, "We have no law."[23]

Congressional civil rights legislation had other important consequences as well. The Civil Rights Act and debates surrounding its adoption had a powerful influence on black consciousness, convincing the former slaves that they were citizens who were entitled to equal rights and impartial justice. In October 1866, for example, a Freedmen's Bureau agent stationed in Staunton, Virginia noted that blacks in his district were well informed on the civil rights question, adding that "news of that kind spreads through the country very quickly." "I am acquainted with one colored man who takes the 'Washington Chronicle,'" he explained, "and regularly imparts the news to his color."[24] The presence of federal officials encouraged former slaves to demand their rights and to challenge arbitrary white authority. Indeed, the records of bureau agents, which contain tens of thousands of complaints that blacks brought against whites during the three years after the war, demonstrate that black men and women understood their rights and were not reluctant to defend them. The informal procedure that bureau agents used in adjudicating these complaints was also important. It enabled blacks, most of whom were illiterate and had no experience with judicial proceedings, to become familiar with the legal process as a means of asserting their rights.

Nevertheless, the bureau's authority was fragile. Because it was an agency of the War Department, its officials fell under the authority of the president. Convinced that the rebel states had legitimate governments and were entitled to restoration, Johnson used his authority to limit the bureau's power to try cases involving blacks. In 1865, he had restricted bureau judicial authority, preventing it from adjudicating cases unless state officials persisted in denying blacks the right to testify. As state governors and legislatures relaxed restrictions on black testimony during late 1865 and early 1866, Johnson pressed the bureau to surrender to state courts jurisdiction over blacks. By mid-1866, bureau officials in most states had complied.

The Freedmen's Bureau Act of 1866, which became law in July, offered some hope, giving the bureau authority to intervene when state officials denied blacks their rights. The act provided that the bureau should exercise this authority under regulations approved by the president. When Bureau officials drew up such regulations, however, Johnson refused to approve them. Lacking authority to try cases involving blacks, bureau agents resorted to bluff. They cajoled local officials, demanding that they attend to complaints made by blacks, and threatened to intervene if they refused to guarantee blacks justice. When blacks complained that employers had cheated them, agents investigated, conducted hearings, and frequently ordered offending employers to pay their workers. Without legal authority to try cases and impose penalties, however, most were reluctant to take further action when local officials or private citizens refused to comply.

The Civil Rights Act also offered blacks limited protection. Bureau officials initiated several successful prosecutions against state officials who enforced laws that expressly discriminated against blacks. Although few in number, these prosecutions deterred most state functionaries from enforcing discriminatory statutes. Where officials persisted in enforcing discriminatory laws, bureau officials succeeded in having cases involving blacks removed from state to federal courts. In Kentucky, for example, most judges persisted in enforcing the state law that prohibited blacks from testifying against whites, clearly denying blacks one of the rights guaranteed by the Civil Rights Act. Invoking its authority under the act to try cases involving persons who were denied equal rights in state law, the United States District Court in Louisville assumed jurisdiction over hundreds of cases in which whites were accused of murdering, assaulting, robbing, and otherwise maltreating blacks, thereby giving blacks access to impartial justice.

In most states, however, antebellum testimony statutes had been modified to permit black testimony, and most officials refrained from enforcing the discriminatory provisions of the black codes. Moreover, throughout the South, state law made it a crime to murder, assault, or rob any person, regardless of race, and permitted all persons to recover damages for breach of contract, trespass, personal injury, and the like. In theory, therefore, blacks "enjoyed full and equal benefit of all laws and proceedings for the security of persons and property," as demanded by the Civil Rights Act. They were denied justice, not by enforcement of discriminatory laws, but rather by discriminatory law enforcement. Prejudiced local officials refused to prosecute whites who beat, murdered, raped, robbed, or cheated blacks, or, if they did, all-white juries refused to convict white defendants, regardless of the evidence against them. Nevertheless, many conservative United States district judges and district attorneys—men who had been appointed by Johnson—read the act narrowly. They refused to take jurisdiction over cases involving blacks unless they were denied justice by enforcement of a blatantly discriminatory law.

Other problems hampered enforcement. Because the federal courts had previously possessed limited jurisdiction, there were few of them; in fact, no southern state had more than two United States district judges assigned to it. Consequently, federal courts were not easily accessible. The Civil Rights Act anticipated this problem, authorizing federal judges to appoint a United States commissioner for each county in their district. Although commissioners were not authorized to try cases, they could hold preliminary hearings and order offenders to appear before district courts, making it easier to initiate proceedings under the act. Yet this offered no panacea. Commissioners were usually white southerners who had little sympathy for blacks and were reluctant to risk their neighbors' wrath by initiating cases against whites. None of these problems were irremediable. A president more sympathetic to the act than Johnson could have directed his attorney general to press district attorneys to interpret the act more favorably to blacks. A Supreme Court decision sustaining a broad interpretation of the act would have brought conservative district judges into line. But as things stood throughout 1866, justice remained elusive for African-Americans.

The consequences were disastrous. Realizing that blacks had little chance of winning redress, planters took advantage of the situation. Their widespread cheating of workers, combined with a poor harvest, meant that most black agricultural workers remained impoverished and economically dependent on white landowners. It was not uncommon for a black family to end the year's labor breaking even or owing the planter for food and supplies advanced over the course of their year's employment. Moreover, throughout the southern countryside whites terrorized blacks without fear of punishment by local officials. "Murders and all sorts of depradations are committed by the wholesale," noted a Freedmen's Bureau agent from Arkansas. "You cannot imagine how terrified the [black] people are. They are aware in case . . . murderers are arrested the criminal laws are so defective that in most cases they get clear, revenging themselves on those who have testified against them."[25]

From Legal Rights to Political Equality

In early 1867, Republican leaders agreed to extend to southern blacks the right to vote, embracing a policy that they had rejected as too radical one year earlier. The events of 1866 had convinced Republicans that whatever rights states might formally extend to blacks, state officials could easily nullify in practice. But if blacks possessed the ballot, Republicans believed that they could elect state and local officials who would be more responsive and would enforce the law impartially. Republican leaders also aimed to minimize the need for intrusive federal involvement in state affairs by giving the freedmen the ability to protect themselves through state political and legal institutions. In many ways the Republican position was terribly naive. As radicals pointed out, it offered an impoverished people recently freed from slavery a paper shield to protect themselves from former masters who controlled the region's economic resources, rejected blacks' claim to civil equality, and remained committed to white supremacy. Republican support for black suffrage was, nevertheless, a radical step. In no other slave society in the world did former slaves win the ballot so quickly. In addition, blacks would use the ballot with remarkable effectiveness, altering the political and social landscape of the South and challenging white hegemony.

Republicans embodied their new program in the Reconstruction Act, which they passed over a presidential veto in March 1867. Resting on the war power (which Republicans claimed Congress might exercise within the rebel states until they were restored), the act divided the ten unrestored states into five military districts and directed the president to appoint a major general to command each. District commanders might permit existing state officials to maintain law and order, but, if necessary, might use military personnel to make arrests and try offenders in military courts. Military authority would be short-lived, however. States were to hold elections for delegates to constitutional conventions, and black adult males would be permitted to vote in these contests. After the conventions had met and drafted new constitutions enfranchising black men, voters had ratified these documents, and state legislatures elected under the new constitutions had ratified the Fourteenth Amendment, Congress would seat southern senators and representatives, thereby restoring the rebel states to the Union.

A political revolution swept the South during 1867, as military officials registered voters in preparation for election of convention delegates. Blacks viewed the ballot as both an emblem of first-class citizenship and a means of breaking the chains that officials of the presidentially reconstructed governments had forged to limit their freedom. Consequently, they joined political clubs like the Union League, where they learned about the political process and debated political issues, and registered to vote at a rate that alarmed white southerners. With the political mobilization of the black community, a powerful Republican party emerged across the Confederate South. Although blacks made up the overwhelming majority of the party's rank and file, Republican organizers, aware that black majorities existed in only three states, also wooed white voters. They attracted northerners who had settled in the South after the war (*carpetbaggers*), as well as a significant number of southern whites (derisively known as *scalawags*), most of whom had been wartime Unionists. Native whites constituted perhaps twenty percent of the party's supporters (although their strength varied considerably from state to state), making them crucial to Republican success.

Because they denied the legitimacy of black suffrage, most southern whites not only spurned the Republican party but refused to vote in elections for constitutional conventions held in the late summer and fall of 1867. Consequently, Republicans won overwhelming majorities in the conventions, gaining control over the process of constitution-making, and were able to write into state constitutions provisions asserting the equality of all men, guaranteeing equality before the law, establishing universal male suffrage, and repealing property-holding requirements for jury service and office holding. They also mandated establishment of public schools, a step viewed as essential to black advancement. Except in the South Carolina and Louisiana conventions, radicals failed to win acceptance of provisions prohibiting segregation in schools or public accommodations. Nevertheless, none of the new constitutions condoned racial segregation. Only the South Carolina convention took meaningful action to help blacks become landowners, establishing a state land commission to purchase land and to sell it on liberal terms to the landless. Elsewhere Republican constitution makers clung to free labor orthodoxy, empowering state government to promote economic growth, thereby hoping to attract more white supporters and to expand economic opportunity for blacks and whites alike. Like the party's congressional leaders, then, southern Republicans defined equality primarily in civil and political rather than economic terms.

During the first half of 1868, southern voters went to the polls to ratify the new constitutions and to elect state officials and congressional representatives. In seven of the ten unrestored states, the constitutions received a majority of the votes cast, and newly elected Republican legislatures ratified the Fourteenth Amendment. In June 1868, with a presidential election at hand, congressional Republicans, eager to show progress toward restoration, voted to restore all seven states. Only Mississippi (where a provision calling for widespread disfranchisement of former rebels led voters to reject the new constitution) and Virginia and Texas (where intraparty divisions slowed constitution-making) remained unrestored by summer's end. Within eighteen months, these three had also ratified new constitutions and gained restoration.

Although white Republicans won the lion's share of the offices in most states, white southerners viewed the new regimes as revolutionary. As leaders of a party that relied on black votes, white office holders supported civil and political equality for the freedmen, drawing the wrath of most of their white neighbors. While black Republicans did not win a share of offices equal to their strength in the party, some were elected to serve as United States senators and representatives, state legislators, sheriffs, county commissioners, and justices of the peace. Thus for the first time African-Americans were elevated to positions of prestige and power, a phenomenon most whites viewed as intolerable. And as blacks' assertiveness and political sophistication increased, they gained a stronger voice in party affairs and won a greater share of offices.

The Republican revolution also produced a significant shift in public policy that affected the ongoing struggle between the races over the meaning of emancipation. During the early years of Reconstruction, southern whites had mobilized the power of the state to reassert their dominance over the former slaves and to guarantee white planters and farmers a continued cheap, tractable labor supply. But Republican legislatures denied whites this weapon, repealing the remnants of the black codes and giving blacks a voice in the legal process by admitting them to the jury box. They also attempted to strengthen the position of the vast majority of blacks who worked as agricultural laborers, sharecroppers, and tenant farmers. Republicans gave agricultural laborers and sharecroppers more effective legal means to secure payment of their wages and also afforded tenants greater protection against landlords. In addition, Republican homestead laws exempted small amounts of personal property (farming tools and livestock, for example) from seizure by creditors. This afforded at least some protection to poor sharecroppers and tenants who relied on planters and merchants for credit while making their crops and who were thus in danger of losing everything in the event of a poor harvest.

Practice changed as well as policy, a fact that was brought home to blacks and whites by their day-to-day experiences. When they attended trials in the county courthouse—a recreation popular among persons of both races—they were struck by the presence of black jurors. Because jury service was a mark of respect in rural communities in the nineteenth century and jurors made decisions that directly affected the well-being of the community, nothing conveyed more graphically the revolutionary nature of Reconstruction. But the presence of blacks on juries was not merely symbolic. By giving blacks a voice in matters that directly affected their lives, jury participation broke another of the bonds of white authority that had circumscribed their lives. With blacks present, juries were more likely to consider seriously black testimony and cases initiated by freedmen. And they were less likely to indict or convict blacks merely because whites accused them of crimes. This made blacks less vulnerable to white authority, shielded them from capricious prosecutions that threatened their liberty, and afforded them greater personal security.

Planters had to deal with local officials—sheriffs, district attorneys, judges, and justices of the peace—who were responsive to blacks. Under Republican rule, arrests and prosecutions of blacks for vagrancy were almost unheard of, and planters and farmers lost an effective tool for compelling blacks to enter contracts on terms favorable to employers. They also found that local officials no longer automatically prosecuted black workers at the behest of their employers. When a group of planters in Greenwood, South Carolina brought charges against blacks who took discarded fence rails to use for firewood, for example, a Republican justice of the peace dismissed the case, noting that the rails "are of no use to any but to assist the poor in the way of fuel." "I believe in justice," he explained, "and if they [the planters] do not like it they can lump it."[26] For planters accustomed to rely on law and government to reinforce their control over workers, the presence of such officials was a devastating blow.

Planters were also outraged when local officials proved responsive to blacks' complaints against them. Republican justices of the peace frequently fined employers who assaulted their employees and offered black workers redress against planters and farmers who attempted to defraud them of the fruits of their labor. Whites expected deference from blacks and bitterly resented being called to account by their former slaves. Unwilling to admit that their former slaves had a right to obtain redress against them, they denounced Republican officials as troublemakers who needlessly encouraged blacks to challenge their employers. "If a negro [sic] should sustain any ill feelings against a white man and can muster the slightest shadow of a case against him," seethed one wealthy South Carolinian, "he rushes off immediately to Beaufort [the county seat] and there he finds a ready and willing mill to grind the respectable portion of the community to ashes." Local officials' responsiveness to former slaves, complained another planter, led to loss of control over workers and "the disorganization of labor."[27]

Bewildered by a world turned upside down and angered by growing black influence that threatened their dominance, the vast majority of southern whites denied the legitimacy of the new order. They contended that black suffrage—on which the Republican state constitutions and governments rested—had been imposed unconstitutionally on the South by Congress and had given political power to "ignorant, stupid, demi-savage paupers.'' The natural result, they charged, was that scheming Republican politicians—the *Daily Arkansas Gazette* characterized them as men whose ''putridity stinks in the nostrils of all decency''—won office through demagogic appeals to ignorant black voters. This, they argued, guaranteed corrupt, rapacious governments that rode roughshod over the rights of upstanding citizens like themselves. Indeed, when Republican legislators raised taxes significantly to fund public education and economic development projects, white Democrats claimed that white property holders, who paid most of the taxes but who were politically impotent, were being ''robbed by the no-property herd.'' And when evidence of corruption surfaced in a number of southern governments, their rage became white-hot. ''This is the rule of the proletariat,'' Mississippi Democrats shrieked, ''it is naked communism—and negro communism at that.''[28]

Because most southern whites considered the Republican regimes bogus and viewed black political power as a threat to the social order, many were willing to condone violence as a legitimate means to throw off the Republican yoke. Between 1867 and 1870 paramilitary groups, most notably the Ku Klux Klan, surfaced in virtually every southern state. Directed from the grass roots rather than by national or state leaders, these organizations unleashed a campaign of terror designed to deter blacks from voting, to destroy the Republican party, and to reestablish white dominance. Aware that leadership was necessary to mobilize black voters and to deliver the vote, the Klan singled out local Republican leaders for special attention, beating and killing them, assaulting members of their families, and burning their homes. But it did not stop there. Klan members also brutalized thousands of rank-and-file Republicans, hoping to convince them to sever their ties with the party, and frequently lashed out at blacks who challenged the authority of their employers or who were insufficiently deferential to whites.

Klan violence finally helped convince Republican leaders that a constitutional amendment was needed to protect the voting rights of blacks. Because the Reconstruction Act applied only to the states of the former Confederacy, it left blacks in the border states and in most of the North without the franchise. Abolitionists, northern blacks, and Radical Republicans, having long argued that suffrage was an inherent right of citizenship, repeatedly called attention to the inconsistency of conferring suffrage on southern blacks while denying it to their northern counterparts. Mainstream Republicans were sensitive to such charges, finding it increasingly difficult to reconcile tolerance of discriminatory voting laws with their commitment to equal rights. In the four years following the war, Republicans in eight northern states had placed before the voters state constitutional amendments establishing equal suffrage. Although these amendments were approved by voters in only two states (Minnesota and Iowa), the vast majority of Republican voters in the other six states supported them. Yet party leaders, unwilling to jeopardize their chances of winning the White House, held back a strong effort to include a plank supporting a suffrage amendment in the party's 1868 platform. But events in the South during the campaign made the demand for an amendment irresistable. Klan terror decimated the Republican turnout in most of the South, putting Georgia and Louisiana in the Democratic column. If this trend continued, Republicans feared, southern Democrats would regain dominance and repeal state constitutional provisions guaranteeing black suffrage.

By early 1869, congressional Republicans agreed that a suffrage amendment was necessary. But as they proceeded, they disagreed sharply over how to word the amendment. Many supported a narrow amendment barring the United States or the states from denying any person the right to vote on the basis of race, color, or previous condition of servitude. Radicals and many moderates sharply criticized this formulation, arguing that states could easily circumvent it by adopting property and literacy requirements that would effectively disfranchise most former slaves, who were poor and illiterate. These Republicans championed a broader version prohibiting state and national officials from denying persons the ballot on the basis of nativity, property, education, creed or race. Although this attracted substantial support, many Republicans feared that it would not win approval by the requisite number of states. Massachusetts and Connecticut had enacted literacy requirements to prevent immigrants from voting, and Rhode Island had established a property requirement for naturalized (but not native-born) citizens. In the Far West, where anti-Chinese sentiment ran deep, the nativity provision would almost certainly result in rejection. In February 1869, after bitter debate, congressional Republicans finally adopted an amendment prohibiting the states or the United States from denying anyone the right to vote on the basis of race and authorizing Congress to enforce this guarantee. Within a year it won the approval of three-fourths of the states and became the Fifteenth Amendment.

Adoption of the suffrage amendment brought to a fitting end a turbulent decade of revolutionary changes in the American Constitution. Because of a complex interplay of principle and expediency, Republicans had transformed a war for the Union into a war to create a more perfect Union, a Union free of the blight of slavery. Identifying the war effort and their party with freedom, Republicans were pressed by events during and after the war to explore the meaning of freedom. Radicals complained that the party moved too cautiously, yet they succeeded in convincing moderates that blacks were entitled to civil and political equality. Although intent on preserving federalism, mainstream Republicans had supported a series of constitutional amendments and a Civil Rights Act that gave the national government broad authority to guarantee equality. In many respects, then, by 1870 the demands made by blacks and abolitionists in the antebellum years had been incorporated into American constitutionalism, an achievement few had thought possible at the beginning of the decade. Nevertheless, bitter resistance to the new order continued, suggesting that even more sweeping changes were necessary to secure the fruits of the Reconstruction revolution.

4

Equality Deferred, 1870–1900

Located in the rich Brazos River Valley some eighty miles northwest of Houston, Washington County, Texas, was part of the nineteenth-century South's cotton kingdom. Although fall usually focused the attention of the county's residents on the harvest and the price of the fleecy staple, the fall of 1886 was different. Politics displaced cotton as the prime subject of discussion at the Barrel House, a popular black bar in Brenham, the county seat; at Routt's bustling cotton gin in nearby Chappell Hill; and at dozens of other gathering spots throughout the county. With the support of the county's slight black majority, Republicans had controlled local government from 1869 until 1884, when Democrats had reclaimed the county courthouse in a closely contested election. For Democrats, the victory had been sweet, bringing to an end fifteen years in which black men and their white allies had governed the county. But Democrats were worried as the 1886 canvass approached. Republican leaders were formidable opponents, and the county's blacks remained politically active and determined to return the county to Republican control. Republicans were equally apprehensive. They recalled that two years earlier their opponents had used violence to reduce the black turnout and believed that local Democrats would resort to whatever means were necessary to guarantee white rule.

Republicans' fears were not misplaced. In three heavily Republican precincts located in the predominantly black eastern portion of the county, masked men clad in yellow slickers seized ballot boxes from election officials at gunpoint. The raids accomplished their purpose, destroying enough Republican ballots to give Democrats a narrow victory in the closely contested canvass. Yet all did not go according to plan for the Democrats. Anticipating foul play, a group of black Republicans in the Flewellen precinct remained at the polling station as election officials tallied the ballots. When masked intruders burst into the room to seize the ballot box, Polk Hill, one of the black observers, opened fire with his shotgun, instantly killing one of the bandits, Dewees Bolton, the son of the Democratic candidate for county commission.

Although Hill fled, local officials arrested eight black men who had been present at the shooting and charged them with murder. In jailing the blacks, they did more than satisfy whites' demands that Bolton's killing be avenged. Democratic leaders, including the county judge, Lafayette Kirk, had orchestrated the election-day fraud and feared that Hill's companions had seen too much. By identifying young Bolton's comrades, they might provide evidence that would enable Republicans to contest the election and put the Democratic conspirators behind bars. On the night of December 1, after Republican lawyer F. D. Jodon had initiated habeas corpus proceedings on behalf of the imprisoned blacks, a band of disguised men broke into the county jail in Brenham. Easily overpowering the jailer, they went to the cells where the black men were being held and asked for Shad Felder, Alfred Jones, and Stewart Jones. After identifying the three, they dragged them out of jail, took them to the bank of nearby Sandy Creek, and hanged them. Two days after the lynching, as an angry mob of whites gathered in Brenham, prominent Democrats informed Stephen Hackworth, James Moore, and Carl Schutze, three of the county's leading white Republicans, that they must leave town. Fearing for their lives, all three quickly departed.

Hackworth and his comrades refused to accept exile, however, and turned to the national government for redress. They found ready allies among Senate Republicans, who had long advocated stronger federal criminal sanctions against election fraud and violence. In mid-February 1887, William Evarts of Massachusetts, a Republican member of the Senate Committee on Elections, initiated hearings on the Washington County affair. During the ensuing three weeks, several dozen Washington County citizens—black and white, Republican and Democrat—made the long trip to the nation's capitol and gave committee members their versions of the 1886 election and its violent aftermath. Running to almost 700 pages of small print, the testimony vividly detailed the fraud and violence that plagued southern elections, offering strong support for advocates of federal regulation of elections. Democrats now controlled the House of Representatives and the White House, however, and Republicans themselves were divided over the wisdom of more vigorous protection of their southern allies. Consequently, Republican leaders were unable to translate indignation over the highhandedness of Washington County whites into legislation providing more effective protection for beleaguered black voters.

Washington County Republicans did not pin all their hopes on congressional intervention. As the Senate hearings got under way, United States Attorney Rudolph Kleberg won an indictment against Lafayette Kirk and eight other prominent Washington County Democrats in the United States district court in Austin. Framed under federal election laws adopted during Reconstruction, the indictment charged the defendants with conspiring to interfere with election officials and to steal ballots at an election at which a congressional representative was elected. Despite his own affiliation as a Democrat, Kleburg threw himself into the case, conducting a thorough investigation and vigorously presenting his case to the jury. Nevertheless, after a lengthy trial in August 1887, jurors were unable to agree on a verdict, and the judge declared a mistrial. Undaunted, Kleberg brought the case to trial again in April 1888, only to have the jury return a verdict of not guilty. In both trials, the government had produced strong circumstantial evidence that Washington County Democratic leaders had engineered the theft of the ballot boxes. Yet because three key Republican witnesses had been lynched and other potential black witnesses were reluctant to give testimony that might cost them their lives, the district attorney did not have a ''smoking gun.'' Not surprisingly, therefore, he was unable to convince juries composed mainly of white Texans to return a guilty verdict against the respectable white defendants. Federal officials could harry Washington County Democrats, but they could not bring them to justice.

The April 1888 acquittal brought an end to the Washington County affair. Because murder was a state, not a federal offense, the Washington County sheriff was responsible for investigating the lynching of the three black men and bringing the guilty parties to justice. Although the identities of the lynch mob's leaders were common knowledge among local whites, community leaders showed no interest in prosecuting the guilty parties. ''[M]ost good citizens regret the hanging,'' the *Brenham Daily Banner* piously noted, ''but in the present state of public feeling it is regarded as one of those occurrences that could not well be avoided.''[1] Not surprisingly, Sheriff N. E. Dever, a white Democrat, made no effort to arrest the guilty parties. This forgive-and-forget attitude did not extend, however, to Polk Hill. Dever and his deputies conducted a manhunt that led to Hill's arrest in late 1886. Hill was transferred to the Milam County jail for safekeeping, a step that probably saved him from the fate of his late neighbors Shad Felder, Alf Jones, and Stewart Jones. Subsequently, he was convicted of manslaughter by an all-white jury and sentenced to twenty-five years in prison.

Events in Washington County were symptomatic of developments elsewhere in the South during the last decades of the century. Despite an unparalleled extension of federal authority during the early 1870s, by 1877 southern Democrats had reclaimed control of state government from the Republicans throughout the South. While the new regimes steadily chipped away at the rights blacks had won during Reconstruction, Democrats' counterrevolutionary designs met determined resistance. Blacks refused to abandon the dream of citizenship and equality and skillfully used the political and legal avenues opened to them during Reconstruction to defend their newly won rights. Moreover, while the national government's vigor in protecting civil rights waned after the mid-1870s, neither Congress, the Justice Department, nor the federal courts completely abandoned blacks during the late 1870s and 1880s. Yet as the demise of Washington County Republicanism suggests, southern blacks were only able to slow, not stop, the counterrevolution. By the end of the century, northern Republicans paid little more than lip service to protection of black rights, the federal courts had transformed the Reconstruction amendments into mere platitudes, and conservative Democrats had successfully employed terror and economic reprisals to overcome black resistance and reestablish white supremacy. It took three decades to accomplish, but by 1900, southern Democrats had reversed the Reconstruction revolution.

Securing the Republican Revolution

Even as Republicans celebrated ratification of the Fifteenth Amendment in February 1870, they recognized the vulnerability of the dramatic civil rights gains they had achieved in the 1860s. Across the South, the Ku Klux Klan and kindred groups had launched a campaign of terror designed to destroy the fledgling Republican regimes and reverse the Republican commitment to equality. State and local officials proved either unwilling or unable to challenge the Klan. Confronting a large,

well-armed terrorist group, Republican sheriffs were reluctant to risk
igniting a race war by mobilizing their supporters (most of whom were
black) into posses to arrest Klansmen. Furthermore, when fearless local
officials made arrests and initiated prosecutions, it was difficult to win
convictions. Witnesses, fearing for their lives, frequently refused to
testify against Klansmen, and many jurors were too intimidated or (in the
case of whites) too sympathetic to the Klan to return guilty verdicts.

In early 1870, with Klan violence spreading and state officials unable
to check it, congressional Republicans considered bold new legislation to
enforce the Fourteenth and Fifteenth Amendments. As they had done
during the Civil War, Republicans viewed the Constitution as a source of
power, arguing that it gave Congress discretion to choose the means
necessary to protect the rights of citizens. "The people know that
. . . the Constitution is created for the people, and not the people for the
Constitution," argued Mississippi Republican George McKee, "and I
would rather trust the clear, simple judgement of the people than that of
any legal quibbler who ever split a constitutional hair on either side of this
House."[2]

Some Republicans argued that the national government had an inherent right to legislate to protect its citizens, whether they were threatened
by state or private action. "I desire that so broad and liberal a construction be placed upon its provisions as will insure protection to the humblest
citizen," explained Joseph Rainey, a black congressman from South
Carolina. "Tell me nothing of a constitution which fails to shelter
beneath its rightful power the people of a country."[3]

Most Republicans, however, feared that giving Congress such open-
ended authority threatened the federal system. Carried to its logical
conclusion, they argued, it would empower the national government to
enact a general code of laws governing crime, property, contracts, family
relations, and other matters that properly lay within state jurisdiction.
Consequently, theirs was a more restrictive view of federal power. They
acknowledged that the Fourteenth and Fifteenth Amendments were
designed to prevent states from denying individual rights rather than to
give Congress primary responsibility for defining and protecting individual rights. Nevertheless, they pointed out that the amendments gave
Congress authority to enact "appropriate legislation" to enforce their
guarantees, thereby conferring broad discretion to choose the means best
suited to that end. They also pointed out that states could, through
inaction, deny the rights guaranteed by the amendments. In other words,

states might just as effectively deny individuals equal protection of the laws by failing to punish murderers as by enacting blatantly discriminatory statutes. Most Republicans concluded that when states, through inaction, denied black citizens rights guaranteed by the Fourteenth and Fifteenth Amendments, Congress could provide the remedies against private action that the states failed to afford.

Acting on this theory, congressional Republicans passed the Enforcement Act in May 1870, dramatically expanding federal protection for individual rights. Designed primarily to enforce the Fifteenth Amendment, the act made it a federal crime for state officials to deny otherwise qualified voters the right to register or to vote. It also established criminal penalties for private citizens who used force, violence, intimidation, bribery, or economic coercion to deny any person the right to vote. At the behest of their black and white southern colleagues, who were particularly sensitive to the problem of violence, congressional Republicans went beyond protection of voting rights. They established stiff criminal penalties (fines of $5,000 and imprisonment for ten years) for those who conspired to deny persons rights guaranteed by the Constitution or federal laws. The act thus broke new ground, affording individuals federal remedies against private acts of violence, something that previously had been the exclusive responsibility of the states.

Less than one year later, in April 1871, congressional Republicans took even firmer action, passing a measure popularly known as the Ku Klux Klan Act. The law made it a federal crime for two or more persons to conspire to deprive any person of equal protection of the laws. Invoking Congress's authority to regulate federal elections, it also established criminal penalties for persons who used force or intimidation to prevent citizens from supporting candidates of their choice in congressional elections. More to the point, it gave the government additional tools with which to combat terrorism. When terrorist groups prevented state authorities from guaranteeing persons equal protection of the laws, the president might use the army or the militia to assist in arresting offenders. And when such organizations were "so numerous and powerful as to . . . set at defiance the constituted authorities," the chief executive might suspend habeas corpus, allowing the military to hold those whom they arrested without initiating formal charges against them.[4]

Between 1870 and 1873, federal officials used the new legislation to mount an impressive and effective campaign against the Ku Klux Klan.

Consider the government's effort in western South Carolina, where a powerful Klan organization (in York County more than three-quarters of adult white males were members) declared war on local blacks during late 1870 and 1871, murdering several dozen black Republicans and severely beating hundreds of others. Federal officials conducted a thorough investigation of Klan violence in the region, gathering a massive amount of evidence against Klansmen. At the urging of Attorney General Amos T. Akerman, who had gone to South Carolina to consult with federal investigators and prosecutors, President Ulysses Grant invoked his broad authority under the Klan Act. In October 1871, he suspended habeas corpus in nine South Carolina counties and authorized the army to assist federal marshals in making arrests. Although many Klan members fled (some went as far as Canada), marshals made hundreds of arrests, and hundreds of other Klansmen, convinced that they could not escape the dragnet, surrendered. By year's end, 195 York County Klansmen resided in the county jail, popularly known as the "United States Hotel." After filling the Spartanburg County jail, federal officials had to rent two additional buildings to house men arrested in that county.

During late 1871 and 1872 trials began in federal courts in Columbia and Charleston. Because federal officials had carefully assembled evidence and the juries impaneled contained black majorities, prosecutors were successful in winning convictions. The trials, however, were time-consuming; the first five cases that went to trial took more than one month to complete. And the creaky federal judicial system was ill-equipped to deal with large numbers of lengthy criminal trials. With only two federal judges assigned to the state and two attorneys responsible for all of the prosecutions, federal officials soon realized that they could bring to trial only a small portion of those whom they had arrested. Consequently, they concentrated on the worst offenders, hoping that the mass arrests and the few dozen convictions they were able to win would demonstrate federal resolve and deter further terrorism. Their strategy worked. Although the government won convictions in only about 150 cases (most of which resulted from guilty pleas rather than jury trials) and ultimately dismissed more than 1,000 cases, it effectively destroyed the Klan in South Carolina.

In no other state did the president suspend habeas corpus; nor did federal officials make as many arrests or win as many convictions elsewhere. Nevertheless, the government's law officers were active, winning indictments against more than 1,200 persons in North Carolina, more than 750 persons in Mississippi, and some 350 persons in Alabama. They did not bring most of these persons to trial, but the mass arrests did convince Klansmen that the government meant business. In North Carolina and Alabama, government attorneys won 63 convictions. In Mississippi, where only one case went before a jury, federal officials obtained guilty pleas in almost 600 cases, trading promises of suspended sentences for confessions. While this meant that most Mississippi Klansmen avoided punishment, they knew that they would go to prison if they were implicated in further Klan activity. As in South Carolina, the government's strategy worked; Klan activity virtually ceased in these states. The Klan had taken its toll, helping to drive Republicans from power in North Carolina, Tennessee, and Georgia in 1869 and 1870; but the government's firm action restored at least temporary peace to most of the South and helped Republicans in other states to retain power.

Not only did the president and the Congress act boldly against the Ku Klux Klan, but federal judges were also willing to interpret broadly the Fourteenth and Fifteenth Amendments. From North Carolina to Mississippi, they rejected claims by defendants that key provisions of the Enforcement and Klan Acts were unconstitutional. And several opinions strongly endorsed Congress's authority to punish private individuals who violated citizens' rights. In an 1871 case, *United States* v. *Hall,* Circuit Judge William B. Woods ruled that the Fourteenth Amendment empowered Congress to protect the fundamental rights of American citizens, including those guaranteed by the Bill of Rights. He also brushed aside arguments that the Enforcement Act was unconstitutional because Congress could only provide remedies against violations of citizens' rights by states, but not private individuals. Echoing the views of congressional Republicans, he pointed out that state officials might deny citizens' rights by failing to protect them against wrongs committed by private individuals. When this occurred, he concluded, Congress might provide appropriate remedies, acting directly against offending individuals if necessary.[5]

Congressional Republicans also confronted the prickly problem of segregation. Although there were wide variations in the depth and vehemence of race prejudice and legally imposed segregation was rare, the years immediately following the war witnessed white resistance to integration of public places. In the South, most hotels and restaurants denied service to blacks; public schools, asylums, and parks generally excluded blacks; and theaters, railroads, streetcars, and steamboats frequently segregated blacks or excluded them altogether. In the North, where segregation had been common in the antebellum years, there was intense prejudice against blacks, but it was neither as broad nor as deep as that which existed in the South. The result was a more confusing, complex pattern of race relations: blacks were denied service at most hotels and restaurants, while others accommodated the few well-to-do blacks who sought admission; most public school systems insisted that blacks attend separate schools that were generally inferior to those provided for whites, but schools were integrated in New England and some other places; railroads, steamboats, and streetcars frequently, but not always, segregated blacks.

In the North, the postwar years witnessed a renewal of the antebellum campaign against segregation. Energized by the triumph over slavery, northern blacks intensified their demands for an end to discrimination in public accommodations. With memories of blacks' wartime service still vivid and support for civil and political equality growing, many white northerners became more responsive to these demands. This shift in northern temperament was by no means universal, however. Most whites remained reluctant to mingle with blacks, and many were violently opposed to permitting any breech in the color line. In postwar Philadelphia, for example, blacks mounted an impressive campaign against segregated streetcars, forcing themselves into whites-only cars where they were routinely assaulted by company employees and white customers and arrested by city police officers. Yet it was not until 1867—after the streetcar companies, city officials, and state judges had resolutely resisted their demands for two years—that blacks secured legislation banning segregation in public transportation. Although white opposition was equally strong elsewhere and segregation remained customary in many parts of the North, blacks did win other notable victories in the late 1860s and early 1870s. Massachusetts (1865), New York (1873), and Kansas (1874) passed laws banning discrimination in public accommodations; Michigan, Connecticut, Rhode Island, Iowa, Minnesota, Kansas, Colorado, and Illinois prohibited school segregation; and school boards in Chicago, Cleveland, and Milwaukee operated integrated schools and even employed a few black teachers.

Southern blacks also challenged the color line. In Charleston, New Orleans, Louisville, and Savannah they used sit-ins to compel streetcar companies to end discrimination. Although white Republicans feared that integrationist policies would alienate the party's white supporters (who provided the crucial margin of victory in many states), black leaders demanded public accommodations laws protecting blacks' right to non-discriminatory service on railroads and steamboats as well as in hotels, theaters, and restaurants. Texas, South Carolina, Louisiana, Mississippi, and Florida enacted such legislation, but it had little effect. Some railroads permitted blacks who could afford the fare to ride in first-class cars with whites, but most continued to demand that all blacks ride in second-class cars with poor whites and those who wished to smoke or chew tobacco. Hotels and restaurants continued to exclude blacks, and theaters persisted in assigning them to balconies. A few blacks sought legal redress under state public accommodations laws, but most, fully aware of the depth of white resistance to integration, wished to avoid insult, and simply avoided places where they were not welcome.

Separation of the races also became the norm in state-operated facilities. Southern Republican regimes ended the policy of excluding blacks from public schools and from institutions for the blind, the deaf, and the insane. They also devoted roughly equal resources to the education of black and white children and created professional opportunities for blacks by hiring thousands of black teachers. Yet with the exception of the New Orleans school board, southern Republicans operated separate schools for blacks and whites and segregated residents in institutions for the blind, the deaf, and the insane. Although some black leaders criticized these policies, most welcomed the opportunity that public schools offered to black pupils and teachers and were more concerned that black schools receive adequate support than that black children attend integrated schools.

Dissatisfied with their slow progress, integrationists turned to the national government. In 1870, Charles Sumner, the radical senator from Massachusetts who had championed school desegregation in antebellum Boston, introduced new civil rights legislation that prohibited racial discrimination in public transportation, hotels, restaurants, schools, churches, cemeteries, and juries. Sumner and his allies, both within and outside Congress, argued that the measure would banish the last vestiges of caste and fulfill the promise of equal rights. "Is it not strange," asked Republican Congressman Ellis Roberts, "that it should be a matter of debate whether there should be . . . legislation guaranteeing to a certain class of our citizens their common law rights? . . ."[6] Having successfully used law to destroy slavery, a powerful institution that had seemed invulnerable little more than a decade before, radicals were confident that law could end discrimination.

Opponents charged that Sumner's bill was both unconstitutional and impractical. By attempting to regulate the practices of private businesses, they charged, it exceeded Congress's authority under the Fourteenth Amendment, which was limited to providing remedies against discriminatory state action. Critics also argued that while government might legitimately guarantee legal and political equality, it had no business enforcing "social equality." Individuals had a right to associate with persons of their choice, they insisted, and to avoid contact with those whom they found objectionable. Indeed, nothing could be more futile than the attempt to legislate "social equality." "[W]here local sentiment is hostile to a statute," the *Baltimore American* asserted, "it becomes inoperative and void."[7]

The bill's Republican supporters offered a thoughtful response. *Harper's Weekly* argued that by forcing whites to change their behavior, the bill would gradually moderate their attitudes. Other supporters challenged the notion that the law interfered with purely personal associations, pointing out that it merely sought to end discrimination in public places. "[I]t is not social rights that we desire," explained John Lynch, a black congressman from Mississippi. "What we ask is protection in the enjoyment of public rights. Rights which are or should be accorded to every citizen alike." Civil rights advocates also contended that the Fourteenth Amendment sanctioned the law. "If an inn, having its right to exist by state authority, being a creature of the state, in fact regulated by it, [engages in discrimination]," explained black abolitionist George Downing, "it may be said that the *state* does the discriminating." Moreover, they reminded opponents that the Thirteenth Amendment authorized the legislation. Tolerating discrimination in public accommodations, explained Senator Frederick Frelinghuysen, "would be perpetuating that lingering prejudice growing out of a race having been slaves which it is as much our duty to remove as it was to abolish slavery."[8]

Despite Republican majorities in Congress, Sumner's bill met stiff resistance. Although the Massachusetts senator introduced it during every session until his death in 1874, he did not live to see his civil rights bill become law. Some northern Republicans argued that the bill was unpopular and would be a political liability. White Republicans from the

South contended that the provision mandating integrated schools would cripple the party by driving away white supporters. It would also, they insisted, destroy the region's fledgling public school system by undermining white support for it. It was not until 1875, when almost half the Republicans in the House were lame ducks and the provisions concerning schools, churches, and cemeteries had been deleted, that the bill finally passed. The hesitation and trimming that marked its long incubation suggested that there were limits to the party's commitment to equality. Nonetheless, passage of the Civil Rights Act of 1875, with its assertion that the national government had a responsibility to assure all citizens equality in public accommodations, marked the high tide of the Reconstruction revolution. "[I]t is the capstone . . . of the reconstruction edifice," the *Springfield Republican* proudly asserted.[9]

The Counterrevolution Gains Force

Even as Republican radicals struggled with the capstone, cracks appeared in the foundation. During the mid-1870s, with federal judges supportive and the Klan on the run, Republicans backed away from vigorous federal intervention in the South. In part this was a response to the success of the 1871–1872 campaign against the Klan and the concomitant decline in terrorism. There were deeper reasons for the party's new posture, however. Most Republicans viewed law enforcement as a state, not a federal, responsibility, considered the campaign against the Klan extraordinary, and were not prepared to continue it indefinitely. They were also concerned about the political consequences of further federal intervention. In a society that worshipped the self-reliant individual, was skeptical of active government, and had long viewed a strong central government as suspect, there was little enthusiasm for continuation of a large-scale federal enforcement program. Furthermore, Democrats charged that tales of Klan terror were nothing more than Republican propaganda, denounced the enforcement program as a ruthless effort to prop up unpopular, incompetent governments with federal bayonets, and portrayed President Grant as a latter-day Caesar. Aware that these charges effectively appealed to Americans' fear of military despotism, Republicans agreed that they must curb federal intervention in the South.

During 1873, Republican leaders began to distance themselves from the mailed-fist policies that had proved so effective in South Carolina.

Under George Williams, who succeeded Akerman as attorney general in late 1871, the Justice Department became more cautious about initiating new civil rights cases. While Williams did not order district attorneys to halt new prosecutions under the Enforcement and Klan Acts, he neither encouraged them to undertake vigorous action nor allowed them the resources necessary for large-scale prosecutions. In fact, the administration became more conciliatory toward white southerners, perhaps hoping that this would moderate their opposition to the new order and bring to an end charges of bayonet rule. Beginning in 1873, President Grant pardoned many of the Klansmen who remained in prison, and the attorney general ordered federal attorneys in the South to dismiss prosecutions against thousands of Klansmen who had been indicted between 1870 and 1872.

Events of 1873–1874 reinforced Republican cautiousness. Members of Grant's inner circle and prominent Republican congressmen implicated in financial scandals were the subjects of congressional investigations during 1873. With the scent of corruption trailing it, the party was also saddled with blame for the severe economic depression that struck in September 1873. Facing a hostile electorate as the 1874 congressional races approached, Republicans were reluctant to add to their woes by undertaking potentially unpopular action in the South. When the dust settled after the election, the party had been routed and a 110-vote Republican majority in the House had become a 60-vote margin for the Democrats. Shell-shocked and fearing further losses in important state elections in 1875, party leaders became even more reluctant to renew large-scale intervention in the South.

Taking advantage of Republican cautiousness, southern Democrats launched a new offensive against their adversaries between 1874 and 1876. By making active support for the Democratic party a test of racial solidarity, they increased the white turnout significantly. They also developed new techniques of intimidation that effectively reduced Republican turnout without reviving northern support for federal intervention. Armed Democrats regularly disrupted Republican meetings, demanding equal time to expose Republican ''lies'' or shouting down Republican speakers. Seeking to impress on blacks the perils of political involvement, armed bands rode through the countryside at night during the weeks preceding elections, firing small arms and sometimes even canon, and patrolled polling places on election day. And when they did resort to beatings and murders, they usually defined their targets carefully and struck quickly rather than inaugurating an ongoing campaign of terror. Democrats also mastered the technique of the "race riot." They provoked altercations between their own supporters and Republicans and, under the pretext of self-defense, launched punishing attacks against their opponents. At the beginning of the 1875 election campaign in Mississippi, for example, white Democrats in Clinton precipitated a fight at a Republican rally in which several blacks and whites were killed. Alleging that the Republicans had initiated a war of the races, Democrats swept the surrounding countryside during the next two days, killing between twenty and thirty blacks and beating hundreds of others.

Despite his recent policy of conciliation and caution, Grant did not ignore the resurgence of violence. He authorized the War Department to station small squads of troops in areas where Democratic intimidation was most pronounced, hoping the presence of bluecoats would cow whites and reassure blacks. Under instructions from Washington, more-over, district attorneys, supported by troops, occasionally arrested persons charged with intimidating voters. The government's effort, however, was far too modest and ultimately proved woefully inadequate. There were too few troops available (by October 1874 only 7,000 bluecoats remained in the South) to make a show of force in more than a few trouble spots. And because the overwhelming majority were infantry, they possessed limited mobility and were not effective against mounted adversaries. Then, too, the number of prosecutions initiated under the Enforcement Act by federal attorneys was too small to serve as a deterrent. What was needed was a large-scale campaign of arrests and prosecutions patterned after the South Carolina effort of 1871–1872. Republican leaders, however, fearing that they lacked popular support for such a campaign, did not meet the Democratic challenge.

The results were disastrous for southern Republicans. Democrats were able to regain control of state government in Texas (where only one-third of the population were blacks) and Arkansas and Florida (where bitter factional disputes doomed Republicans) without resorting to widespread violence. In the rest of the unredeemed South, however, the new techniques of terror were crucial. In 1874, Alabama Democrats carried statewide elections, in part by employing violence and intimidation in key black belt counties, while Louisiana Democrats smashed Republican organizations in many rural parishes, winning control of the state assembly. The following year white Mississippians mounted an impressive campaign of terror to carry the state legislature. With that accomplished, they swiftly impeached Republican Governor Adelbert Ames. In 1876, Democrats in Louisiana and South Carolina effectively used violence to carry state elections, completing the process of redemption. By 1877, then, the Democratic counterrevolution had recaptured the South, ending Republican control in every state in the region.

Although freedmen continued to vote in large numbers and Republicans still held office in some predominantly black counties after 1877, southern Democrats relied on fraud and intimidation of black voters to cling to power. As a prominent Mississippi Democrat admitted in 1890, "we have been stuffing the ballot boxes, committing perjury, and . . . carrying the elections by *fraud* and violence" since 1875.[10] The consequences of Democratic hegemony were momentous. While blacks remained eligible to serve on juries, in most areas local officials manipulated jury selection procedures to exclude them. Consequently, black plaintiffs and defendants once again found justice elusive as they confronted all-white juries. Blacks also felt the economic consequences of redemption: Democratic legislatures repealed measures that the Republicans had enacted to protect agricultural laborers; state supreme courts developed legal doctrines that reinforced the authority of landowners against sharecroppers; sheriffs again used vagrancy statutes to compel reluctant black workers to accept unfavorable contracts with planters; and justices of the peace turned a deaf ear to complaints that black workers lodged against their employers. Absence of effective legal protection, combined with a steady decline in the price of cotton, left black sharecroppers and agricultural workers impoverished, reinforcing their economic dependence on whites. Black children also suffered as state legislatures cut support for public education and local officials reduced the proportion of school funds that went to black schools.

As southern Democrats moved ahead with the counterrevolution, the United States Supreme Court circumscribed national authority to protect civil rights. Most members of the Court were conservative northern Republicans who were not hostile to civil rights but had never shared the radicals' passion for equality. Like most of their contemporaries, they were committed to preserving a decentralized federal system and believed that this required strict limits on national authority and sharp delineation of state and national functions. It is difficult for Americans living in the late twentieth century to appreciate this commitment to federalism. We are the heirs of more than fifty years of steady growth of federal authority and believe that the scope of national power is virtually limitless. Nineteenth-century Americans were products of a much different world, however. The federal government played little role in their day-to-day lives, and, with the exception of the local postmaster, they rarely encountered a federal official. Moreover, as products of a political tradition that equated centralized authority and tyranny, they believed that self-government demanded that local communities enjoy substantial autonomy. It is hardly surprising, therefore, that they viewed expansion of federal authority with suspicion.

Federalism was a principle that mattered, not merely a cover for hostility to blacks, as historians have sometimes suggested. Indeed, the concern for preserving state authority was reflected in decisions giving the states broad discretion to regulate business and restrict the rights of property owners in order to promote the general welfare. This is not to say that race did not matter. Had the justices been more sensitive to blacks' needs and more intent on protecting blacks' rights, they would have abandoned other principles that stood in the way; however, they were neither hostile nor indifferent to protection of black rights nor unwilling to expand federal civil rights authority. Rather, they were insufficiently committed to the rights of blacks to accept the truly radical expansion of federal power necessary to meet the exigencies of blacks.

The first indication of the Supreme Court's position came when it decided *The Slaughter-House Cases* in 1873. The cases were brought, ironically, not by former slaves, but by white butchers in New Orleans who challenged a state law that restricted their freedom to practice their trade. The butchers charged that the liberty to pursue a lawful occupation was a fundamental right of citizenship and therefore one of the privileges and immunities of United States citizenship protected by the Fourteenth Amendment. The implications for blacks were quite clear. If the Court accepted the butchers' argument, Congress and the federal courts would enjoy authority to protect a wide range of individual rights, thus enhancing their ability to guarantee the rights of blacks.

In a severe blow to civil rights advocates, a sharply divided Court rejected the butchers' position by a 5–4 margin. Writing for the majority, Justice Samuel Miller argued that the Fourteenth Amendment recognized dual citizenship, expressly stating that Americans were citizens of the United States *and* the state in which they resided. He inferred from this that they possessed two separate and distinct sets of rights, one set deriving from national and the other from state citizenship. Defining the former as those ''which owed their existence to the national government,'' Miller suggested that they were of decidedly limited scope. They included the right to habeas corpus, to assemble to petition the government for redress of grievances, to come to the nation's capital, to unfettered use of the nation's ports and navigable rivers, and to protection by the government while abroad. More basic rights, such as the right to pursue a trade, were among the rights of state citizenship and thus not protected by the Fourteenth Amendment. Since Miller made no reference to them, presumably the guarantees of the Bill of Rights were not included among the privileges and immunities of United States citizens and remained merely limitations on the authority of the national government.

Miller's opinion was greeted by sharp dissent, with Justice Noah Swayne charging that the majority had ignored the intent of the framers, transforming ''what was meant for bread into a stone.'' Other dissenters argued that by making national citizenship primary, the Fourteenth Amendment had transformed the federal system, transferring responsibility for protecting fundamental rights to the national government. Although this analysis was persuasive, it threatened the federal system by transferring primary authority to define and protect individual rights from the states to Congress and the federal courts. Indeed, Miller feared that a broad construction of the amendment would lead to a ''great departure from the structure and spirit of our institutions,'' ''fetter and degrade'' the states, and ''radically change the whole theory of the relations between the State and federal government to each other and of both . . . to the people.''[11] The threat of such revolutionary consequences prompted the Court's majority to slow the juggernaut of constitutional change, even if it had to do so through a strained interpretation of the amendment.

By holding that the privileges and immunities of United States citizens included only a few rights that were of limited importance to most persons, the decision trivialized the provision that contemporaries viewed as the heart of the Fourteenth Amendment. (Indeed, the privileges and immmunities clause remains a dead letter in the late twentieth century.) Nevertheless, in dismissing the claims of the butchers, Miller emphasized that Congress had passed the postwar amendments in order to guarantee full freedom and genuine equality for blacks. The ''pervading purpose'' of the admendments, he emphasized, was ''the freedom of the slave race, the security and firm establishment of that freedom, and the protection of the newly-made freeman and citizen from the oppressions of those who had formerly exercised unlimited dominion over him.'' Thus Miller suggested that the Court would look favorably on assertions of national power designed to protect the rights of the former slaves. And while the *Slaughter-House* decision meant that the privileges and immunities clause would be of limited value, the Thirteenth Amendment and the equal protection clause of the Fourteenth Amendment might easily support legislation aimed at rooting out racially motivated violations of individual rights.[12]

The Court brought the implications of *Slaughter-House* into sharper focus in 1876, when it decided *United States* v. *Cruikshank*. William Cruikshank was one of a well-armed band of more than 100 whites who attacked blacks who had gathered outside the courthouse in Colfax, Louisiana in April 1873 to support local Republican officials whose claims to office had been challenged by Democrats. After their initial attack forced approximately 150 freedmen to take refuge in the courthouse, the whites torched the building, killed dozens of blacks as they fled the blaze, and subsequently shot in cold blood between 30 and 40 blacks who had surrendered. In all, perhaps 100 freedmen died in the massacre. In 1874, Cruikshank and two other participants were convicted in federal circuit court in New Orleans for violation of the Enforcement Act of 1870, which made it a crime to use force or intimidation to deprive citizens of rights granted by the Constitution or laws of the United States. Specific charges in the indictment accused the defendants of using violence to deny their victims the right to bear arms (protected by the Second Amendment), the right of assembly (protected by the First Amendment), and the right to equal protection of the laws and due process of law (protected by the Fourteenth Amendment).

In a complicated ruling that focused on the indictment under which the defendants had been convicted (rather than the constitutionality of the Enforcement Act), the Supreme Court reversed the convictions and dealt a severe blow to the government's civil rights authority. Chief Justice Morrison Waite noted that the right to bear arms, freedom of assembly, and the other guarantees of the Bill of Rights were merely limitations on the national government, not rights that were enforceable against states and private individuals. Following the logic of *Slaughter-House*, he suggested that they were among the rights of state citizenship. Consequently, Waite concluded that they were not rights granted by the Constitution and that violation of them by private citizens was not punishable under the Enforcement Act (which punished infringements on rights granted by the Constitution). The Court was now harvesting the bitter fruit of *Slaughter-House*. It had circumscribed the rights of United States citizens, rights that could be said to be granted by the Constitution and therefore were within Congress's power to protect. As *Cruikshank* tragically demonstrated, this seriously compromised the government's authority to protect individual rights.

The chief justice also rejected those parts of the indictment that accused the defendants of depriving citizens of equal protection and due process of law. This amounted to charging the defendants with murder, he concluded, a crime that came within the purview of state authority. The due process and equal protection clauses of the Fourteenth Amendment, according to Waite, added "nothing to the rights of one citizen . . . against another," but were merely restrictions on state action. They authorized Congress to provide remedies against denial of equal protection or due process by states and their officers, but did not empower it to punish private citizens who violated the rights of others. Thus the Court implicitly rejected the more expansive reading of the equal protection clause offered by Judge Woods in *United States* v. *Hall*, making it more difficult for the national government to protect blacks against wrongs inflicted by private citizens. With southern state governments now firmly in the hands of Democrats, who were not inclined to afford blacks personal security, this left blacks largely at the mercy of their white neighbors.[13]

When it decided *The Civil Rights Cases* in 1883, the Court used the state action theory to strike down the provisions of the Civil Rights Act of 1875 banning discrimination in hotels, restaurants, theaters, and public transportation. Justice Bradley, who wrote the Court's opinion, denied that the Fourteenth Amendment's equal protection clause sanctioned the law. It merely prohibited discrimination by state authorities, he held, not by private individuals and businesses. Bradley also denied that the Thirteenth Amendment authorized the statute. He admitted that it abolished all "badges and incidents" of slavery and decreed "universal civil and political freedom throughout the United States." He also conceded that the Thirteenth Amendment, unlike the Fourteenth, was not directed exclusively at state action, and that Congress's power to enforce it included authority "to enact all necessary and proper laws for the obliteration and prevention of slavery with all its badges and incidents." Bradley denied, however, that discrimination against blacks by proprietors of hotels and restaurants, which had been common in the free states during the antebellum years, was a badge of servitude. "It would be running the slavery argument into the ground," he concluded, "to make it apply to every act of discrimination which a person may see fit to make as to the guests he will entertain, or . . . take into his coach . . . or admit to his . . . theater. . . ."[14]

Bradley's opinion did not go unchallenged. The black press likened it to Taney's infamous *Dred Scott* opinion, and one week after it was announced, Frederick Douglass denounced the decision at a mass protest meeting in Washington, D.C. On the Court itself, Justice John Marshall Harlan, a Kentucky Republican who had once owned slaves, penned an eloquent dissent. Hearkening back to the idealism that had animated the Republican party's civil rights program, he characterized Bradley's analysis as "entirely too narrow and artificial," charging that its "subtle and ingenious verbal criticism" sapped "the substance and spirit of the recent Amendments." "Constitutional provisions, adopted in the interest of liberty, and for the purpose of securing . . . rights inhering in a state of freedom, and belonging to American citizenship," he explained, "have been so construed as to defeat the ends . . . which they attempted to accomplish. . . ."[15]

Although the Court narrowed the scope of national power under the postwar amendments, it by no means abandoned the framers' commitment to equality. In *Strauder* v. *West Virginia* (1880), it held that a law that restricted jury service to white men violated the Fourteenth Amendment's equal protection clause. In the process, it reaffirmed that the amendment had been designed to protect the former slaves from hostile state action and to guarantee that "all persons, whether colored or white, shall stand equal before the laws of the States." Moreover, the Court suggested that it would not tolerate laws establishing racial classifications. As Justice William Strong explained,

> The words of the [Fourteenth] Amendment . . . are prohibitory, but they contain a necessary implication of a positive immunity, or right, most valuable to the colored race—the right to exemption from unfriendly legislation against them distinctively as colored; exemption from legal discriminations, implying inferiority in civil society . . . and discriminations which are steps towards reducing them to the condition of a subject race.[16]

The justices also proved willing to provide remedies against state officials who were guilty of enforcing nominally impartial laws in a discriminatory fashion. In *Ex parte Virginia*, decided at the same term as

Strauder, the Court upheld the prosecution of a Virginia judge charged with systematic exclusion of blacks from juries in his court. Justice Strong noted that the Fourteenth Amendment was designed "to take away all possibility of oppression by law because of race or color," but denied that its reach was limited to formal enactments of the legislature. "Whoever, by virtue of a public position under a state government, . . . takes away the equal protection of the laws, violates the constitutional inhibition; and as he acts in the name and for the State, . . . his act is that of the State," he explained. "This must be so or the constitutional provision has no meaning."[17] In 1880, in *Neal* v. *Delaware*, the justices indicated that blacks might prove discrimination even if they did not introduce testimony showing that officials had consciously intended to keep blacks off juries. In reversing the conviction of a black man who had been indicted by an all-white grand jury and tried by an all-white petit jury, the Court held that the fact that no black had served on a jury in a state that was fifteen percent black constituted adequate proof of discrimination.

The Court's clearest indication that it would not tolerate discrimination came in 1886 when it decided *Yick Wo* v. *Hopkins*. The case was brought by a Chinese laundry operator who challenged a San Francisco ordinance that prohibited persons from operating laundries in wooden buildings without a permit from city officials. Although ostensibly designed to prevent fires, Yick Wo charged that the law's real purpose was to exclude Chinese from the laundry business. Indeed, he demonstrated that all applications for permits by Chinese had been denied while only one non-Chinese had been refused a permit. The Court, noting that the "actual operation" of the law was "directed . . . against a particular class," declared it a violation of the equal protection clause. "Though the law itself be fair on its face and impartial in appearance, yet if it is applied . . . with an evil eye and an unequal hand . . . the denial of equal justice is still within the prohibition of the Constitution," concluded Justice Stanley Matthews.[18]

The Court also upheld federal authority to protect blacks' political rights. In *United States* v. *Reese*, decided in 1876, the Court struck down two provisions of the Enforcement Act of 1870, one punishing state officials and the other private individuals who denied any otherwise qualified person the right to vote. The problem, according to the Court, was that while the Fifteenth Amendment prohibited interference with the right to vote on account of race, the sections of the Enforcement Act under consideration went beyond this, authorizing prosecution of persons who denied any qualified voter the right to vote for any reason whatsoever. Significantly, however, Chief Justice Waite did not invoke the state action theory to strike down the provision that punished private individuals. And he asserted that the Fifteenth Amendment "has invested the citizens of the United States with a new constitutional right which is within the protecting power of Congress[:] . . . exemption from discrimination in the exercise of the elective franchise on account of race. . . ."[19] Waite's analysis suggested that the government had authority to prosecute both private individuals and state officials who used force, violence, intimidation, or economic coercion to deny citizens the right to vote because of race. Indeed, a year later, sitting as circuit justice in South Carolina, Waite sustained indictments against whites who were prosecuted for acts of violence against blacks during the 1876 campaign.

In *Ex parte Yarbrough*, decided in 1884, a unanimous Supreme Court endorsed Waite's position. Jasper and Dilmus Yarbrough and seven other white Georgians (all members of the Pop and Go Club, a Democratic terrorist organization) had been convicted for violation of the Enforcement and Klan Acts for their part in violence against blacks who had voted in a hotly contested congressional election in 1882. The defendants appealed, contending that under the Court's rulings in *Cruikshank* and *The Civil Rights Cases*, the federal government did not have authority to punish private citizens for civil rights violations. Justice Miller unequivocally rejected their argument. He pointed out that Article I, section 4 of the Constitution gave Congress power to regulate the election of its members and justified legislation (like the provision of the Klan Act under which Yarbrough was prosecuted) punishing persons who attempted to control congressional elections by fraud and violence. According to Miller, Congress had ample authority to protect the Republic by guaranteeing that "the votes by which its members . . . are elected shall be the *free* votes of the electors, and the officers thus chosen the free and uncorrupted choice of those who have the right to take part in that choice."[20]

The Court's ruling in *Yarbrough* recognized that the government had broad authority to protect blacks against political terrorism. Although it merely upheld the government's authority to punish violence at congressional elections, federal and state elections were generally conducted at the same time. As a practical matter, therefore, the ruling enabled federal officials to police most state elections. In fact, Miller's opinion strongly suggested that the government had authority to use the Enforcement Act against persons who attempted to intimidate black voters in any election, regardless of whether candidates for national representative were on the ballot. He expressly reaffirmed the constitutional guarantee of exemption from racially motivated discrimination against voters. In addition, because he held that Congress possessed authority to protect this right from infringement by private individuals as well as by state officials, the opinion strongly suggested that the national government could prosecute parties who sought in any election to intimidate voters because of their race.

While hardly a champion of blacks, the Court thus supported limited federal protection of civil rights, especially in the area of voting rights. Sections of the Enforcement Act of 1870 and the Klan Act punishing infringement of the right to vote, intimidation of voters, and election fraud remained on the books and, in fact, had been reenacted by Congress in 1874 as part of *The Revised Statutes*. Encouraged by the Court's rulings in *Reese* and *Yarbrough*, the Justice Department vigorously enforced these measures throughout the 1880s and the early 1890s. Indeed, for attorneys general and their subordinates, Reconstruction did not end in 1877; prosecuting voting rights cases and ensuring ''a free ballot and a fair count'' continued to be a high priority. Federal attorneys and marshals in the South won indictments against thousands of election officials who refused to permit blacks to register or vote, stuffed ballot boxes, and engaged in other types of skullduggery aimed at neutralizing the votes of blacks and their allies. They also prosecuted hundreds of individuals who resorted to violence to keep blacks away from the polls or to punish those who had dared to vote.

Despite this effort, the Justice Department won few convictions. Defendants were generally regarded by their white neighbors as heroes persecuted by meddling outsiders. Communities contributed generously to their defense funds, and when cases went to trial, federal attorneys faced batteries of highly skilled defense lawyers. In order to put together cases that experienced defense counsel could not pick apart, harried federal attorneys needed the services of detectives to help them assemble evidence. They also required the assistance of experienced trial lawyers who could help them develop strategies for prosecution and present cases effectively in court. These hotly contested cases frequently involved large numbers of witnesses and lengthy trials, thus resulting in substantial expenses for summoning witnesses and jurors. Congress, however, facing considerable pressure to reduce federal spending, consistently denied the department adequate resources. While federal attorneys' overall caseloads quadrupled during the last quarter of the nineteenth century, Justice Department appropriations only doubled. Consequently, department officials frequently denied prosecutors' requests to hire detectives and additional attorneys. In fact, they occasionally ordered federal attorneys to dismiss cases because they did not have sufficient funds to cover the costs of prosecution.

Juries proved an even greater obstacle to success. Although federal juries continued to be racially mixed, they also included white Democrats who sympathized with defendants and denied the legitimacy of the prosecutions. Because a guilty verdict required the assent of the entire jury, prosecutors had to convince some jurors who were not only skeptical, but often downright hostile. Moreover, because blacks were often eyewitnesses to or victims of the crimes and because community pressure prevented most whites from coming forward to testify against defendants, federal attorneys had to rely heavily on black testimony. Convincing hostile white jurors to change their minds on the basis of evidence offered by blacks was not easy. As one distressed federal attorney explained, "The law is plain—the facts are plainer, but I can't make a white democratic juror believe colored witnesses nor force him to vote [for conviction]. I can't keep politics out of the human mind and I can't make the jury commissioners select more impartial men."[21]

Although it produced few convictions, the Justice Department's effort was not completely without effect. It served notice that northern Republicans had not abandoned support for civil rights and suggested that any systematic effort to deny blacks the right to vote through literacy tests and poll taxes would meet resistance. To underscore this, Republicans in Congress conducted regular investigations of southern election fraud and violence. Combined with opposition from poor whites, who feared that poll taxes and literacy tests would disfranchise them, the government's campaign to protect the voting rights of blacks helped keep the disfranchisers in check during the 1870s and 1880s. Before 1890, only Georgia and Virginia (which experimented with poll taxes in the 1870s) and South Carolina (which in 1882 established a complicated system of balloting effectively disfranchising illiterate blacks) had enacted legislation designed to disfranchise blacks.

As long as they were not legally barred from voting, southern blacks refused to be pushed out of politics. Equating the franchise with freedom, personal dignity, and equal citizenship, they were well aware that political decisions had a significant bearing on their lives. Consequently, in most states of the former Confederacy, blacks continued to vote at a high rate and occasionally mounted serious challenges to Democratic hegemony. In a number of heavily black counties, redemption did not bring an end to Republican control; candidates elected by former slaves continued to serve as state legislators, local officials, and sometimes even congressmen. In addition to retaining power in black belt enclaves, Republicans mounted periodic challenges that threatened Democratic control at the state level. In Tennessee, where Unionist whites in the mountainous eastern counties joined with blacks in the central and western counties to support Republican candidates, the party remained a threat to Democratic control. Indeed, the Republican gubernatorial candidate won election in 1880, when the Democrats divided, and the party won more than forty percent of the vote in statewide elections during the remainder of the decade. In North Carolina, support from mountain Unionists in the west and blacks in the east enabled Republicans to come within a whisker of regaining control of the state in 1880. During the next two decades, Republicans would remain a force to be reckoned with in North Carolina politics.

In other states, Republicans forged alliances with dissident Democrats. During the late 1870s and throughout the 1880s, independent political movements, backed mainly by poor white farmers who were alienated by the economic policies of conservative Democratic leaders, emerged throughout the region. By joining forces with the dissidents, Republicans were able to mount serious challenges in Florida, Arkansas, and Texas. In Virginia, disaffected Democrats known as the "Readjusters" (they advocated reducing or "readjusting" the state debt, most of which was held by outside investors) formed an alliance with Republicans that shook the Old Dominion. Uniting white farmers and blacks, the Readjusters controlled the state between 1879 and 1883, when Democrats regained control in a campaign won through violence and fraud.

There were also other indications that blacks were not resigned to second-class citizenship in the years following the end of Reconstruction. Even in the South, where Democrats dominated the legislatures and the courts and protesters risked violent reprisals, blacks continued to challenge discrimination through legal and political action. When Democrats resegregated the New Orleans public schools in 1877, the city's blacks turned to the courts, arguing that segregation denied them the equal protection guaranteed by the Fourteenth Amendment. Although they were not successful, their action suggests that they did not accept second-class citizenship and continued to use the legal process to assert their rights. In other parts of the South, where segregated schools had emerged during Reconstruction, most blacks accepted the redeemers' continuation of dual school systems; however, black conventions protested unequal funding of black schools and demanded that state governments devote equal resources to black and white schools. In Kentucky and North Carolina, where Democratic legislatures provided that taxes paid by members of each race be used to support their own schools, blacks used legal and political action to have the laws reversed and to secure more equitable funding.

It was in the North, however, that blacks made the greatest gains against segregation during the 1880s. While in 1883, the Supreme Court had ruled that Congress lacked authority to ban discrimination in places of public accommodation, it left the way open for individual states to enact such measures. Indeed, comments by Justice Bradley in his opinion in *The Civil Rights Cases*, as well as the Court's well-established tolerance of state legislation to promote the public welfare, suggested that states enjoyed broad authority to enact antidiscrimination measures. Making the most of this, blacks who met in Washington, D.C. in 1883 to protest the Court's decision urged civil rights advocates to press for state legislation to replace the federal law struck down by the Court. The North's tiny black community (blacks comprised only about two percent of the region's population) responded energetically. In Ohio, for example, blacks formed a network of equal rights leagues to demand civil rights legislation. Between 1884 and 1887, Ohio and twelve other northern states passed laws prohibiting discrimination in hotels, restaurants, public transportation, and places of amusement. During the late 1880s and the 1890s many of these states expanded the list of places covered by the acts, and four additional states passed antidiscrimination measures. Moreover, in enforcing these laws, state courts refused to permit businesses to make any distinction on account of color. In the three states where the issue arose, they ruled that restaurant and theater owners could not segregate blacks within their establishments.

Northern blacks also continued their campaign for integrated schools. Blacks had won admission to white schools in most of New England prior to the Civil War, and during the late 1860s and 1870s they had used effectively political and legal action to end school segregation in seven other states. Yet school boards in a number of northern states maintained separate schools for blacks, and state courts in Nevada, Ohio, California, and Indiana had ruled that separate schools did not violate guarantees of equality contained in the Fourteenth Amendment and state constitutions. During the 1880s and 1890s blacks and their white allies won legislation mandating integrated schools in seven additional northern states, including laws reversing the effects of prosegregation court decisions in California and Ohio. Throughout the North black litigants enjoyed frequent success in cases they brought against school boards that operated separate schools for blacks. In deciding these cases, state courts usually relied on state constitutional provisions and statutes to strike down segregation and, with one exception, held that the Fourteenth Amendment did not require integration. Nevertheless, as a result of litigation and political action, there were few segregated schools in the North by 1900.

Northern blacks' continued success in the battle against discrimination did not mean that racism was dead in the North. Social contact between whites and blacks was rare, aversion among whites to contact with blacks in public places was still widespread, and most whites denied that blacks were their equals. If anything, northern racism became stronger during the 1880s and 1890s, as respected biologists and social scientists placed the imprimatur of science on the myth of black inferiority by asserting that blacks had not reached the same intellectual or moral level as whites. Given the persistence of racism, northern blacks continued to suffer discrimination and, despite the new public accommodations laws, were frequently denied admission to white theaters, hotels, restaurants, and amusements. The public accommodations laws gave blacks remedies against such abuses, and they frequently sued those who discriminated against them; however, because confrontations with hostile proprietors were unpleasant and lawsuits were expensive, many blacks chose to avoid places where they knew they were not welcome. White prejudice also consigned most blacks to menial, low-paying jobs, depriving them of the opportunities offered by an expanding economy. And whether or not they were willing to sue, state law offered no redress against employment discrimination.

Nevertheless, northern blacks' political and legal victories were not meaningless. In practical terms, they gave black children access to white schools, which were better funded and offered greater educational opportunities than were available in the South's separate and unequal schools. Even though discrimination continued, greater fluidity in race relations existed in the North. Consequently, northern blacks, unlike their southern counterparts, were not subject to constant and blatant reminders that they were regarded as an inferior caste, unfit to associate with whites. Furthermore, the victories of the 1870s and 1880s established the principle of colorblind citizenship as part of the North's dominant public philosophy. As the Michigan Supreme Court noted in 1890, "there must be and is an absolute, unconditional equality of white and colored men before the law. . . . Whatever right a white man has in a public place, the black man has also."[22] This marked a significant change from the antebellum era, when most Republicans had assured their constituents that they did not support black suffrage, much less blacks' right to equal access to public accommodations. While the principle of colorblind citizenship often amounted to little more than empty rhetoric, it nevertheless upheld a standard that blacks could press whites to honor in practice as well as in name. And given the political and legal techniques they had learned and the confidence they had gained in over half a century of agitation for reform, blacks would not be bashful about holding whites to their promises.

The Triumph of Racism

While northern blacks' campaign for civil rights accelerated during the years after Reconstruction, southern blacks' gains were swept away by a rising tide of white supremacy. During the late 1870s and 1880s southern blacks had refused to accept the Democratic counterrevolution, using political and legal means to defend their rights. Yet while they had won occasional victories, their position generally had deteriorated. Beginning in the late 1880s and stretching into the first two decades of the twentieth century, southern Democrats launched a ferocious new offensive that reduced blacks to second-class citizenship.

Despite Democrats' efforts to deter them, blacks had continued to vote at a high rate in most states during the 1870s and 1880s. Indeed, they had frequently joined with poor white farmers who had bolted the Democratic party because of dissatisfaction with its economic policies, forming coalitions that forced the dominant Democrats to resort to even greater violence and fraud in an effort to maintain their power. This pattern continued in the 1890s, as many economically distressed white farmers left the Democratic party to join the Populists. The new party pledged itself to use the power of government on behalf of working people, advocating nationalization of the railroads, a vigorous campaign against big business, wholesale reform of the financial system, and establishment of producer-operated cooperatives that would free farmers from dependence on merchants. Like the independent parties of the 1870s and 1880s, the Populists hoped to attract black voters to their cause, uniting poor whites and blacks in a coalition that would drive the Democrats from power. In North Carolina, where Populists fused with the Republican party, the strategy worked, at least temporarily; and in a number of other southern states, only widespread violence and unprecedented fraud by the Democrats defeated it.

Shaken by this challenge, southern Democrats moved to undercut the opposition by disfranchising blacks. Aware that the Fifteenth Amendment prohibited them from openly denying blacks the right to vote, Democrats sought to accomplish their objective indirectly. By requiring voters to pay poll taxes (small annual head taxes usually amounting to less than three dollars per year), they could reduce the black electorate substantially. The great majority of southern blacks were desperately poor agricultural laborers and sharecroppers. Trapped in a vicious credit system that kept many in debt from year to year, precious little cash passed through their hands. Consequently, a tax of only three dollars could put the ballot beyond their reach. The literacy test offered disfranchisers an even more effective tool. Given the legacy of slavery and the meager support for black schools in the aftermath of Reconstruction, illiteracy among blacks was widespread. In 1890, more than half of the adult black males in the South could not read, and many others were barely literate. Fairly administered, literacy tests (which required prospective voters to prove that they could read a provision of the state or federal constitution) would deny the ballot to most black men; applied by partisan white officials who were bitterly opposed to black suffrage, they would cut even further into the black electorate.

For Democratic leaders, literacy tests and poll taxes had an added attraction. Although publicly they emphasized the effect these measures would have on blacks, Democrats were well aware that they would also take their toll on poor whites. The region's depressed agricultural economy affected whites as well as blacks, leaving many white farmers on the brink of ruin and forcing many others into the poverty of tenancy and sharecropping. Poverty also bred illiteracy; in 1900, twelve percent of southern whites could neither read nor write. The new voting requirements, therefore, would exclude many whites from voting, and happily for Democratic leaders, these would be the men who had defected from the party during the 1880s and 1890s.

Although blacks and dissident whites bitterly opposed disfranchisement, conservative Democrats achieved their objective. Beginning with Florida and Tennessee in 1889 and Mississippi in 1890 and concluding with Georgia in 1908, measures designed to prune the electorate were adopted throughout the South. Each of the eleven states of the old Confederacy made payment of a poll tax a requirement for voting, and five heightened the effect of the tax by making it cumulative (i.e., requiring voters to pay poll taxes for previous years as well as for the year of the election). Seven of these states coupled the poll tax with a literacy test, and seven adopted the secret ballot, which served as a de facto literacy test because illiterates were unable to read it. Except for Florida, each of these states supplemented the poll tax with a literacy test or the secret ballot or both. In five states, Democratic leaders established loopholes for whites—a concession necessary to obtain sufficient support for passage of the disfranchisement measures. Several states exempted from the literacy test those who owned a certain amount of property (usually $300) or enacted understanding clauses that enfranchised those who could explain a passage of the constitution when it was read to them by the registrar. Several states supplemented these with grandfather clauses that waived literacy tests for those who were descendents of persons who had been qualified to vote prior to 1867 (the year southern blacks gained the ballot) or who had fought for the Union or Confederacy.

The new requirements had a dramatic effect on the southern electorate; in the years following their enactment, registration among blacks plummeted. By 1910, black registration had decreased to fifteen percent in Virginia and to less than two percent in Alabama and Mississippi. Although loopholes and discriminatory administration of the laws allowed many whites to dodge the effects of the literacy requirements, the new laws took their toll on whites as well. Many were too proud to admit that they could not read and declined to exploit the loopholes, while others were excluded from voting because they were too poor to pay their poll taxes. Therefore while white registration remained at approximately eighty percent in Virginia and Alabama, it decreased to approximately fifty percent in Louisiana and to sixty percent in Mississippi. As J. Morgan Kousser, the leading student of suffrage restriction had noted, the disfranchising measures "insured that the Southern electorate for half a century would be almost all white; yet . . . [they] did not guarantee all whites the vote."[23]

Passage of legislation mandating segregation—the Jim Crow laws[24]—coincided with disfranchisement. Separation of the races in churches, schools, public transportation, hotels, and restaurants had become customary in the decades following the war. During the late 1870s and 1880s, however, some states began to codify custom, mandating segregation in prisons and public schools. Beginning in the late 1880s and continuing through the first two decades of the twentieth century, southern legislatures and city councils went to work with a new fervor, enacting a mountain of laws and ordinances to formalize and to put the force of law behind what had been largely customary arrangements.

The move to give white supremacy the force of law was a natural product of a turbulent era. As white Democrats launched their disfranchisement campaigns, they stoked the fires of racial prejudice white hot in order to focus attention on blacks (rather than poor whites) as the primary targets and to convince those who were concerned about the impact on poor whites that disfranchisement was necessary at all costs. The disfranchisers repeatedly denounced blacks as ignorant, lazy, criminally inclined, and venal, a race demonstrably unqualified to exercise political rights. In an atmosphere poisoned with racial hatred, it is hardly surprising that laws designed to further degrade blacks attracted broad support. Continued black assertiveness and activism in the decade after Reconstruction also contributed to the emergence of segregation. It reminded southern whites that they had not fully established white supremacy, the goal of the redeemers. In fact, many whites feared that a new generation of blacks who had never known slavery was coming to maturity and that they might pose an even stiffer challenge to white supremacy than had their parents. Frustrated by their failure to restore black deference and concerned about the future, the establishment of legally sanctioned segregation offered white southerners a powerful means of asserting their power and dominance. Moreover, given the deep racism that existed throughout the South, adoption of segregation statutes by one or two states led legislators in neighboring states to follow suit, quickly spreading the laws across the region.

Jim Crow came to the South in three waves. Between 1887 and 1891 most states of the former Confederacy adopted laws requiring railroads to provide separate but equal accommodations for the two races. Then, beginning in 1901 with Virginia, most southern states passed laws requiring urban street railroads to separate black and white passengers. Finally, during the 1910s, states and localities created a complex web of regulations designed to extend the logic of separation to all spheres of southern life. A number of states forbade whites and blacks to be taught together, even in private schools, and barred teachers and nurses from serving students or patients of another race. States and cities established separate parks and mandated residential segregation. Some states required manufacturers to designate different entrances for white and black employees, to maintain separate pay windows, toilets, and water buckets, and to separate workers by race on the job. Not content with segregating school children, North Carolina and Florida required that public school textbooks used by children of different races be stored separately. And, though not required by law, many courts kept separate Bibles for swearing black and white witnesses.

The results of the segregation campaign were devastating for southern blacks. Since the end of the Civil War they had lived in a world increasingly separate from whites. Yet the triumph of Jim Crow infused this separateness with deeper meaning and force. By the early twentieth century, southern blacks lived in a world circumscribed by signs designating ''white'' and ''colored'' facilities. Separate Bibles in courtrooms as well as separate waiting rooms in train stations served as constant reminders that whites considered them a degraded caste. The signs, together with the intricate set of laws establishing segregation, made blacks adapt to ludicrous rules that varied from state to state and city to city, further underscoring whites' power.

In the face of the white onslaught, a growing number of black leaders—most notably Booker T. Washington, president of Alabama's Tuskegee Institute—renounced the battle for political and social equality. Blacks should be concerned not with integration and political rights, they argued, but with obtaining the education and skills that would enable them to advance economically and, gradually, to earn political rights and social acceptance by whites. In communities across the South, however, many blacks rejected accommodationism as a dead end. As a powerless, proscribed group, they argued, blacks would be even more vulnerable to white aggression and would find their efforts at advancement continually thwarted. Viewing segregation and disfranchisement as an effort ''to humiliate, degrade, and stigmatize the negro,'' more militant leaders urged resistance "in order to maintain our self-respect."[25] In at least twenty-seven cities, blacks launched boycotts of segregated streetcars between 1900 and 1910, some lasting as long as two years. Black leaders also turned to the courts, charging that Jim Crow legislation violated the letter and the spirit of the Fourteenth and Fifteenth Amendments. Without the aid of a national organization to raise funds and develop legal strategy, a number of southern black communities raised money locally to support litigation aimed at derailing the movement for white supremacy.

Blacks' constitutional claims, however, were unequivocally rejected by the Supreme Court. During the 1870s and 1880s the Court had been dominated by northern Republicans who, although quite conservative, nonetheless had come of age at the height of the struggle against slavery and who shared their party's commitment to emancipation and equal rights. Their rulings had narrowed the compass of the postwar amendments, restricting the government's authority to punish civil rights violations by private citizens. However, they had emphasized that the postwar amendments had been adopted to guarantee the former slaves equal rights and that they clearly barred discriminatory state action, whether it was carried out through blatantly discriminatory laws or by more subtle means. The six new justices who came to the Supreme Court between 1888 and 1894 were of a different generation. Although most were northern Republicans, they had come of age at a time when northern interest in Reconstruction was dimming and scientists were giving respectability to racism. Consequently, the new justices were less inclined than their predecessors to protect the constitutional rights of blacks.

The first major test of the new justices' position on civil rights came in 1896, when the Court decided *Plessy* v. *Ferguson*. The case had been initiated by the American Citizens Equal Rights Association, a group organized by New Orleans blacks to challenge an 1890 Louisiana law requiring railroads to provide separate but equal accommodations for blacks. The association was represented by Albion Tourgee of New York, who had served on the front line of the Reconstruction-era battle for equality as a Republican leader in North Carolina and who had remained an eloquent advocate of the cause after returning to the North. Hewing to the arguments developed by abolitionist legal theorists and Reconstruction-era Republican congressmen, Tourgee denied that the law's guarantee of equivalent facilities satisfied the requirements of the

Fourteenth Amendment's equal protection clause. The entire purpose of the postwar amendments, he emphasized, was to eradicate caste and establish a colorblind Constitution. By separating blacks from whites, he concluded, the Louisiana statute stigmatized and degraded blacks, subjected them to invidious discrimination, perpetuated the spirit of caste, and therefore was patently unconstitutional.

The Court's response suggested that the arguments of Reconstruction-era Republicans rang hollow to the new justices. Justice Henry Brown, a Michigan Republican who in 1890 had replaced Justice Samuel Miller, wrote the Court's opinion, sustaining the law's constitutionality. Reading the scientific racism of the 1890s back into the 1860s, Brown asserted that the amendment's framers must have understood that there was a deep natural aversion to racial intermingling. Consequently, he asserted, they had merely intended to guarantee "the absolute equality of the races before the law," not social equality. Brown concluded therefore that the amendment was satisfied by the Louisiana statute's requirement of equal but separate facilities. Blind to the campaign of racial hatred that was then raging in the South, he denied Tourgee's assertion that the statute "stamps the colored race with a badge of inferiority." "If this be so," the justice blithely explained, "it is not by reason of anything found in the act, but solely because the colored race chooses to put that construction upon it." Only John Marshall Harlan, a veteran of Reconstruction-era political battles who had served on the Court for nearly twenty years, dissented, predicting that "the judgment this day rendered will . . . prove to be quite as pernicious as . . . the *Dred Scott case.*"[26]

Three years later, when it decided *Cumming* v. *School Board of Richmond County, Ga.*, the Supreme Court suggested that it would not be overly scrupulous in guaranteeing that segregated facilities were actually equal. The case was brought by Augusta, Georgia blacks to challenge the school board's decision to close the county's only black high school. Since the board continued to support several white high schools, the plaintiffs charged that it had deprived black children of opportunities afforded whites, thereby denying them equal protection. A unanimous Court turned aside their argument, however, signaling that under the guise of separate but equal blacks might be consigned to grossly unequal schools, services, and accommodations.

The Court also sustained disfranchisement. While the new voting requirements disfranchised many poor whites, they were directed principally at blacks. Not only did many states include understanding clauses, property tests, and grandfather clauses offering whites ways around the literacy tests, but the new laws had a much more drastic effect on blacks than on whites. Moreover, the rhetoric accompanying disfranchisement suggested that southerners were determined to eliminate blacks from politics. Despite the fact that the disfranchisement laws were racially neutral on their face, therefore, a good case could be made that they violated the Fifteenth Amendment.

In 1898, when it decided *Williams* v. *Mississippi*, the Court rejected such an argument. Justice Joseph McKenna, a California Republican who had recently joined the Court, admitted in his opinion that the Mississippi Supreme Court had openly suggested that the state's poll tax and literacy test were designed to disfranchise blacks. Indeed, it had been quite candid in discussing the purpose of the measures:

> Within the field of permissible action under the limitations imposed by the Federal Constitution, the [state constitutional] convention swept the circle of expedients to obstruct the exercise of suffrage by the negro race. . . . By reason of its previous condition of servitude and dependencies, this race had acquired or accentuated certain peculiarities of habit . . . which clearly distinguished it as a race, from the whites—a patient, docile people; but careless, landless, migratory within narrow limits, without forethought; and its criminal members given to furtive offenses, rather than to the robust crimes of the whites. Restrained by the Federal Constitution from discriminating against the negro race, the convention discriminates against its characteristics. [27]

Nevertheless, McKenna concluded that "nothing tangible can be deduced from this," adding that the state's voting requirements did not deny anyone the right to vote on the basis of race. In sum, states might devise clever strategies to defeat the spirit of the Fifteenth Amendment so long as they did not expressly violate its provisions. [28]

By the end of the century, then, the postwar amendments' revolutionary promise of a colorblind Constitution that empowered the national government to guarantee its citizens civil equality lay unfulfilled. Given the ferocity of southern resistance, most white Americans' unwillingness to centralize power in the national government, the waning of concern for black rights in the North, and the resurgence of racism nationwide, the nation reneged on promises made in the heat of the Civil War and Reconstruction. During the 1870s and 1880s the Supreme Court had significantly restricted the scope of national power to protect individual rights, effectively curtailing (although not destroying) the revolutionary potential of postwar amendments and civil rights laws. With the addition of new members to the Supreme Court in the 1890s, the Court capitulated to the racist fury that was sweeping the South. Placing form above substance, ignoring the purpose of the postwar amendments, and demonstrating a perverse ignorance of southern legislators' intent, the Court accepted segregation and disfranchisement.

Consequently, blacks entered the new century stripped of the promise of the Reconstruction revolution. Northern blacks were in a better position than black southerners, but with no thanks to federal Constitutional guarantees. Through political and legal action they had been able to win passage of legislation guaranteeing them equal civil rights, and state courts, relying on state constitutional provisions and statutes, had handed down decisions protecting these rights. Despite the law, however, racism remained powerful among northerners, as evidenced by the behavior of northerners who served on the Supreme Court, and frequently undercut the rights to which blacks were entitled. It was in the South, however, where ninety percent of the nation's blacks lived in 1900 that the capitulation to racism was most evident. There blacks were subjected to a humiliating system of segregation in all aspects of their lives, a system that, despite the legal fiction of separate but equal, consigned them to schools and other facilities that were separate and visibly unequal. They were also systematically denied the ballot, the principal symbol of citizenship in the Republic. Marked by the law as members of an inferior caste and denied political power, they were left by the law to the tender mercies of their white neighbors.

5

The Age of Segregation, 1900–1950

Born in 1895, the year Frederick Douglass died, Charles Hamilton Houston would combine Douglass's passion for equality with sharply honed legal skills to rekindle the struggle for equality—a struggle that had been all but abandoned by the time of Douglass's death. Unlike Douglass, who was born a slave, Charles Houston was the only son of a lawyer and a teacher. He attended Washington's M Street School, perhaps the best black high school in the nation, and, after graduating first in his class, he went on to Amherst College, where he was elected to Phi Beta Kappa and was valedictorian of the class of 1915. After graduation, he taught in Washington and served in the army during World War I, saving enough money to attend Harvard Law School. There he became the first black to serve on the *Harvard Law Review* and caught the eye of future Supreme Court Justice Felix Frankfurter, the human dynamo who was an inspiring teacher, an exacting scholar, an avid civil libertarian, and an active public servant who urged his students to use their talents in service to the public. After graduating fifth in his class in 1922, Houston devoted one year to graduate work with Frankfurter and then traveled to Spain and Italy for additional advanced study.

Houston was clearly an exceptional young man, leading a seemingly charmed life. Nevertheless, he was a black man in Jim Crow America, and he could not insulate himself from the barbs of white racism. While Houston was at Amherst, President Woodrow Wilson, a native Virginian, brought segregation to the federal civil service, something that undoubtedly stung Houston since many family friends worked in the federal bureaucracy. During World War I, he fought in a Jim Crow army that was supposed to make the world safe for democracy, and he and other black soldiers returned from France in 1919, not to a hero's welcome, but to a series of ugly race riots that swept across the nation. As he practiced law, he was repeatedly reminded of the color line. One incident was recalled by Herbert Wechsler, a white lawyer who would go on to a distinguished career at Columbia Law School. During 1931, while clerking for Justice Harlan Fiske Stone, he encountered Houston, with whom he had become acquainted during his stay in Washington, D.C. outside the Supreme Court's chambers. "I proposed that we have lunch in the Capitol," remembers Wechsler, "and he said no, we couldn't do that. . . ."[1] Washington, D.C. was a Jim Crow town, and the Capitol restaurants were segregated.

Houston entered practice with his father and, despite the indignities of segregated Washington, could have made a good living for himself. Perhaps because of personal experiences, perhaps because of Frankfurter's example, he had a burning desire to bring his legal skills and intellectual ability to the service of black America. In 1929, Howard University's president, Mordecai Johnson, offered him the opportunity to do just that, asking him to become dean of the Howard Law School and to revitalize a program that had floundered for years and had recently lost its accreditation. Houston accepted and during the next six years rebuilt the law school. Recruiting the best black legal talent in the nation, he created a rigorous program designed to produce top-notch lawyers. Thurgood Marshall, the future Supreme Court justice who was Houston's most prominent student, recalled:

> He was hard-crust. First off, you thought he was a mean so-and-so. He used to tell us that doctors could bury their mistakes but lawyers couldn't. And he'd drive home to us that we would be competing not only with white lawyers but really well-trained white lawyers. . . . I'll tell you—the going was rough. There must have been thirty of us in that class when we started, and no more than eight or ten of us finished up. He was so tough we used to call him "Iron Shoes" and "Cement Pants" and a few other names that don't bear repeating. But he was a sweet man once you saw what he was up to. He was absolutely fair, and the door to his office was always open.[2]

But Houston was interested in more than turning out first-rate lawyers. He instilled in his students a commitment to public service and created the nation's first program in public interest law. "He kept hammering at us all those years that, as lawyers, we had to be social engineers or else we were parasites,'' explains Oliver Hill, who graduated in 1934, one year behind Marshall. Howard offered the first civil rights course in the country, and its law library became a treasure-trove of books, memos, reports, lawyers' briefs, and other materials on segregated education, transportation, and housing; voting rights; and discriminatory law enforcement. Houston and his colleagues demanded that the nation fulfill its long-delayed promise of equality, insisting that all they asked was that ''the United States respect its own Constitution and laws.'' And they set out to create a generation of black lawyers who shared their commitment to equal rights and to using the law as a tool to effect social change. ''Frankly, the purpose there was to learn how to bend the law to the needs of blacks,'' noted one Howard graduate. Moreover, like the abolitionists, Houston viewed lawsuits not only as a means to challenge legal rules that held blacks in thralldom but also as opportunities for rallying broad-based support in the black community for the struggle for equality.[3]

During the following decades, Houston would continue to play a major role in that battle. In 1935 he became chief counsel for the National Association for the Advancement of Colored People (NAACP). In that post, which he held until 1938, he began a methodical campaign of litigation designed to undermine Jim Crow and to nurture grass-roots civil rights consciousness. After health problems forced him to return to private practice, he remained active in civil rights litigation throughout the 1940s. His greatest contribution, however, was at Howard University, where he created a first-rate law school that helped produce a generation of black lawyers who would reassert constitutional principles of equality, using them as a hammer to demolish the edifice of segregation.

Black America in the Age of Segregation

By the time Charles Houston left Amherst in 1915, the position of blacks in America was approaching its nadir, especially in the South. Disfranchisement and segregation shaped the contours of life for black southerners during the first half of the twentieth century, leaving them vulnerable to arbitrary white authority and sharply constricting their options. Segregated schools and whites' monopoly of political power had an especially devastating effect on black children. In 1910 the eleven states of the former Confederacy spent three times more per capita on white students than on their black counterparts. Although absolute levels of spending increased during the following thirty years, per capita spending on black students remained one-third of that for whites on the eve of World War II. The results were predictable: black schools were run-down, overcrowded, and often without heat in the winter; buses were unavailable to transport black children to school (a major problem since the majority of black southerners lived in rural areas); and student–teacher ratios were far higher than in white schools. Opportunities to go beyond elementary school were limited. By the mid-1930s, only nineteen percent of southern black children between the ages of fourteen and seventeen attended high school; the comparable figure for whites was fifty-five percent. Black teachers also suffered. In 1935, they taught classes that were thirty percent larger and took home paychecks that were forty percent smaller than those of their white peers.

If blacks lost, whites gained from the system. Underfunding of black schools spared taxpayers the considerable expense that would have been required to maintain separate and genuinely equal schools. In addition, tax dollars that should have gone to black schools were available to enhance educational opportunities for white children. The system also guaranteed that most blacks remained poorly educated and therefore unable to compete with whites for higher-status, higher-income jobs. Finally, whites (confusing achievement with ability) cited blacks' low level of intellectual development as proof of their inferiority. This, they claimed, justified disfranchisement, segregation, and low levels of spending on black education. The cycle was complete and self-perpetuating.

The caste system also narrowed employment opportunities for southern blacks, especially access to white-collar and professional jobs. Black poverty and white prejudice guaranteed that white-owned businesses dominated the southern economy. These establishments—from the local dry goods store to large firms like Coca-Cola—refused to hire blacks as clerks, secretaries, or salespersons, much less as managers. With government controlled by men committed to white supremacy, blacks were excluded from managerial and clerical positions in state and local bureaucracies as well as from elective office. A few blacks became physicians, dentists, and lawyers, but opportunities in these fields were limited. Whites shunned black professionals, and most blacks, being poor, sought medical and legal services infrequently. Those blacks who could afford a lawyer often hired white attorneys, aware that they would have greater credibility with white judges and jurors. With medicine and law offering promising careers to only a few, white-collar and professional employment was, for all practical purposes, limited to teaching in black schools, preaching in black churches, and owning or working in black-owned businesses that served the black community. Consequently, blacks' opportunity to achieve middle class status—the opportunity that defined the American Dream—was sharply restricted.

The situation was no better for blue-collar workers. Blacks were virtually excluded from jobs in textiles and oil and gas, the South's fastest growing industries. They won a significant number of jobs in the construction, tobacco, railroad, iron and steel, turpentine, lumber, fertilizer, and mining industries, but these were unskilled, menial, dirty, hot, dangerous, and low-paying positions—jobs that whites considered "Negro work." Other black workers took service positions in hotels, restaurants, laundries, and private homes, which paid meager wages for long hours and which most whites considered beneath their dignity. With good nonagricultural jobs closed to them, however, a majority of southern blacks continued to work the land, their fate tied to the cotton and tobacco economies. Given the low prices of these commodities and the fact that, as in industry, blacks were segregated into the least desirable, lowest-paying, most vulnerable positions (laborers and share-croppers rather than owners and renters), rural blacks knew little but grinding poverty.

Regardless of their economic position, blacks were members of a despised caste and stood outside the protection of the law. Virtually all law enforcement officials, justices of the peace, judges, and jurors were white men who shared their society's commitment to the principles of white supremacy. Most believed that the word of a white person, any white person, was superior to that of a black, that blacks were lazy, shiftless, and given to lying and theft, and that white men must have adequate authority to keep blacks in a position of subservience. The effect on the southern legal system was utterly corrosive. Law enforcement officers had little reason to fear complaints made against them by blacks, and consequently, police brutality and disregard for the rights of blacks suspected of crime were pervasive. When blacks were charged with crimes against whites, judges and jurors discounted the testimony of black witnesses and readily convicted black defendants, even when the evidence against them was weak. Law enforcement officials generally refused to prosecute whites who assaulted or murdered blacks, especially if the perpetrators claimed that blacks had provoked the attacks by insolence or lack of deference. Finally, white officials showed little concern about crime within the black community, failing to prosecute or imposing light punishments on blacks who assaulted, murdered, or robbed other blacks.

Lynching was the most terrible example of the way white supremacy made a mockery of the rule of law. Blacks accused of especially heinous offenses against whites (especially murder or rape) or who flouted the conventions of white supremacy too conspicuously were frequently seized by angry mobs, subjected to gruesome torture, and executed, often before throngs of cheering whites. In 1911 a white mob in Livermore, Kentucky dragged a black man accused of killing a white to a local theater and hanged him before an audience of white townspeople who paid admission. Those paying for orchestra seats were invited to empty their pistols into the victim's swinging body, while patrons in the balcony were each permitted one shot. State and local officials generally proved unable or unwilling to halt mobs or to prosecute participants, whose identities were widely known. Although the number of lynchings declined after the 1890s, an average of sixty-seven blacks were lynched each year during the first two decades of the twentieth century. The horror of these grizzly spectacles underscored black powerlessness and was deeply etched in blacks' consciousness. Indeed, it found expression in black music, most notably in the ballad, "Strange Fruit," popularized by the great jazz singer, Billie Holiday:

> Southern trees bear strange fruit,
> Blood on the leaves and blood at the root,
> Black body swinging in the southern breeze,
> Strange fruit hanging from the poplar trees.

> Pastoral scene of the gallant South,
> The bulging eyes and the twisted mouth.
> Scent of magnolia, sweet and fresh,
> And the sudden smell of burning flesh.

> Here is a fruit for the crows to pluck,
> For the rain to gather, for the wind to suck,
> For the sun to rot, for a tree to drop,
> Here is a strange and bitter crop.

Although there was overwhelming support for segregation among white southerners, some of these men and women were appalled by the flagrant denials of basic human rights they witnessed. Sometimes their vision of a more humane, more paternalistic form of white supremacy helped to curb the system's excesses. During the 1930s, for example, the Association of Southern Women for the Prevention of Lynching, led by Jessie Daniel Ames, publicized the horrors of lynching, warned southerners that it had tarnished the region's image in the eyes of the nation, and pressed local officials to protect blacks from the mob. While the efforts of these women of good will contributed to a significant decline in lynching, the pangs of conscience felt by paternalistic southerners did little to stop the day-to-day injustices that were part of the fabric of black life. To most whites, blacks simply did not count, indeed were invisible. This made it easy for whites to ignore the problems blacks encountered and the barbarities of the caste system. And those whites who were in positions to curb the excesses—especially lawyers, judges, and politicians—generally feared the social, political, and professional consequences of speaking out against injustice and remained silent.

Injustice persisted not only because of the reluctance of most whites to risk taking a stand against it, but also because whites derived substantial benefits from the status quo. By degrading blacks, the legal system assured that even whites of the lowest social and economic position were superior to blacks. White taxpayers also benefitted from the steady stream of blacks who were convicted of petty crime and sentenced to serve on county chain gangs if they could not pay their fines and court costs. Manacled, clothed in striped suits, and supervised by armed guards who had carte blanche to extract labor through flogging and other forms of violence, county convicts worked on roads and bridges, saving taxpayers millions of dollars annually. Planters and farmers also found the system useful. Blacks convicted of petty crimes provided a steady source of cheap labor. Eager to avoid the chain gang, they were in no position to reject labor contracts offered by whites who agreed to pay their fines. When labor was scarce, local officials obligingly used the threat of prosecution for vagrancy to prod blacks who supported themselves through odd jobs to come to terms with planters. The system also encouraged black deference to white authority, creating outwardly pleasant relations between the races and placing a thin veneer over its oppression. Blacks realized that only a white patron or a reputation among whites as a ''good Negro'' could protect them should they get into trouble or fall into the toils of the law. Outwardly at least, most southern blacks, especially those in rural areas and small towns, accepted the conventions of white supremacy and were reluctant to challenge a system that brutally exploited them.

The oppression experienced by southern blacks, combined with the crisis of the cotton economy brought on by the boll weevil and falling cotton prices, drove successive waves of them to northern urban centers. More than 200,000 migrants trekked north between 1890 and 1910. The Great Migration of the 1910s saw one half-million blacks leave the South for northern cities, and more than one million more followed in the next two decades. By 1940, more than twenty percent of the nation's blacks lived in the North, with most concentrated in overcrowded ghettos in the region's great metropolises.

This migration produced new social tensions, increasing racial prejudice among northern whites. As southern blacks moved into northern cities, they entered white working class neighborhoods in search of low-cost housing. Proximity did not lead to greater understanding. Working class whites—native-born as well as recent European immigrants—often greeted the new arrivals with suspicion, viewing them as competitors for jobs. Suspicion turned to hatred when white employers occasionally hired blacks as strikebreakers, and hatred sparked violence. During the first two decades of the twentieth century, serious race riots erupted in New York (1900), Springfield, Illinois (1908), East St. Louis, Illinois (1917), and Washington, D.C., Omaha, and Chicago (1919). In Chicago the fighting lasted thirteen days and left 38 dead, more than 500 injured, and 1,000 black families homeless.

But racism was not the special preserve of working-class whites, and it was not only they who attacked blacks in these melees. Prominent scientists purported to show that blacks were inferior to whites, popular writers trumpeted the superiority of the Anglo-Saxon over darker-skinned peoples, historians depicted Reconstruction as a tragic era in which ignorant, venal black voters plunged the south into corruption and chaos, and the advertising and movie industries inundated Americans with images of childlike, irresponsible, lazy blacks. In this milieu, middle and upper-class whites responded to the new immigrants with hostility, viewing them as a potential threat to their neighborhoods, schools, and communities.

Although race relations remained considerably more fluid in the North than in the South, northern blacks encountered increasing discrimination during the 1910s and 1920s. Residential segregation was the norm in most northern cities. As blacks settled in areas where low-cost housing was available, working-class whites began to move out. More recent black arrivals, drawn to areas where their relatives lived and where black churches and community organizations had been established, took their places. If residential segregation emerged as a result of black settlement patterns, whites employed legal and extra-legal devices to preserve it. White homeowners adopted restrictive covenants[4] barring sale of their property to non-whites. Adoption of these agreements was so widespread that by 1940, between twenty-five and fifty percent of Chicago's South Side was closed to blacks. Realtors' associations in many cities established guidelines prohibiting their members from showing homes in white neighborhoods to prospective black buyers, and lending institutions, afraid that integration would lead to white flight and lower property values, refused to make loans to blacks who wished to purchase homes outside the ghetto. If these devices were not sufficient to deter them, blacks who moved into white neighborhoods frequently encountered hostility and violence.

Most northern states did not require separate schools and many even had laws prohibiting school segregation. Consequently, there was racial mixing in many northern schools, and black teachers occasionally taught white children. Nevertheless, residential segregation made neighborhood schools predominantly white or black. Race-conscious white school officials also contributed to segregation by drawing school district boundaries to maximize racial separation and by offering transfers to white children whose residences fell within heavily black districts. Officials in some northern cities went even further, creating separate classes for those blacks who attended racially mixed schools or even creating all-black schools in violation of state law. In states like Kansas and Indiana which permitted (but did not require) segregation, some school boards established openly segregated schools.

Blacks also encountered discrimination in employment and in public accommodations, although this discrimination was neither as pervasive nor as blatant as in the South. "Whites only" signs were rare in theaters, hotels, and restaurants, and some employers, notably the Ford Motor Company, offered black immigrants skilled jobs at good wages. Nevertheless, many white-owned businesses refused to serve blacks, and laws (enacted in the 1880s and 1890s) barring discrimination in public accommodations offered little relief from such indignities. In order to enforce their rights under these measures, victims of discrimination had to sue, a time-consuming and expensive proposition. As a result, the laws were seldom enforced, and most blacks, unwilling to risk humiliation, avoided theaters, restaurants, and hotels that catered to whites. Employers generally refused to consider blacks for white-collar and professional positions, fearful that their presence would anger white employees and alienate customers and clients. The blue-collar world was little different. Most of the unions affiliated with the American Federation of Labor (primarily craft unions which represented skilled workers) excluded blacks, effectively denying them good jobs in union shops. When employers managed to keep unions out, blacks fared no better. Because of their own prejudice or because they feared unrest among white workers, most employers considered blacks only for the most menial jobs, keeping them stuck at the bottom of the occupational ladder. The situation in Boston was typical of cities across the North: "As late as 1940, 6 out of 7 [blacks] worked in manual occupations," notes the historian Stephan Thernstrom, "more than half were still confined to typical 'Negro jobs' as laborers, janitors, porters, servants, or waiters."[5]

The Attack on Discrimination Begins: 1910–1930

Although the North was not the promised land, it offered blacks significant advantages. Economic and educational opportunities, while constricted, were greater than in the South, and northern blacks could vote. Although fear of white reprisals had a chilling effect on black militance in the South, northern blacks encountered little opposition from whites when they organized to demand equal rights. As they had done in the antebellum era, therefore, northern blacks took the lead in the struggle for equality, organizing a host of protest organizations between 1890 and 1910. Groups such as the Afro-American League (led by T. Thomas Fortune, the militant New York editor), the Negro Fellowship League (organized by Ida Wells-Barnett, the fiery antilynching critic who had been driven out of Memphis by a white mob which demolished her newspaper), the New England Suffrage League (presided over by William Monroe Trotter, editor of the *Boston Guardian*), and the Niagara Movement (formed by the scholar and writer, W. E. B. DuBois) urged blacks to demand that the nation honor the pledges of equality contained in the Declaration of Independence and the Reconstruction amendments.

Northern blacks were not alone in this endeavor. Although racism became more pronounced in the North in the early twentieth century, some whites remained committed to the abolitionist vision and worked with the black militants. The most long-lived and fruitful product of black–white collaboration was the NAACP, founded in 1909 in New York City. Organizers included white descendants of the abolitionist tradition, including Oswald Garrison Villard (grandson of William Lloyd Garrison and editor of the *New York Post*) and Moorfield Storey (the distinguished Boston attorney who had served as Charles Sumner's clerk during Reconstruction); white social workers such as Mary White Ovington, Henry Moskowitz, and Jane Addams; white socialists William English Walling and Charles Edward Russell; and prominent black leaders such as DuBois, Wells-Barnett, Trotter, Mary Church Terrell, and Francis Grimke. Although the dominant role that whites played in the NAACP's early leadership gradually declined during the 1920s and 1930s, the organization retained its commitment to integration and biracial action on behalf of equality.

From the beginning, black and white leaders agreed that the goal of the new organization would be to end disfranchisement and Jim Crow and to guarantee black Americans their rights as citizens. Like the abolitionists, NAACP leaders found inspiration in the Constitution. They insisted that it was a document intended to guarantee equality and called on Americans to reassert its equalitarian principles. "Besides a day of rejoicing, Lincoln's birthday in 1909 should be a day of taking stock of the nation's progress since 1865," declared Oswald Garrison Villard in calling the meeting that created NAACP. "How far has it gone in assuring to each and every citizen, irrespective of color, the equality of opportunity and equality before the law which underlie our American institutions and are guaranteed by the Constitution?"[6] In their effort to reclaim blacks' Constitutional rights, NAACP leaders came to the aid of individual blacks who were victims of racism and lawlessness. They also relied heavily on exposing and publicizing the horrors of racism, believing (like the Progressive Era's muckraking journalists) that they could bring about reform by pricking the nation's conscience. The ultimate goal of NAACP leaders, however, was to secure legislation and court decisions that would expand protection for the rights of blacks.

During the 1910s and 1920s, as NAACP officials initiated their campaign of publicity, lobbying, and litigation, they found victories hard to achieve and progress slow. They were concerned by the upsurge in lynching and mob violence that accompanied World War I, aware that lynching was of the utmost importance to northern and southern blacks, and confident that a campaign against lynching would attract black members to the new organization. Consequently, they made passage of federal antilynching legislation a top priority. As the 1910s progressed, the NAACP investigated lynchings and published articles, pamphlets, and studies exposing the horrors of lynching. Hoping to convince the public that federal antilynching legislation was necessary, the organization sponsored a well-publicized conference on lynching at New York's Carnegie Hall in 1919. The 2,500 persons who attended heard addresses by such prominent figures as Moorfield Storey, Charles Evans Hughes, and Anna Howard Shaw of the National American Woman Suffrage Association and passed resolutions demanding that lynching be made a federal crime. Reviving Reconstruction-era ideas of national power, NAACP leaders also challenged the widespread belief that the state action doctrine precluded Congress from punishing civil rights violations perpetrated by private individuals.

James Weldon Johnson and Walter White of the NAACP staff worked closely with Leonidas Dyer, a St. Louis Republican, to capitalize on the change in public sentiment created by the antilynching campaign. In 1918 Dyer introduced in the House of Representatives legislation providing broad sanctions against lynchers as well as public officials and communities that tolerated lynching. Although the Republican party had grown tepid in its support of black rights, its traditions and its interest in keeping the growing number of northern blacks in the fold led it to give grudging support to Dyer's measure. In 1922, after four years of pressure, the House Republicans overcame solid Democratic opposition to pass the Dyer bill. Nevertheless, the threat of a southern filibuster[7] in the Senate, along with lukewarm support from the Republican leadership, killed the measure in the upper house.

Although antilynching advocates would not mount another sustained effort for federal legislation for another decade, the campaign of 1918–1922 was not without positive results. It exposed the ugliest side of American race relations, and began the long process of destroying whites' complacency. The publicity generated by the campaign appalled and embarassed some influential southern whites and prompted them to work against lynching. Debate over the Dyer bill also revived the tradition of broad construction of the Fourteenth Amendment, an essential step if the amendment were to be rescued from the narrow, formalistic interpretation given it by the Supreme Court in the 1880s and 1890s. Finally, the battle for the Dyer bill laid the groundwork for an alliance between blacks and Jews (who themselves had been victims of prejudice, discrimination, and violence) on behalf of more vigorous national protection for civil rights. Louis Marshall of the American Jewish Committee, Felix Frankfurter of Harvard Law School, Herbert Lehman the New York banker who was prominent in state Democratic party circles, and the Council of Jewish Women all supported the Dyer bill, beginning a fruitful and long-lived partnership on behalf of equal rights.

NAACP leaders also carried the struggle to the courts. As they did so, there were indications that the United States Supreme Court was ready to give substance to the guarantees of the Reconstruction amendments. During the first decade of the twentieth century, a number of prominent journalists exposed the evils of peonage (or involuntary servitude for debt). Offended by the brutality of the new slavery and concerned that it would retard the New South's economic progress, federal attorneys and judges in the South initiated a vigorous campaign against peonage, using a little-known 1867 federal statute that prohibited laws and practices that held persons in service for debt and established penalties for anyone "who shall hold, arrest, or return . . . any person . . . to a condition of peonage."

In a series of decisions between 1905 and 1914, the Supreme Court sustained the antipeonage campaign. In *Clyatt* v. *United States* (1905), a unanimous Court upheld the 1867 statute as a legitimate exercise of Congress's authority to enforce the Thirteenth Amendment's ban on involuntary servitude. Six years later, in *Bailey* v. *Alabama* (1911), the Court struck down an Alabama law that stipulated that an employee who received an advance from an employer and left before paying it back would be presumed to have taken the money with intent to defraud and would be subject to criminal penalties. Typical of statutes in other states, the law was used by planters and others to prevent indebted employees from leaving their service. The Court held that, because fraud was presumed, the law actually made breach of a labor contract a crime and thus compelled involuntary servitude. Finally, in *United States* v. *Reynolds* (1914) the Court banned southern criminal surety laws. These measures provided that persons convicted of petty crimes might sign contracts to labor for anyone who agreed to pay their fines, and they punished workers who fled before their contracts expired. Aware that many of the victims of these laws had often been convicted on trumped up charges of vagrancy or disturbing the peace and that they had accepted contracts in order to avoid the horrors of the chain gang, the Court ruled that these agreements compelled involuntary servitude and were not enforceable.[8]

Despite the Court's vigorous stand against practices and laws that sustained peonage, it did not root out the new slavery. Most victims of peonage were held in servitude through private terror and the extra-legal action of local officials rather than through enforcement of criminal fraud or criminal surety laws. While the *Clyatt* case gave federal prosecutors authority to punish persons engaged in such activity, United States attorneys were often reluctant to undertake time-consuming prosecutions on behalf of poor blacks. And even if federal attorneys were eager to attack peonage, it was no easy task to uncover instances of forced labor in hundreds of out-of-the-way rural communities throughout the South. Not only did they lack the staff to investigate, but the victims, who were often ignorant of federal remedies or terrorized by their employers, rarely filed complaints. Despite the Court's rulings, then, many southern blacks continued to live in "the shadow of slavery."[9]

Despite their limited effect, the peonage cases encouraged NAACP activists to turn to the courts. Their initial venture into litigation came in 1915, when the United States Supreme Court considered a challenge to the Oklahoma grandfather clause. Like similar provisions adopted by a number of southern states, it required prospective voters to pass a literacy test but waived the requirement for persons whose forebears had been entitled to vote on January 1, 1866, or who had resided in a foreign country on that date. Because only a few thousand blacks who had resided in six northern states could vote in 1866, the obvious purpose of the law was to establish a literacy test that could be used to disfranchise blacks but not illiterate whites. Because Republicans needed black votes to carry the state, the United States attorney for Oklahoma (an active Republican) moved promptly to prevent its enforcement. Charging that the grandfather clause violated the Fifteenth Amendment and was therefore void, he prosecuted state officials who enforced it, winning convictions in federal court.

When the case, known as *Guinn* v. *United States*, reached the Supreme Court in 1913, the government was represented by John W. Davis, the solicitor general. At this point, the NAACP, viewing the case as an opportunity to challenge disfranchisement, authorized Morefield Storey to file an *amicus curiae*[10] brief. Although the Court had upheld other disfranchising measures, in 1915 it heeded Davis and Storey and struck down the grandfather clause in a unanimous decision written by Chief Justice Edward D. White of Louisiana. White ruled that the measure was a transparent attempt to establish an obstacle to voting that applied to blacks but not to whites and therefore violated the Fifteentl, Amendment. While the victory was clear-cut, it was quite limited. Other states had adopted the grandfather clause as a temporary loophole; indeed, Georgia's, adopted in 1908, was the only one that had not expired when the Court heard *Guinn*. Moreover, White explained that the Court would not scrutinize the motive of states in enacting voting requirements that were not on their face racially discriminatory and noted that literacy tests without grandfather clause loopholes were valid. Therefore the case left literacy tests and poll taxes, which were the essential tools of disfranchisement, in place.[11]

The NAACP also mounted a vigorous campaign against residential segregation laws that spread across the South between 1910 and 1916. Although the ordinances varied, typically they barred whites who owned property on blocks that were more than fifty percent white from selling to blacks and vice versa. Although two Baltimore ordinances were successfully challenged in the Maryland Supreme Court by that city's NAACP chapter, the most important attack on residential segregation came in *Buchanan* v. *Warley*, a case initiated by the Louisville NAACP chapter and carried to the United States Supreme Court in 1917 by Moorfield Storey.

The case presented a daunting challenge for the distinguished attorney. Not only had the Court consistently sanctioned segregation, but Chief Justice White and most of his colleagues shared the race prejudice dominant in white America as the nation entered World War I. Storey made the best of a bad situation. He not only contended that the Louisville ordinance denied blacks equal protection by effectively restricting them to the least desirable areas of the city, but he exploited the justices' willingness to use the Fourteenth Amendment to protect property rights. Since the late 1890s, the Court had accepted the doctrine of liberty of contract, ruling that state laws that imposed unreasonable restrictions on contractual relations denied persons liberty without due process of law in violation of the Fourteenth Amendment. Storey grasped the opportunity that the new doctrine offered, arguing that the Louisville ordinance denied property owners liberty without due process of law by placing arbitrary and unreasonable restrictions on their right to sell their property.

Storey's strategy was far more successful than he could have imagined. A unanimous Court struck down the Louisville ordinance in a surprisingly broad opinion written by Justice William R. Day of Ohio. Day held that the ordinance was a "direct violation of the fundamental law enacted in the Fourteenth Amendment . . . preventing state interference with property rights except by due process of law." Although ultimately he rested the decision on conservative due process grounds, Day gave civil rights advocates an unanticipated boost. At a time when the Court seemed to have forgotten that the Fourteenth Amendment had anything to do with protection of the rights of former slaves, Day quoted liberally from *The Slaughter-House Cases* and *Strauder* v. *West Virginia*, reminding his readers that the "chief inducement to the passage of the Amendment was the desire to extend federal protection to the recently emancipated race from unfriendly and discriminating legislation by the states." He further suggested that the Louisville ordinance violated the Civil Rights Act of 1866, which guaranteed "fundamental rights in property . . . upon the same terms to citizens of every race and color."[12]

Despite this improvement in the Court's memory, the victory was pyrrhic. *Buchanan* broke the back of efforts to legislate residential segregation, but it said nothing about the use of restrictive covenants, which were becoming an increasingly popular means of maintaining segregated housing, especially in northern cities. NAACP leaders were well aware of the problem and challenged the constitutionality of judicial enforcement of restrictive covenants (without which they would not be binding) in *Corrigan* v. *Buckley*, a case heard by the United States Supreme Court in 1926. The Court dismissed the case, however, rejecting the argument that restrictive covenants denied individuals liberty to buy and sell property without due process of law. The covenants were merely private agreements, the Court noted, and did not come within the prohibitions of the Fifth and Fourteenth Amendments, which were merely restrictions on government action.[13] The case legitimized restrictive covenants and encouraged white property owners and real-estate developers to use them to keep minorities out of their neighborhoods.[14]

NAACP lawyers did win a significant victory in *Moore* v. *Dempsey*, a 1923 case growing out of the Phillips County, Arkansas riot. In the fall of 1919, violence erupted in the county when a deputy sheriff was killed as he and a posse tried to break up a meeting of a sharecroppers' union. The killing sparked a rampage by local whites in which dozens of blacks were murdered. Although none of the whites were prosecuted, twelve blacks were convicted of murdering the white deputy after hasty trials that were a charade of justice. All were sentenced to die in the electric chair. Some sixty-seven other blacks pled guilty to a variety of charges and received prison terms of as much as twenty years. Moore and the five other blacks who were parties to the Supreme Court appeal were among those sentenced to die. Moorfield Storey represented the defendants before the high court. He contended that they had not had the charges against them fully explained, had been denied adequate representation, and had been convicted at trials permeated by a lynch mob atmosphere. This made a fair trial impossible, Storey argued, and denied his clients due process of law in violation of the Fourteenth Amendment. The Court agreed, explaining that public passion and prejudice against the defendants had flawed the trial and had denied Moore and his codefendants due process of law.[15]

The decision marked a new departure in civil rights law. Since the adoption of the Fourteenth Amendment, the Court had consistently refused to employ the due process clause as a restriction on state criminal procedure. It had denied that due process required states to honor the provisions of the Bill of Rights and had refused to reverse convictions when defendants had been denied the right to indictment by grand jury, the right to trial by jury, the right to confront witnesses against them, and the right to protection against self-incrimination. *Moore*, of course, did not hold that any of the guarantees of the Bill of Rights applied to the states. Nevertheless, it did mark an important departure, indicating that the Court would scrutinize state criminal proceedings to guarantee defendants justice, a matter of special concern to blacks, who were frequently the victims of kangaroo-court proceedings.

The Attack Broadens: The 1930s

The Great Depression of the 1930s brought economic privation to tens of millions of Americans as unemployment, bank failures, and foreclosures swept across the land. Black Americans bore a disproportionate share of the pain: they were more likely to be fired than whites, lost their hold on jobs that had previously been too menial and low-paying to attract whites, and, especially in the South, encountered sharp discrimination in public-welfare programs. Nevertheless, the decade brought new hope to blacks. The economic crisis of the 1930s shook the foundations of the American political order and in the process increased blacks' political leverage, once again making civil rights an important political issue.

During the 1930s most black voters abandoned the party of Lincoln, which had offered them little but platitudes for thirty years. Courted by urban Democratic political machines in the North, impressed by the New Deal's commitment to working people, and heartened by President Franklin D. Roosevelt's openness to them and Eleanor Roosevelt's outspoken support for civil rights, blacks transferred their political loyalty to the Democratic party. Although they had voted heavily for Hoover in the Democratic landslide of 1932, by 1936, according to the Gallup Poll, seventy-six percent of black voters cast their ballots for FDR.

As black voters entered the Democratic fold, their leaders forged alliances with important elements of the Democratic coalition, alliances that increased blacks' political influence during the 1930s and beyond. Perceiving the growing black vote as crucial to their success, northern urban Democratic politicians proved willing supporters. Black leaders also found powerful allies among the leadership of the influential Congress of Industrial Organizations (CIO). The CIO unions—the United Mine Workers, the United Auto Workers, and the United Steel Workers, among others—brought all workers, skilled and unskilled, in a given industry into one organization. Consequently, most CIO unions had significant black membership, and their leaders were forthright advocates of civil rights. Blacks also received firm support from liberal intellectuals, whose strength in party councils far outweighed their numbers. Influenced by new research in biology, psychology, and anthropology which debunked the myth of white supremacy, and sensitized to the consequences of racism by the spread of fascism in Europe, these men and women worked closely with black leaders on behalf of civil rights. Blacks also strengthened their ties with Jews, whose own experience with discrimination provided common ground for cooperation with blacks in the struggle for equality.

Growing militance further enhanced blacks' political influence, making it more difficult for political leaders to duck their demands. Eager to win black support, the Communist party attacked the NAACP for its faith in gradual change through lobbying and litigation and began an uncompromising, outspoken campaign against racism. Noncommunist radicals such as Howard University political scientist Ralph Bunche and W. E. B. DuBois (who in 1934 broke with the organization he had helped to found) also criticized NAACP leaders for their reliance on litigation, their lack of concern for working class blacks, and their faith in gradualism. Fearful that the radicals would steal its thunder, the NAACP responded by adopting new tactics. While refusing to abandon its program of lobbying and litigation, the organization devoted increasing attention to economic matters and encouraged direct action against discrimination. The Communists' boldness, combined with traditional civil rights leaders' growing militance, led to an upsurge of black protest activity. Blacks in thirty-five cities conducted "Don't Buy Where You Can't Work" campaigns, boycotting and picketing white businesses that refused to hire blacks. Demonstrations by Ohio blacks prodded the state employment service to encourage businesses to hire minorities. In a dozen cities blacks marched to protest segregated schools, and in many others they picketed theaters that showed racist films. Although this grass-roots militance flourished primarily in northern cities, it gave a new urgency to black demands and helped put civil rights on the national agenda.

Blacks' growing political influence produced significant changes in federal policy. FDR appointed more blacks to significant governmental positions than had any president since Grant. He named William Hastie of the NAACP to the bench, making him the first black federal judge, and William Houston, the father of Charles Houston, became the first black to serve as an assistant attorney general. In addition, New Dealers named more than 100 blacks to administrative positions in federal agencies and opened professional positions in the federal bureacracy to several thousand others. Democratic lawmakers wrote into law the principle of nondiscrimination, adding clauses prohibiting "discrimination on account of race, creed, or color" to more than twenty bills establishing federal programs. While it proved difficult to translate principle into practice, there was some progress. FDR created an interdepartmental committee popularly known as the "Black Cabinet" to monitor discrimination in federal programs and to assess how effectively those programs served blacks. By the late-1930s, important New Deal agencies which provided work for the unemployed, job training, and loans for family farms had substantially eliminated discrimination from their programs. Attorney General Frank Murphy (a former member of the NAACP Board of Directors) revived the Justice Department's long dormant interest in civil rights, creating a Civil Liberties Unit to afford "aggressive protection of fundamental rights inherent in a free people."[16]

While the New Deal marked a break with the past, it neither eliminated discrimination from federal programs, won enactment of federal civil rights legislation, nor made civil rights issues a top priority. Southern Democrats controlled key congressional committees and were a force to be reckoned with on Capitol Hill. Consequently, many New Deal administrators were reluctant to root out discrimination in relief and recovery programs in the South because they feared antagonizing powerful committee chairmen who controlled their agencies' appropriations. Southern legislative power—especially skillful use of the filibuster—also thwarted efforts by liberals to enact federal legislation outlawing lynching and the poll tax. Moreover, northern Democrats refused to make civil rights a top priority. FDR's relations with southern Democrats deteriorated during the mid-1930s. Nevertheless, during his first administration and later, between 1939 and 1941, as the nation moved toward war, he relied too heavily on southern support to lay down the gauntlet on civil rights. Even more important, civil rights failed to become a top priority for the president and for northern Democrats because it was overshadowed by problems of economic recovery and, after 1939, the outbreak of war in Europe.

Like the president and the Congress, the Supreme Court took important, albeit halting, steps to expand national protection of civil rights during the 1930s. In a series of cases growing out of flagrant denials of justice to black defendants, the Court enlarged the due process rights of criminal defendants. In the process, it expanded the beachhead established by *Moore* v. *Dempsey* (1926) and provided greater checks on criminal justice officials who had long abused blacks. The Court decided these cases with a surprising degree of consensus considering how bitterly divided the justices were on the questions of economic regulation and federal power that preoccupied them during the decade; however, members of the Court's conservative bloc were judicial activists who were not reluctant to strike down state and federal policies they believed to be misguided. Indeed, they had long employed a broad, substantive definition of due process to strike down state and federal regulation of business that they considered arbitrary and unreasonable. Several of the conservatives followed the logic of this view to join their more liberal brethren in using the due process clause to expand the rights of the criminally accused.

The Court took its first step in this direction in 1932, when it decided *Powell* v. *Alabama*, one of the most highly publicized cases ever to come before the justices. Ozie Powell was one of nine black youths who were tried in Scottsboro, Alabama in 1931 for the rape of two white women. With crowds of whites demanding that white womanhood be avenged, the nine went on trial for their lives, defended by an alcoholic white attorney who had only met with them twice and who was so poorly prepared that he offered no closing statement to the jury. The testimony of the alleged victims was contradictory (within the year one of the women would admit that there had been no assault) and the statements offered by the examining physicians strongly suggested that the women had not been raped. Nevertheless, white jurors found the defendants guilty; eight were sentenced to death, and the ninth, who was only thirteen years old, received a sentence of life imprisonment. The International Labor Defense, a Communist organization, hired lawyers to appeal the convictions and tirelessly publicized the ''legal lynching'' that was about to take place. Through newspaper and magazine articles, scores of rallies and marches, petitions, a demonstration outside the White House, mock trials, and even plays, the party fixed national attention on Scottsboro, making it a byword for racial oppression.

When Ozie Powell's appeal came before the Supreme Court, the justices reversed the convictions in a 7–2 decision written by George Sutherland, a member of the Court's conservative bloc. Sutherland agreed that the trial court had denied the defendants due process of law by failing to provide effective, meaningful representation. The right to counsel was an essential part of due process, Sutherland held, expanding the meaning of due process as it affected criminal proceedings. Moreover, he asserted that in capital cases, states must provide indigent defendants with effective representation.[17]

In the years following *Powell* the Court announced decisions in a series of cases brought by black defendants that further curbed the arbitrary authority of state and local officials. In *Brown* v. *Mississippi* (1936) the justices considered an appeal by three blacks who had been convicted of murdering an elderly white man. The only evidence of their guilt was confessions that had been beaten out of them. Indeed, when the three men had appeared at their trial the bruises and lacerations inflicted by the county sheriff and his deputies had been clearly visible on their bodies. Although the Court had ruled in 1908 that ''exemption from compulsory self-incrimination in the courts of the States is not secured by any part of the Federal Constitution,''[18] it now unanimously reversed the convictions. ''It would be difficult to conceive of methods more revolting to the sense of justice than those taken to procure the confessions of these petitioners,'' wrote Chief Justice Charles Evans Hughes, "and the use of the confessions thus obtained [as evidence] . . . was a clear violation of due process.''[19] Four years later, in *Chambers* v. *Florida* (1940), the Court considered the appeal of a black man who had been convicted of murdering a white man on the basis of a confession obtained after an interrogation that lasted five days and culminated in an all-night grilling. Again, use of evidence obtained through coercion, whether physical or psychological, was deemed a violation of basic principles of justice and therefore a denial of due process of law.

The Court's rulings in *Powell*, *Brown*, and *Chambers* dealt with general issues of criminal procedure and were applicable to white as well as black defendants. Nevertheless, they had a special relevance to blacks. They began the process of transforming the due process clause into an effective means of guaranteeing procedural fairness in state criminal trials. By doing so, they expanded federal courts' ability to supervise the actions of state and local criminal justice officials and established a check on the repressive methods typically employed against blacks. Justice Hugo Black (who had once been an Alabama police court judge and was familiar with the grim realities of southern justice) caught the racial implications of these rulings in his *Chambers* opinion. Due process, he explained, was designed to bar "secret and dictatorial proceedings" of the sort employed by "tyrannical governments . . . to make scape-goats of the weak, or of helpless political, racial, or religious minor-ities.''[20]

The Court also challenged exclusion of blacks from juries, a wide-spread practice that lay at the root of the South's racially oppressive criminal justice system. The Scottsboro affair again produced the pivotal case, *Norris* v. *Alabama* (1935). After the Supreme Court had reversed their initial convictions, the Scottsboro boys had been retried and convicted by all-white juries. The trial judge, who was convinced of their innocence, set aside the verdicts and ordered a new trial. A third round of trials produced the same result, as lily-white juries once again found the nine guilty. The youths' repeated convictions made it clear that pro-cedural rights, effective representation, and mountains of evidence meant little as long as judgment was passed by white jurors. In *Norris*, defense lawyers appealed the latest round of convictions, charging systematic exclusion of blacks from the juries that had indicted and tried their clients. This, they argued, had denied them the equal protection of the laws in violation of the Fourteenth Amendment. The Court agreed in a unanimous decision written by Chief Justice Hughes. His opinion rejected the state's claim that proof of discrimination required evidence that local officials had consciously and intentionally excluded potential black jurors on account of their race. Instead, he ruled that the evidence produced at the trial—which showed that for decades no blacks had served on juries in the counties in which the defendants had been indicted and tried—was sufficient proof of discrimination.[21]

Four years later, in *Smith* v. *Texas* (1940), the Court extended its ruling in *Norris*. Although the Harris County, Texas grand jury that had indicted Smith was all-white, token numbers of blacks had served as grand jurors in the county during the 1930s. Defense lawyers pointed out that while more than twenty percent of the county's residents were blacks, only six blacks had served on the thirty-two grand juries that sat in Harris County between 1931 and 1938. This token representation, they contended, was proof of systematic discrimination that denied their client equal protection. The justices unanimously accepted this argument and reversed Smith's conviction. By doing so, they suggested that mere token representation of blacks on juries did not get local officials off the hook and might, in fact, be used to prove discrimination.[22]

The most important legal development of the decade resulted from the NAACP's campaign against segregated education. In the early 1930s the organization's legal staff had envisioned an ambitious program of litigation challenging segregation in elementary and secondary education. When Charles Houston became chief counsel in 1935, however, he realized that the organization lacked adequate resources to implement the original plan. Consequently, Houston and his protégé, Thurgood Marshall, who joined the staff in 1936, attacked segregation at the periphery. Emphasizing the equality requirement implicit in the separate but equal rule established by *Plessy*, they initiated suits challenging unequal pay for black teachers and discrimination in graduate and professional education.

These suits were attractive for several reasons. First, discrimination in these areas was blatant; most states maintained graduate and professional programs for whites but not for blacks, and school districts' salary schedules clearly showed that black teachers received substantially lower pay than whites with comparable training and experience. Consequently, limited research would be required to prove discrimination, making the cases inexpensive to litigate. Second, the salary cases would revitalize moribund NAACP chapters by drawing black teachers into the organization and would thus help raise civil rights consciousness at the grass-roots. Third, by winning precedents requiring absolute equality under segregation, Houston and Marshall would, at the very least, improve the quality of black schools and might even make segregation too expensive for the South to maintain. Especially at the graduate level, states might find it more practical to admit blacks to white schools than to establish expensive programs for the small number of blacks who sought advanced education. And this would be the first crack in the South's wall of segregation.

Houston and Marshall scored their first victories in two law school cases. In 1935 they represented Donald Murray, a graduate of Amherst College who had been denied admission to the University of Maryland's all-white law school. Like most other southern states, Maryland had no graduate or professional programs in its black colleges. Instead, it had established tuition grants to black residents who were admitted to programs in other states. The legislature, however, had not funded the program, so no money was actually available. Houston and Marshall charged that the state clearly had denied Murray an equal opportunity for legal study. Even if the tuition-grant program were funded, they contended, it would not give Murray the same rights as whites. While white students would be able to attend school in Maryland, their client would have to incur the inconvenience and expense of leaving the state to obtain a legal education. Both the trial court and the Maryland Supreme Court, which heard the case on appeal in 1936, agreed, ordering Murray's admission to the state's white law school.[23]

A Missouri case offered the opportunity to bring these issues before the United States Supreme Court. After graduating in 1935 from Lincoln University, the state's Jim Crow college, Lloyd Gaines applied for admission to the University of Missouri Law School. Because the school did not admit blacks, university officials rejected Gaines's application. They advised him that the state met the needs of blacks by providing grants for them to attend law school in another state and by offering to establish a law school on demand at Lincoln University. With the aid and encouragement of the St. Louis chapter of the NAACP, Gaines sued, demanding admission to the all-white law school. The black St. Louis lawyers who filed the case promptly called on Houston's expertise, and he argued the case when it went to trial in Missouri and later, in the United States Supreme Court. In 1938, when the high court announced its decision in *Missouri ex rel Gaines* v. *Canada*, it handed Houston a major victory. "The admissability of laws separating the races in the enjoyment of privileges afforded by the State rests wholly upon the equality of the privileges which the laws give to the separated groups within the State," noted Chief Justice Hughes. But Missouri fell short of this standard. The promise to establish a legal program at Lincoln remained a "mere declaration of purpose," while the subsidy program denied blacks a right enjoyed by whites, the right to obtain a legal education without leaving the state.[24]

Gaines did not end segregation in graduate education, and many southern states attempted to hold the line against integration by establishing graduate and professional programs at their all-black colleges. Its implications, nevertheless, were far-reaching. By rejecting Missouri's subsidy program—which offered blacks legal education at out-of-state schools that were fully equal to the University of Missouri—the Court suggested that segregation must be accompanied by absolute equality. Even if it were financially feasible for southern states to establish graduate and professional programs that would pass the Court's muster, *Gaines* spelled trouble for the South. The standard of absolute equality presumably applied to all levels of education, and southern states would be financially hard-pressed to bring black elementary and secondary schools up to the level of white schools.

Litigation demanding an end to separate and unequal salary schedules for black teachers suggested that the courts would carry *Gaines*'s demand for genuine equality beyond the level of graduate education. Between 1936 and 1940, Thurgood Marshall worked with local groups of black teachers in Maryland, initiating lawsuits to demand equal pay for black and white teachers with similar qualifications. In most counties, school officials agreed to salary equalization before the cases went to trial. And in Anne Arundel County, where the school board refused to settle, the U.S. district court ruled in 1939 that the substantial discrepancies between the salaries of black and white teachers was based on race and therefore violated the equal protection clause.[25] As the Maryland cases moved toward a successful conclusion, Marshall was already working with teachers in Virginia. In 1940, close on the heels of his victories in Maryland, he convinced the Fourth Circuit Court of Appeals to strike down Norfolk's discriminatory salary structure in *Alston* v. *School Board of Norfolk*. The victory was particularly noteworthy because the United States Supreme Court declined to hear the case when the school board appealed, thereby affirming the lower court's decision. By 1940 the federal courts had clearly suggested that they would accept segregation only if it were accompanied by absolute equality.[26]

Jim Crow at the Crossroads: The 1940s

As the nation moved toward war in 1940–1941, blacks' demand for equality became more insistent. Their expectations raised by promising developments in the 1930s, black leaders were outraged that the so-called arsenal of democracy marched to war to a beat laid down by Jim Crow. As defense orders revived industry and brought millions of the unemployed back to work, blacks encountered systematic discrimination by employers and government-training programs that were established to remedy the shortage of skilled workers needed in defense plants. Discrimination also permeated the armed forces. The Army practiced segregation and maintained a quota that sharply restricted black enlistment, the navy accepted blacks only as messmen, and the marines and the air corps excluded them altogether. Black leaders and journalists unleashed a barrage of criticism, demanding a swift end to discrimation. "Our war is not against Hitler in Europe, but against Hitler in America," thundered the black columnist George Schuyler. "Our war is not to defend democracy, but to get a democracy we never had." Fearing a defection by black voters in the 1940 election, FDR moved quickly to mollify blacks. He directed federal agencies which supervised the defense industry to develop plans guaranteeing nondiscrimination in employment and training; ordered the War Department to issue a statement that "colored men will have equal opportunity with white men in all departments of the Army;" created a new air corps training unit for blacks; and promoted Colonel Benjamin Davis, a black career officer, to brigadier general.[27]

Disappointed that Roosevelt had left Jim Crow in place and had not established concrete policies to end discrimination in the defense industry, blacks turned up the pressure. The NAACP announced that it would represent any black who wished to challenge discrimination by the armed forces, and black community groups protested employment discrimination in cities across the country. But it was the March on Washington Movement (MOWM), spearheaded by the black union leader and socialist, A. Philip Randolph, that galvanized black protest and forced FDR to take meaningful action. In early 1941 Randolph announced that on June

24 blacks would stage a mass march on Washington. During the ensuing months, MOWM chapters emerged in communities across the country, and march leaders confidently predicted that 100,000 would join the protest. Fearing that a confrontation between marchers and whites might spark violence and further divide the nation as it prepared for war, the president reached an agreement with Randolph and other black leaders. He promised to issue an executive order barring discrimination in employment and training programs in the defense industry. He also pledged to establish an administrative agency, the Committee on Fair Employment Practices (FEPC) to investigate complaints, provide redress for victims of discrimination, and recommend policies to achieve equal employment opportunity. In return, black leaders agreed to call off the march.

These concessions were significant. FEPC secured greater economic opportunity for black workers, and the demonstration of black political power emboldened blacks. In the aftermath of Pearl Harbor black leaders threw their support behind the war effort, but they insisted that the nation defend freedom and democracy at home as well as abroad. ''Prove to us,'' Walter White demanded, ''that you are not hypocrites when you say this war is for freedom.'' Phillip Randolph, who transformed MOWM into a permanent organization, was more specific, demanding an end to ''Jim Crow in education, in housing, in transportation, and in every other social, economic, and political privilege; full enforcement of the Fourteenth and Fifteenth amendments; abolition of all suffrage restrictions and limitations; and of private and government discrimination in employment; and expansion of the role of Negro advisors in all administrative agencies.''[28] Moreover, as support for the march on Washington suggested, there was growing assertiveness at the grass-roots. The NAACP grew from 355 branches with 50,000 members in 1940 to 1,073 branches with a membership of almost one half million in 1946. And southern as well as northern blacks participated in this growing militance. In South Carolina, for example, NAACP membership grew from 800 to more than 14,000 during the war years, and by the end of the war the Progressive Democrats, a black group formed to end disfranchisement, claimed almost 50,000 members.

Although the war postponed action on the civil rights agenda, blacks won important victories in the postwar years. In many northern states the New Deal coalition of blacks, big city politicians, labor leaders, Jews, and liberals secured important new civil rights laws. The new measures were a milestone in the history of civil rights, attacking discrimination in housing and employment. During the late 1940s, eleven states and twenty cities passed laws against discrimination by employers, and nine states barred discrimination in public housing. Moreover, most of the measures established effective means of enforcement. Rather than relying on lawsuits initiated by individuals—which were too expensive for most citizens to undertake—the new laws created administrative agencies to enforce the rights they proclaimed. Victims of discrimination could file complaints with these agencies; they, in turn, had authority to investigate and issue cease-and-desist orders which were enforceable by the courts if they found evidence of discrimination.

Blacks also achieved important victories at the national level. Joined by their white allies, they pressed Harry S. Truman to use the power and prestige of the presidency on behalf of equal rights. Concerned that black voters in northern cities were drifting back to the Republicans (Governor Thomas Dewey of New York, the likely Republican presidential nominee in 1948, had a strong civil rights record), Truman became the first president in the twentieth century to urge passage of a comprehensive civil rights program. In February 1948, he sent a long message on civil rights to Capitol Hill requesting antilynching legislation, tough federal action against employment discrimination and segregation in interstate transportation, and measures to guarantee blacks the right to vote. In addition, he promised to end Jim Crow in the armed forces by executive order.

Some important results came from Truman's initiative. The Justice Department filed an *amicus curiae* brief in an NAACP suit challenging the constitutionality of restrictive covenants, thus ending the government's neutrality in civil rights litigation and bringing it into the fray on behalf of equal rights. In July 1948 the president issued an executive order calling for "equality of treatment and opportunity" in the armed forces and established a committee to supervise desegregation. Although the army bureaucracy doggedly resisted implementation and only accepted full integration after the outbreak of the Korean War in June 1950, Truman's action marked the first time that the federal government had challenged segregation since enactment of the Civil Rights Act of 1875.

Equally important was the fair employment practices bill that the administration sponsored in Congress, a measure that harnessed recently expanded federal commerce power on behalf of civil rights. During the mid-1930s, the Supreme Court's slender conservative majority had used

a narrow definition of Congress's power to regulate interstate commerce
to strike down New Deal legislation regulating industry, agriculture, and
labor relations. In 1937, under the threat of FDR's court-packing
proposal, the Court underwent a change of heart. It had accepted the
government's contention that the commerce clause gave Congress full
authority to regulate any activity that affected interstate commerce. In the
following years, as consevatives left the bench and New Dealers replaced
them, the Court used the new view of federal commerce power to justify a
wide range of federal regulatory activity. This shift in doctrine had
important implications for civil rights. While the state action theory
might limit Congress's authority under the Fourteenth Amendment to ban
discrimination by private employers and labor unions, the newly invigorated commerce power offered the means to regulate the activities of
private individuals and organizations that were involved in interstate
commerce. The Truman administration's fair employment bill drew on
this reservoir of power, banning discrimination by employers and labor
unions involved in interstate commerce and establishing a federal commission with authority to issue cease-and-desist orders against violators.

The accomplishments of the Truman administration, however, fell far
short of its promises. The administration's civil rights package, including
the fair employment bill, died in Congress. Republican control on
Capitol Hill limited Truman's influence, and southern senators used the
filibuster to stall civil rights legislation. Truman, however, bears some
responsibility for his program's failure. Although the president forth-
rightly supported his civil rights porposals, he neither made them a top
priority nor launched an all-out effort to win passage. Concerned about
other legislative programs and unwilling to risk a complete break with
southern Democrats, he chose not to throw all of his resources into the
civil rights battle. Blacks had gotten the attention of national political
leaders, but they had not yet forced them to make civil rights a top
priority. Until that happened, meaningful civil rights legislation would
continue to die on the vine.

Blacks fared better in the courts than in Congress. Roosevelt appoin-
tees dominated the Court in the 1940s. Most of these men—Hugo Black,
Felix Frankfurter, Wiley Rutledge, William Douglas, and Frank
Murphy—were staunch opponents of segregation, while the others—
Stanley Reed and the mercurial Robert Jackson—were sympathetic to the
cause of civil rights. Truman's four appointees—Fred Vinson, Sherman
Minton, Tom Clark, and Harold Burton—were undistinguished jurists

not known for passionate devotion to human rights. Nevertheless, like Reed and Jackson, they were willing to make concessions to civil rights advocates.

Changes in public opinion encouraged the justices to take a bolder stand on civil rights, assuring them that more liberal rulings would not generate such widespread opposition that they would be unenforceable. Passage of state antidiscrimination laws and President Truman's bold civil rights initiatives suggested that there was growing public support for civil rights. The fight against Nazism had made obvious to many whites the contradictions between segregation and democracy. Moreover, as the Cold War began, many Americans found segregation an embarrassment that threatened the nation's status as the leader of the free world and that gave Soviet propagandists ammunition "to prove our democracy an empty fraud, and our nation a consistent oppressor of underprivileged people."[29] Although few whites became outspoken critics of segregation and most found it convenient to ignore racial discrimination, outside the South, at least, support for Jim Crow was waning.

More liberal civil rights decisions were not simply the result of changes in the Court's membership or shifting white public opinion. The Court acts only when individuals initiate lawsuits and bring cases before it. Black plaintiffs and black lawyers kept civil rights issues before the justices, pushing them to expand earlier rulings and forcing them to choose between adherence to legal precedent and the nations's equalitarian heritage.

Civil rights advocates won two notable victories that expanded the definition of state action and thus increased the reach of the Fourteenth and Fifteenth Amendments and federal civil rights legislation. The first came when the Court ended the twenty-year battle over the Texas white primary. In the one-party South, Democratic primaries were hotly contested, but those who won were assured victory in the general election. Concerned that those blacks who had not been disfranchised by poll taxes, literacy tests, or intimidation might hold the balance of power in close primaries, the Democratic party in most southern states had limited participation to whites. Although black Texans and the NAACP had waged a determined fight against the white primary during the 1920s and 1930s, the Court had ultimately turned aside their objections in *Grovey* v. *Townsend* (1935). According to the Court, the Texas Democratic party was a private organization and was therefore not subject to the Fourteenth and Fifteenth Amendments. Consequently, it was free to deny blacks membership, thereby prohibiting them from participating in the electoral process at the level at which races were actually decided.[30]

Texas blacks refused to give up, however. By the early 1940s changes in the Court's membership and a recent decision holding that primaries were an integral part of the state's election process suggested that *Grovey* was ripe to be overturned. In *Smith* v. *Allwright*, which the NAACP Legal Defense and Education Fund (LDF)[31] carried to the Supreme Court in 1944, Texas blacks renewed the challenge and won an important victory. The Court not only reversed *Grovey*, but indicated that it was willing to take a broad view of state action. Justice Stanley Reed explained that primaries "are conducted by the party under state authority," thereby making the party "an agency of the State in so far as it determines the participants in a primary election." In concluding, Reed emphasized that legal fictions would not be permitted to stand in the way of constitutional rights, noting that the "right to participate in the choice of elected officials without restriction by any State because of race . . . is not to be nullified by a State through casting its electoral process in a form which permits a private organization to practice racial discrimination. . . ."[32]

Black lawyers also pushed the Court to accept a broader view of state action by challenging judicial enforcement of restrictive covenants. Although in 1927 the Court had suggested that these were private agreements that did not come within the purview of the Fourteenth Amendment, NAACP lawyers were eager to bring the issue before the Court again. They got their chance in 1948, when the Court heard *Shelley* v. *Kraemer*, a St. Louis case, and two other restrictive covenant cases that were appealed from Detroit and Washington, D.C. Accepting the organization's analysis, all six members who heard the cases concurred that the agreements were unenforceable. "These are not cases . . . in which the States have merely abstained from action, leaving private individuals free to impose such discriminations as they see fit," wrote Chief Justice Vinson. "Rather, these are cases in which the States have made available to such individuals the full coercive power of government to deny to petitioners, on the grounds of race or color, the enjoyment of property rights. . . ."[33]

The Court also clearly indicated its dislike for segregation in public accommodations. Facing a steady stream of complaints from blacks about the indignities of Jim Crow buses and trains, NAACP strategists mounted an imaginative challenge to segregated transportation. In *Mor-*

An antislavery meeting, Cazenovia, New York, 1845. Frederick Douglass is seated to the left of the table; Thedosia Gilbert is on his right; Gerrit Smith is standing behind him; the Edmundson sisters are on either side of Smith. *Courtesy of the Madison County Historical Society, Oneida, New York.*

THE NATIONAL COLORED CONVENTION IN SESSION AT WASHINGTON, D.C.—Sketched by Theo. R. Davis.—[See First Page.]

"The National Colored Convention in Session at Washington, D.C.," *Harper's Weekly*, February 6, 1869. Meetings like this one had been held at both the state and national level since 1830 and played an important role in forging equalitarian constitutional ideas. *Courtesy of the Special Collections Department, Robert W. Woodruff Library, Emory University.*

'Shall I Trust These Men, And Not This Man?" *Harper's Weekly*, August 5, 1865. This Thomas Nast drawing suggests the way that black military service broadened northern support for equal rights during Reconstruction. *Courtesy of the Special Collections Department, Robert W. Woodruff Library, Emory University.*

"The Lobby of the House of Representatives at Washington, D.C. During the Passage of the Civil Rights Bill," *Harper's Weekly,* April 28, 1866. Note the black lobbyist in the right center of the picture. Blacks came to play an increasingly important role in the political and legal process during Reconstruction. *Courtesy of the Special Collections Department, Robert W. Woodruff Library, Emory University.*

A racially mixed jury. *Harper's Weekly,* November 30, 1867. *Courtesy of the Schomburg Center for Research in Black Culture. The New York Public Library. Astor, Lenox, and Tilden Foundations.*

Blacks in New York march to protest the East St. Louis riot, July 1917. *Courtesy of the Schomburg Center for Research in Black Culture. The New York Public Library. Astor, Lenox, and Tilden Foundations.*

Do not look at the Negro.

His earthly problems are ended.

Instead, look at the seven WHITE children who gaze at this gruesome spectacle.

Is it horror or gloating on the face of the neatly dressed seven-year-old girl on the right?

Is the tiny four-year-old on the left old enough, one wonders, to comprehend the barbarism her elders have perpetrated?

Rubin Stacy, the Negro, who was lynched at Fort Lauderdale, Florida, on July 19, 1935, for "threatening and frightening a white woman," suffered PHYSICAL torture for a few short hours. But what psychological has been wrought in the minds of the white children? Into what kinds of citizens

NAACP antilynching poster. *Courtesy of the Schomburg Center for Research in Black Culture. The New York Public Library. Astor, Lenox, and Tilden Foundations.*

Antilynching parade in Washington, D.C., ca. 1922. *Courtesy of the Moorland-Springarn Research Center, Howard University.*

Signs such as this one designating the colored waiting room in a train station were a normal part of life in the South during the first half of the twentieth century. *Courtesy of the Schomburg Center for Research in Black Culture. The New York Public Library. Astor, Lenox, and Tilden Foundations.*

Black women in Kansas City, Missouri protest a separate and unequal school, 1949. *Courtesy of the Schomburg Center for Research in Black Culture. The New York Public Library. Astor, Lenox, and Tilden Foundations.*

Charles Hamilton Houston in court. *Courtesy of the Moorland-Springarn Research Center, Howard University.*

Students and parents who initiated the Prince Edward County, Virginia, school desegregation case, one of the cases that the U.S. Supreme Court considered with *Brown* v. *Board of Education. Courtesy of the Schomburg Center for Research in Black Culture. The New York Public Library. Astor, Lenox, and Tilden Foundations.*

Spectators in the lobby of the Supreme Court, December 7, 1953, awaiting the second round of arguments in *Brown* v. *Board of Education. Courtesy of the Moorland-Springarn Research Center, Howard University.*

George E. C. Hayes (left), Thurgood Marshall (center), and James Nabrit, Jr. (right), the NAACP attorneys who presented arguments in *Brown* v. *Board of Education,* outside the Supreme Court after the Court announced its landmark decision. *Courtesy of the Schomburg Center for Black Culture. The New York Public Library. Astor, Lenox, and Tilden Foundations.*

gan v. *Virginia*, which reached the Court in 1946, they argued that segregation in interstate transportation was unconstitutional, not because it violated the equal protection clause, but because it impeded interstate commerce. They drew on a long line of precedents voiding state laws and regulations that unduly burdened commerce or dealt with matters that required uniform national regulations. Thurgood Marshall contended that state segregation laws disrupted interstate commerce by forcing passengers to change seats as they went from one state to another and by imposing a multiplicity of complex regulations on interstate carriers. With only one member in dissent, the Court agreed, holding that state segregation statutes unduly burdened interstate commerce and could not be enforced against interstate carriers.[34]

The decision did not apply to travelers within a single state. Nor did it effectively end segregation for interstate travelers. Because *Morgan* struck down state laws, but not carrier-imposed regulations, most southern railroads and bus companies continued to enforce company rules requiring segregation. The decision, nevertheless, presaged the future. Had the justices not been predisposed to whittle away at segregation, they would not have found the NAACP's rather strained argument convincing. Indeed, had the Court followed its recent trend of allowing states greater freedom to regulate businesses involved in interstate commerce, it would have rejected the NAACP's argument. Thus the case suggested that the justices were hostile to segregation and that, while they were not yet ready to take the dramatic step of overruling *Plessy*, its days were numbered.

The NAACP's campaign against segregation in graduate and professional education, which had begun in the 1930s, brought the Court even closer to the precipice. In the years following World War II, Thurgood Marshall, who had succeeded Houston as chief counsel in 1938, moved cautiously toward a direct attack on the separate but equal doctrine. The LDF staff mushroomed in the postwar years, and many of these young black lawyers were impatient with the strategy of working within the confines of the separate but equal doctrine to erode segregation. Marshall himself was keenly aware of the limitations of this approach. During the 1940s, as the campaign to equalize the salaries of black teachers had spread beyond Maryland and Virginia, progress had slowed considerably. School officials in most states had developed systems of rating teachers that allowed white administrators to make subjective judgments about merit and performance, thus perpetuating discrimination through less obvious means. Challenging this more subtle form of discrimination required extensive research and a multiplicity of complicated lawsuits that achieved fewer concrete results. Consequently, Marshall realized that the old strategy of using the separate but equal doctrine to force equalization of black and white schools in hopes of making segregation too expensive was more likely to wear down the NAACP than the South. Yet Marshall was not simply driven to undertake a direct attack by the young turks on his staff or by the failure of the indirect approach. His own reading of the postwar political climate suggested to him that the time was ripe to challenge *Plessy*.

The Texas law school case, *Sweatt* v. *Painter*, offered the best opportunity to present a direct challenge to the separate but equal doctrine. When Heman Sweatt, a black mail carrier, sued to win admission to the University of Texas Law School, the state promptly created a makeshift black law school in Austin, renting three rooms in a building across the street from the state capitol, assigning faculty from the white law school to teach in the new school, and offering black law students access to the state law library, a substantial collection located in the capitol. The black law school, while not fully equal to the university's law school, was not a complete travesty. Indeed, the quality of its faculty and library compared favorably to those of the University of Texas Law School. This made the case more difficult, yet also offered the opportunity to press the Court to reconsider the legitimacy of separate but equal. When the case came before the Supreme Court, Marshall argued that the law school did not meet the requirements of separate but equal: the state law library was open to the public and not designed primarily for the use of students, and the black school had no law review or moot court program; however, he also broadened the argument, contending that even if the two schools were physically equal, the black school could never accord blacks true equality. Intangible factors—the superior reputation of the established white law school, the greater opportunity it offered for developing professional contacts, its wide network of influential alumni—doomed the black school's ability to offer its students opportunities open to their white counterparts. Thus separate but equal in professional education was an oxymoron.

The ball was in the justices' court. Justice Tom Clark, himself a graduate of the University of Texas Law School, urged the justices to confront the issue squarely and to declare that separate but equal had no place in graduate education. "If some say this undermines *Plessy* then let it fall, as have many Nineteenth Century oracles," he urged in a memo to his colleagues. With Chief Justice Vinson and several other justices unwilling to issue an opinion openly questioning *Plessy*, the Court rejected Clark's counsel. Nevertheless, the unanimous decision in *Sweatt*, written by the chief justice, was a severe blow to *Plessy*. Although Vinson found the physical facilities of the black law school inferior, he suggested that the black school would be wanting even if it were physically equal to the white law school:

> What is more important [than the disparity in physical facilities], the University of Texas Law School possesses to a far greater degree those qualities which are incapable of objective measurement but which make for greatness in a law school. Such qualities, to name but a few, include reputation of the faculty, experience of the administration, position and influence of the alumni, standing in the community, traditions and prestige.[35]

This emphasis on intangibles had important implications for the future. "Given the discussions within the Court, invoking the intangibles committed the justices as much as any doctrine could to the position that equality could not be achieved in separate graduate and professional schools," notes Mark Tushnet, the most careful student of the NAACP's legal campaign against segregated education.[36] Once separate but equal fell in the realm of higher education, it was only a matter of time before it fell in secondary and elementary education. Indeed, *Sweatt* (as well as the Court's decision in another 1950 case, *Henderson* v. *United States*, which effectively invalidated carrier-imposed segregation in interstate commerce[37]) heartened NAACP attorneys and encouraged them to launch an all-out offensive against the separate but equal doctrine. By mid-century, then, the stage was set to bring down the legal framework that perpetuated the caste system. Black leaders had developed the arguments, secured the precedents, built the political alliances, and, perhaps most important of all, fostered grass-roots support for civil rights in black communities across the nation. The dream of equality not only remained alive but increasing numbers of African-Americans were confident that it would be realized in their lifetimes.

6

The Civil Rights Movement and American Law, 1950–1969

Rosa Parks, a forty-two-year-old Montgomery, Alabama seamstress, was tired when she left work on Thursday, December 1, 1955. Her neck and shoulders aching after a long day at her sewing machine, she wearily boarded the Cleveland Avenue bus for the long trip home. Like the other black riders, Mrs. Parks moved toward the back of the bus, taking a seat in the first row of the colored section. As more riders boarded at succeeding stops, black passengers stood in the aisles, even though a few seats in the white section remained vacant. By the third stop the last "white" seat was taken leaving one white man standing at the front of the bus. In keeping with company policy (which was to expand the white section row by row as it became filled), the driver brusquely ordered Parks and the other three blacks in her row to surrender their seats. The others complied, but Parks refused to move—even when the driver stopped the bus and threatened to have her arrested for violating the city's bus segregation ordinance. Prolonging the trip home was the last thing Parks wanted, yet she deeply resented the bus company's humiliating policies and had resolved that she would never surrender her seat to a white. Several minutes later, police officers responded to the driver's call for help, arrested Mrs. Parks, and took her to the police station, where she was booked and placed in the city jail. Although the United States Supreme Court had declared segregation unconstitutional one-and-a-half years earlier, Montgomery officials, like most other southern whites, remained determined to preserve Jim Crow.

Mrs. Parks's arrest set off feverish activity in the Montgomery black community. E. D. Nixon, who had worked closely with her in the local NAACP chapter, quickly learned of her arrest, posted bond to secure her release, and drove her home. Later that evening, Nixon conferred with Jo Ann Robinson, a black English professor at Alabama State College and the president of the Women's Political Caucus (WPC). The two had long wished to organize a bus boycott and agreed that Parks's arrest offered the perfect opportunity to mobilize Montgomery blacks. Mrs. Robinson and her collegues in the WPC immediately went to work. They spent the night in the college mimeographing room cranking out thousands of copies of a flier urging blacks to protest Parks's arrest by staying off the buses on Monday. As bleary-eyed WPC members began to distribute the handbills the next morning, Nixon was on the phone, summoning Montgomery's black leaders to assemble that evening to discuss the boycott. Those who attended agreed to endorse a boycott and to convene a mass meeting at the Holt Street Baptist Church on Monday evening to determine whether there was sufficient community support to continue the protest.

On Monday, December 5, the movement developed greater momentum. The first day of the boycott was almost 100 percent effective, despite the fact that most blacks were dependent on city buses for transportation. That afternoon, black leaders met again, endorsing a series of resolutions drafted by Nixon. Acknowledging white intransigence, they demanded, not integration, but a more humane form of segregation. They proposed that blacks could seat themselves from the rear to the front, whites from the front to the rear, and no black, once seated, would be ordered to surrender his or her seat. They also formed a new organization, the Montgomery Improvement Association (MIA), to coordinate the protest and to negotiate with city officials. The group then chose as its president a twenty-six-year-old minister who had recently come to the pulpit of the prestigious Dexter Avenue Baptist Church after completing his Ph.D. in theology at Boston University. His name was Martin Luther King, Jr.

That evening, a huge crowd packed the Holt Street Church, spilling out into the surrounding churchyard. King electrified the throng with a largely improvised speech. In rolling cadences, he assured his listeners that they were not wrong to resist "being trampled over by the iron feet of oppression." "If we are wrong—the Supreme Court of this nation is wrong," he insisted. ". . . If we are wrong—Jesus of Nazareth was merely a utopian dreamer who never came down to earth! If we are wrong—justice is a lie." He urged the audience to employ nonviolent protest to call attention to the evils of segregation and to compel whites to do justice. "First and foremost we are American citizens," he explained. "We are not here advocating violence. . . . The only weapon that we have in our hands this evening is the weapon of protest," and "the great glory of American democracy is the right to protest for right." Moved by King's call for action, the audience roared its approval and agreed to continue the boycott until city officials capitulated.[1]

In the days following Monday's meeting, MIA leaders organized a vast car pool that transported thousands of boycotters, while thousands of other blacks braved the elements and walked to jobs, schools, and stores. Even though the boycott drove the bus company into the red, city officials remained resolute, refusing to accept the MIA's moderate demands. In the face of white intransigence, blacks continued to walk, and MIA leaders filed a lawsuit in federal district court that transformed the nature of their demands. No longer seeking merely to modify segregation, they asked that Jim Crow bus service be declared unconstitutional. As the boycott dragged on, the homes of MIA leaders (beginning with King's) were bombed; black leaders (including King) and car pool drivers were arrested on trumped up speeding charges; and more than 100 boycott leaders were charged with violating an obscure state law outlawing boycotts "without just cause or legal excuse."[2] White retaliation only steeled blacks' resolve, and throughout the spring, summer, and fall of 1956 working class blacks continued the boycott, seemingly oblivious to the great personal inconvenience involved. Although white officials were equally resolute, blacks' persistence ultimately paid off. In June the U.S. disrtict court declared Montgomery's bus segregation statute unconstitutional. When city attorneys appealed to the Supreme Court, the justices unanimously sustained the lower court's ruling.[3] Just before dawn on December 21, 1956, one year and twenty days after Rosa Parks refused to give up her seat, King and other boycott leaders ceremoniously boarded a city bus and took seats near the front as photographers snapped photos and reporters scribbled notes.

The triumph the journalists reported was a portent of the following turbulent decade. Court decisions and statutes attacking the South's caste system would meet massive, determined, ingenious, and often violent resistance from whites determined to preserve their power and privilege. In the face of such resistance, court decisions and laws would not, by themselves, guarantee equality. Blacks would have to mobilize and stand up to whites, challenging the day-to-day operation of the caste system if they were to breathe life into pronouncements from Washington and force cautious national leaders to make civil rights a priority. Yet the success of the Montgomery movement also suggested that community mobilization, while vital, had its limits. After all, it was not until the Supreme Court spoke that city officials capitulated. Neither law nor mass protest was, by itself, sufficient to end the caste system; only a combination of the two would accomplish that monumental task and bring the long deferred promise of equality closer to realization. Martin Luther King, Jr. understood that as he donned the mantle of leadership that December evening in 1955. "Not only are we using the tools of persuasion, but we've got to use tools of coercion," he prophetically told the audience at the Holt Street Baptist Church. "Not only is this thing a process of education, but it is also a process of legislation."[4]

Challenge and Response, 1950–1960

In part, the rumblings of protest in Montgomery were triggered by the successful culmination of the NAACP's long legal battle against segregation. Since the 1930s Thurgood Marshall and his colleagues on the NAACP legal staff had crisscrossed the South, arguing scores of cases designed to chip away at segregation. Their campaign had produced a long string of important victories and had brought the Supreme Court to the verge of abandoning the separate but equal doctrine of *Plessy* v. *Ferguson*. Encouraged by the trend of the Court's decisions and by growing support for black equality, Marshall and his staff sought to push the Court further. During 1951, attorneys from the NAACP Legal Defense Fund, representing black parents in Delaware, Virginia, South Carolina, Kansas, and the District of Columbia who were seeking to have their children admitted to white schools, directly challenged the constitutionality of segregated education. *Sweatt* v. *Painter*'s emphasis on the intangible aspects of education, they argued, meant that segregated schools were necessarily unequal. They cited social science research that demonstrated that segregation had a devastating effect on black children, destroying their self-esteem and their incentive to learn. Therefore, even if physical facilities were equal, the black lawyers contended, segregated schools denied blacks equality.

In 1952 the Supreme Court ageed to hear appeals in these cases, consolidating the four state cases under the title of the Kansas case, *Brown* v. *Board of Education of Topeka*, while addressing the somewhat different constitutional issues posed by the District of Columbia appeal in a separate case, *Bolling* v. *Sharpe*.[5] In doing so, the justices set the stage for a full-scale debate over the constitutionality of segregated education, a debate that forced often anguished consideration of the nature of judicial power. All of the justices except Kentuckian Stanley Reed found segregation distasteful and did not wish to reaffirm *Plessy*. Nevertheless, most had reservations about the wisdom of declaring segregation unconstitutional. They realized that most white southerners passionately supported segregation and would bitterly resist its demise. Southern opposition, they feared, might lead to an endless stream of cases that would drag the Court into day-to-day management of local school districts. And if the Court's mandate were not backed by the president and the Congress, it might prove unenforceable, severely damaging the Court's prestige.

Several of the justices, notably Felix Frankfurter and Robert Jackson, also worried that the Court might exceed the proper limits of its authority if it reversed *Plessy*. They had long criticized conservative judges for using the general language of the due process clause to declare unconstitutional state laws regulating business and to write their personal preference for laissez faire economic policy into the law. In a democracy, they firmly believed, elected officials should make public policy, and judges should invoke the power of judicial review only when legislation clearly violated the Constitution. This philosophy of judicial self-restraint made the *Brown* case a difficult one for Frankfurter and Jackson. Both found racial segregation repugnant; however, the Fourteenth Amendment's equal protection clause did not expressly prohibit it, and there was little evidence that the framers of the Fourteenth Amendment had intended it to do so. In addition, Congress (which had express authority to enforce the equal protection clause) had supported segregated schools in the District of Columbia since the 1860s, suggesting that it did not view segregation as unconstitutional. Furthermore, for fifty-six years the Supreme Court had maintained that segregation and equal protection were not incompatible. Consequently, Frankfurter and Jackson worried that in striking down segregation they would be writing their personal preferences into law and usurping authority best left to legislators—the very things for which they had taken conservatives to task. Although both men would overcome these doubts and Frankfurter would help unify the Court against segregation, in early 1953 neither was firmly committed to reversing *Plessy*.

The Court was thus in disarray as the justices considered *Brown* during the spring of 1953. Justice Reed was committed to upholding segregation, Chief Justice Vinson leaned in that direction, and several other members of the Court were undecided. Because even the staunchest foes of segregation believed that a divided Court would encourage southern resistance, the justices agreed to postpone a decision. In June 1953 they ordered the case held over for reargument, creating a one-year delay that would profoundly affect the outcome. In early September, barely one month before the Court reconvened, Chief Justice Vinson died, and President Dwight Eisenhower appointed Governor Earl Warren of California as his successor. While Vinson had been noncommittal, Warren firmly believed that segregation denigrated blacks and therefore was a clear violation of equal protection. He used his considerable political skills and powers of persuasion to win over doubters and forged unanimous support for a decision declaring segregated schools unconstitutional.

While Warren had no doubt about the proper outcome, he was determined to avoid "precipitous action that would inflame [the white South] more than necessary."[6] This concern rather than abstract legal principles shaped his opinion in the *Brown* case, which was announced on May 17, 1954. To avoid antagonizing whites, Warren refrained from attacking segregation as part of a caste system that was designed to preserve white supremacy and that was on its face a denial of equal protection. Rather than suggesting that *Plessy* had been wrongly decided and that southerners had supported a blatantly unconstitutional institution for more than a half century, he contended that recent developments had made segregation incompatible with the guarantees of equal protection. In recent years public education had become far more important than it had been when the Fourteenth Amendment had been adopted or when *Plessy* had been decided. In fact, it now was "a principal instrument in awakening the child to cultural values, in preparing him for later professional training, and in helping him to adjust normally to his environment." Citing recent social science research, Warren argued that segregation denied black children the full benefit of education and thus put them at a considerable disadvantage. "To separate them from others of similar age and qualifications," he explained, "solely because of their race generates a feeling of inferiority . . . that may affect their hearts and minds in a way unlikely ever to be undone." Therefore, the chief justice concluded, "separate educational facilities are inherently unequal."[7]

An important question remained: how would legal principle be translated into practice? If segregation were unconstitutional, black children presumably had the right to attend nonsegregated schools immediately. Warren and his colleagues were not prepared to issue such an order, however, fearing that if they moved too fast they would unduly antagonize white southerners. They believed that democracy ultimately relied on consent rather than force and were determined to win at least grudging acceptance from southern whites. Massive resistance, they feared, would produce chaos, block compliance with the decision, humiliate the court, and threaten the rule of law. Consequently, Warren's opinion postponed a decision on implementation until the Court's next term, reassuring whites that the Court would not act rashly.

One year later, in May 1955, the Court issued another decision (commonly known as *"Brown II"*), addressing the thorny problem of enforcement. Eager to conciliate whites, Warren's *Brown II* opinion emphasized that implementation would be gradual and would take into account local conditions. He ordered the cases returned to the courts in which they had been tried, giving judges who were familiar with each local situation responsibility for enforcement. While the lower courts were to require school officials to "make a prompt and reasonable start" toward compliance, they were to consider the complex problems involved and give local officials adequate time to deal with them. Judges were to implement *Brown* "with all deliberate speed," Warren concluded. In their desire to defuse white resistance the justices placed responsibility for implementing *Brown* on the lower federal courts but gave them vague and even contradictory instructions (what was "deliberate speed"?) as to how they should proceed.[8]

Hope that the white South would accept *Brown* quickly faded. Although many school districts in the border states grudgingly acquiesced, whites in the Deep South bitterly denounced the decision as an unconstitutional act of judicial tyranny and vowed to resist. In 1955, Mississippi whites organized the Citizens' Council to hold the line against integration. It quickly spread across the Deep South, claiming 250,000 members by 1956 and orchestrating a campaign of economic reprisals against blacks and whites who dared to challenge segregation. Some whites demanded sterner measures. The months following *Brown* witnessed a resurgence of the Ku Klux Klan and a wave of bombings, murders, beatings, and cross burnings aimed at intimidating black activists. In Mississippi three prominent black leaders were murdered during the summer and fall of 1955—one, Lemar Smith, shot to death in broad daylight on the grounds of the Pike County Courthouse. In 1956 mobs prevented black students from enrolling in the University of Alabama and in the public schools of Mansfield, Texas, and Clinton, Tennessee. Nor did the violence quickly subside. In 1957, as Birmingham blacks began efforts to desegregate the public schools, a black man was savagely beaten and castrated by a group of whites who told him, "This is what will happen if Negroes try to integrate the schools."[9]

With the South aflame, state legislatures quickly crafted measures designed to preserve segregation. Several states passed laws prohibiting school officials from obeying court orders to integrate. Others ordered integrated schools closed and offered to pay private school tuition to children in communities that closed their public schools. Less bombastic, but more effective, were the pupil placement laws enacted by most southern states. These measures purported to meet *Brown*'s requirement for gradual desegregation by establishing ostensibly nonracial criteria for assignment of new students to schools and by allowing students already enrolled to apply for transfers to any school in their district. When assigning new students to schools or considering applications for transfers, school officials were directed to consider such things as the academic preparation, moral character, and home environment of the pupil, "the effect of admission of the pupil upon the academic progress of other students, . . . [and] the possibility of . . . disorder among pupils or others."[10] These criteria were flexible enough to permit white officials to assign black children to all-black schools and to deny the applications of those black children who had the temerity to request transfers to white schools. Moreover, the laws established a procedural maze that students must follow to challenge school officials' decisions. The latter requirement was particularly important. Because federal law required persons to exhaust all administrative remedies before suing in federal courts, time-consuming and complicated local procedures were guaranteed to keep all but the most determined blacks out of court.

In the face of determined white resistance, proponents of desegregation received little support or encouragement from the president or the Congress, fulfilling the worst fears of the justices. President Eisenhower worked behind the scenes to promote desegregation in the District of

Columbia and ultimately intervened in Little Rock when he was confronted with a direct challenge to federal supremacy; however, he had (as an aide noted) a "basic insensitivity" toward blacks' aspirations, feared that vigorous support for desegregation would reverse the progress that the Republican party had made in attracting white southerners, and believed that the *Brown* decision was ill-advised.[11] Consequently, the president refused to endorse *Brown* publicly thus declining to use his enormous popularity to reconcile white southerners to the decision. On more than one occasion when he was asked about desegregation, Ike responded that moral beliefs could be changed only by education, not by law. Congress did no more to assist desegregation. Although liberals pressed for adoption of legislation authorizing the Justice Department to bring desegregation suits, an alliance of southerners and northern conservatives blocked its passage.

With the political branches inert, enforcement of *Brown* depended on lawsuits initiated by blacks in hundreds of communities across the South, guaranteeing that widespread desegregation would be a long time coming. Blacks—especially those who lived in rural areas and small towns—invited economic and physical retaliation if they challenged segregation; not surprisingly, most were reluctant to press their rights under *Brown*. In 1955, for example, blacks in five Mississippi towns petitioned for school desegregation, but intense pressure from the Citizens' Council deterred them from going to court. Besides, lawsuits were too expensive for most black communities to undertake. Even when local attorneys volunteered their services or the Legal Defense Fund sent counsel to manage a case, it cost plaintiffs approximately $15,000 (the equivalent of $50,000 in 1990 dollars) to take a desegregation case through the federal courts. Consequently, as late as 1961 few southern school districts in the Deep South had faced school desegregation suits.

Despite the intimidation and expense, southern blacks did bring several dozen school cases before the federal courts during the late 1950s. United States district courts, presided over by a single judge, initially heard most of these. If a plaintiff requested an injunction barring enforcement of an allegedly unconstitutional state law (as was sometimes done in desegregation suits) a special three-judge district court would hear the case instead. Although parties could appeal the decisions of three-judge district panels directly to the Supreme Court, appeals from the decisions of single-judge courts went first to the courts of appeals for consideration. The nation was divided into ten circuits, each supervised by an appeals court consisting of between three and nine judges depending on the circuit's caseload. Five of these tribunals had jurisdiction over at least one southern state (the third circuit included Delaware; the fourth Virginia, the Carolinas, Maryland, and West Virginia; the fifth, Florida, Georgia, Alabama, Mississippi, Louisiana, and Texas; the sixth, Kentucky and Tennessee; and the eighth, Arkansas) and therefore played an important role in supervising desegregation.

The judges who presided over these courts and who enjoyed enormous discretion in overseeing school desegregation under *Brown II* were white southerners. Most had grown up in a society that viewed segregation as necessary and moved in professional and social circles in which segregation was staunchly defended. A few—most notably John Minor Wisdom, John R. Brown, Elbert Tuttle, and Richard Rives of the United States Court of Appeals for the Fifth Circuit, and District Judges Frank Johnson of Alabama and J. Skelly Wright of Louisiana—defied friends and associates to become forceful advocates of integration. Most southern federal judges, however, found integration distasteful and believed that the Supreme Court had decided *Brown* incorrectly. Although only a minority of these men let their personal prejudices prevail over their constitutional duty, most were more inclined to emphasize deliberation than speed in implementing *Brown*. Indeed, given the absence of support from the president and the Congress and the vague instructions dispensed by the Supreme Court, little more could have been expected of them.

Where federal judges' devotion to segregation was stronger than their commitment to carry out their oaths of office, they sometimes effectively blocked desegregation. Consider the tortuous pace of litigation in Dallas. Although black plaintiffs initiated a desegregation suit in September 1955, District Judge William Atwell, an outspoken segregationist, refused to act for two years. After the Fifth Circuit Court of Appeals had twice overruled Atwell's dilatory tactics, it issued a third opinion, in September 1957, ordering the school board to develop a desegregation plan. When no plan was forthcoming two years later, the plaintiffs went back to the district court to compel action. Atwell had retired, but another segregationist, T. Whitfield Davidson, had taken charge of the case. After admonishing blacks to recognize ''that the white man has a right to maintain his racial integrity and it can't be done so easily in integrated schools,'' he directed school officials to ''study this question and perhaps take further action, maybe an election.'' The court of appeals again intervened, directing the school board to come up with a desegregation plan and to do it soon. When the board complied and presented Davidson with a proposal to admit a few black first graders to white schools in the fall of 1961 and to integrate another grade each year until the process was completed in 1973, Davidson rejected it as too radical. "The Dallas Plan," he explained, "would lead . . . to an amalgamation of the races."[12] Once again the court of appeals reversed Davidson's decision. It suggested that the school board's twelve-year plan was too slow and would have to be accelerated, but it ordered the board to begin on schedule. In 1961, after five long and costly years of litigation, token desegregation began in Dallas.

Even when district judges did not engage in outright obstruction, progress was slow, as judges' response to the pupil placement laws suggest. Appeals courts struck down Virginia and Louisiana placement statutes that were part of legislative packages prohibiting integregation; however, they took a more charitable view of those laws that did not openly announce their opposition to integration. Until the early 1960s, the United States Court of Appeals for the Fourth Circuit held that these measures were adequate steps toward desegregation and ruled that blacks could not sue until they had exhausted the administrative appeals established by the acts. The fifth circuit court was somewhat more skeptical of the pupil placement laws. In 1959, a federal district judge in Florida refused to order Dade County (Miami) school officials to present a desegregation plan, ruling that the Florida pupil placement law constituted such a plan. The fifth circuit judges quickly reversed his decision, explaining that such statutes were insufficient if districts remained segregrated. Although the court did not order desegregation, Miami school officials soon began token integration in order to forestall action by the federal courts.

As the Miami case suggests, even when federal judges acted in good faith, the result was generally only token integration. After four years of litigation, District Judge J. Skelly Wright finally imposed a grade-a-year desegregation plan on New Orleans in 1960. Although Wright stood firm in the face of defiance by state officials, the plan brought only five black first graders into white schools when it was implemented in November 1960. The story was the same in Atlanta. In late 1959, under pressure from Judge Frank Hooper, the school board adopted a plan admitting a few black seniors to previously all-white schools and moving down one grade each year thereafter. Although interference from the state legislature blocked implementation in the fall of 1960, the plan took effect the following year, and by September 1962, forty-four black high school students were enrolled in ten previously all-white schools.

As federal judges inched toward implementation of *Brown,* the Supreme Court remained aloof. It routinely affirmed without comment or refused to review lower court rulings that accepted the validity of pupil placement statutes, grade-a-year plans, and token desegregation. The Court's cautiousness is understandable. Justice Frankfurter remained a force to be reckoned with until his death in 1962. While he had played an important role in unifying the justices in *Brown* and remained an opponent of segregation, Frankfurter continued to believe that the Court's power should operate in a narrow compass and was reluctant to become deeply involved in the management of southern schools. Moreover, he and most of his colleagues believed that white resistance and the absence of support for desegregation from the president and Congress dictated caution. Although the lower federal courts were moving slowly, they were nonetheless translating *Brown's* call for desegregation into reality, demonstrating to southerners that the world would not end if blacks went to school with whites, and establishing a beachhead in the fight for integration.

The Court's only major statement on school desegregation came in response to the Little Rock crisis of 1957–1958. Under a desegregation plan approved by a federal court, nine blacks were scheduled to enter Little Rock's Central High School in September 1957. On September 3, the first day of classes, Governor Orville Faubus deployed units of the Arkansas National Guard to block admission of the black students. District Judge Ronald Davies, who continued to supervise the city's school desegregation plan, promptly directed school officials to go ahead with desegregation. On September 4, as several hundred hostile onlookers taunted and spat on the black students, National Guardsmen turned the nine youths away from the school. Intent on preventing Faubus from nullifying federal law, Davies issued an injunction on September 20, ordering the governor and members of the National Guard to desist from further interference with the court-approved desegregation plan. On Monday, September 23, when the nine blacks arrived at Central High, the National Guard was gone, but a mob had taken its place. School officials succeeded in getting the black children past the angry whites and into the school, but integration proved short-lived. Fearing a violent assault on the school, they evacuated the blacks later that day.

Confronted with open violation of federal law and a clear threat to federal supremacy, President Eisenhower finally acted. Invoking his authority to use the military to remove obstructions to national authority, he sent units of the 101st Airborne Division to Little Rock, called the National Guard into federal service, and deployed these forces at Central High to quell resistance to the federal court's desegregation order. Although Eisenhower still declined to endorse *Brown,* he was nonetheless determined to quash open defiance of federal authority. Refusal to intervene, he informed Senator Richard Russell of Georgia, "would be tantamount to acquiescence in anarchy and the dissolution of the union."[13] On September 24, protected by 1,000 troops, the nine black students entered the high school. In the face of continued white harassment and an epic war of wills, eight of them would remain for the entire school year, escorted at all times by the federal troops assigned to guarantee their safety.

In February 1958, with troops still present at Central High and tensions running high, the school board asked that the black children be withdrawn and desegregation postponed until September 1960. Although the district judge accepted this proposal, a unanimous Supreme Court reversed him, ruling in *Cooper* v. *Aaron* (1958) that the black children be allowed to remain. In an unprecedented step, all nine justices signed the Court's opinion, emphasizing their commitment to *Brown* and their determination to stay the course on school desegregation. "The principles announced in that decision and the obedience of the States to them, according to the command of the Constitution, are indispensible for the protection of the freedoms guaranteed by our fundamental charter for all of us," they explained. "Our constitutional ideal of equal justice under law is thus made living truth." The Court also declared its unwillingness to tolerate evasion: "[T]he constitutional rights of children . . . declared . . . in the *Brown* case can neither be nullified openly and directly by state legislators or state executive or judicial officers, nor nullified indirectly by them through evasive schemes for segregation whether attempted 'ingeniously or ingenuously.' "[14]

The Court's strong language neither called for a quickened pace of desegregation nor signaled an end to tokenism. Nevertheless, it was an important step. Reinforced as it was by Eisenhower's action, it warned white southerners that the federal government would not capitulate. The Court reinforced this message, albeit in a less highly publicized fashion, in a series of cases dealing with other civil rights issues. Between 1955 and 1958, prodded by Thurgood Marshall and other Legal Defense Fund attorneys, the Court extended its ban against segregation from education to other public facilities, including parks, buses, golf courses, and beaches.[15] Although in the absence of congressional legislation it did not extend the ban to privately owned businesses, the Court did expand the definition of what constituted a public facility. Thus in 1961, it ruled that a privately owned restaurant that operated in a city parking garage was so closely tied to the city that discrimination by it was tantamount to state action and therefore impermissible under the Fourteenth Amendment.[16] Moreover, it shielded the NAACP from harassment by southern officials, barring them from compelling the organization to reveal the names of its members. Such disclosure, the Court ruled, would subject NAACP members to retaliation and thus inhibit their First Amendment right to freedom of expression and association.[17]

Even Congress took action, cautious though it was, to promote civil rights. With northern voters closely divided between the two major parties in the crucial industrial states, northern Democrats were intent on holding the black vote while Republicans were determined to woo blacks back to the party of Lincoln. Consequently, there was strong bipartisan support for civil rights legislation on Capitol Hill as 1956, an election year, dawned. Eager to place the resources of the Justice Department behind plaintiffs in school desegregation cases, liberals urged that the attorney general be given authority to seek injunctions against all civil rights violations. Their efforts were defeated by a coalition of conservative Republicans and southern and western Democrats. The bill that eventually emerged from Congress, the Civil Rights Act of 1957, was a weak measure concerned principally with voting rights. It elevated the civil rights section of the Justice Department to a division directed by an assistant attorney general for civil rights, provided for appointment of a Commission on Civil Rights to investigate voting discrimination, made it a federal offense to interfere with the right to vote, and authorized the attorney general to prosecute voting rights cases.

Dissatisfied with this half-hearted measure, liberals pressed for bolder action. They demanded a comprehensive civil rights bill that would authorize the Department of Health, Education, and Welfare (HEW) to draft school desegregation plans for communities that refused to do so, empower the attorney general to seek injunctions in all cases involving civil rights violations, and prohibit employment discrimination. Liberals also wanted to put teeth in federal voting rights law. They urged that the Commission on Civil Rights be empowered to investigate complaints of voting discrimination and to dispatch federal officials to register voters in any county in which it discovered evidence of discrimination.

Once again liberals went down to defeat as Congress enacted another mild bill. Like the 1957 law, the Civil Rights Act of 1960 dealt mainly with voting. It required state officials to preserve records of federal elections for at least two years, thus preventing destruction of incriminating records before complaints of fraud could be investigated. It also strengthened the hand of federal judges in voting cases. If they determined that local voter registration officers were guilty of discrimination, judges could dispatch federal referees to supervise registration. Although this involved the time-consuming process of litigation, it offered a potentially effective tool to combat southern officials' often ingenious manipulation of registration requirements to prevent blacks from voting. Finally, the act established criminal penalties for anyone who obstructed federal court orders (a provision aimed at nullificationists like Orville Faubus) or who crossed state lines to engage in bombings or arson.

The Pace of Change Quickens, 1960–1965

If the slow pace of change symbolized by the tepid civil rights bills of 1957 and 1960 frustrated most black leaders, it spurred black college students to challenge the status quo. They had grown up on a steady diet of Cold War rhetoric that extolled the openness of American society and proclaimed the United States the leader of the free world in its struggle against Communist dictatorship. *Brown* (handed down when they were in their early teens) led them to believe that the nation was finally prepared to make good its professions of democracy and equality by breaking down the color line. The slow pace of change in the late 1950s, however, undermined these assumptions, giving birth to a new militance that shook the foundations of the old order and hastened the pace of change.

On February 1, 1960, four neatly dressed black freshmen at North Carolina Agricultural and Technical College in Greensboro, walked into the local Woolworth store, sat down at its segregated lunch counter, and politely asked to be served. When the waitress refused, the young men remained at the counter, studying quietly, until the store closed. During the weeks that followed, more than 1,000 students joined these 4 pioneers, as the sit-ins spread to other Greensboro lunch counters, and local blacks closed ranks with the students, picketing and boycotting

Woolworth and other variety stores that discriminated against blacks. The Greensboro sit-ins sparked a direct action campaign that spread across the South like wildfire. In dozens of towns and cities, in every southern state, black youths defied segregation at lunch counters, restaurants, motels, swimming pools, beaches, libraries, and theaters and staged massive demonstrations. Using the tactics of nonviolent resistance, the demonstrators politely asserted their moral right to equal treatment and turned the other cheek when whites verbally and physically abused them. Thousands of demonstrators were arrested and chose jail over bail (or payment of fines) in order to highlight the repressiveness of the caste system. In Orangeburg, South Carolina, for example, police filled the city and county jails and incarcerated 300 more black student protesters in a hastily improvised stockade.

The sit-ins marked a turning point in the civil rights struggle. In response to the new militance, more than 200 cities began desegregation of public accommodations. Although most towns and small cities in the Deep South refused to budge, students boasted that in six months they had moved the South closer to integration than the federal courts had done in the six years following *Brown*. Even more important, the students demonstrated a new sense of urgency, indicating that they were tired of gradualism and were no longer willing to wait until judges and politicians decided the time was ripe for them to enjoy their rights. "[W]e cannot tolerate, in a nation professing democracy and among people professing Christianity, the discriminatory conditions under which the Negro is living today," Atlanta sit-in leaders proclaimed. "We do not intend to wait placidly for those rights which are already legally and morally ours to be meted out to us one at a time." [18]

This impatience and militance was not a flash in the pan. It was institutionalized in April 1960, when black student leaders formed the Student Non-Violent Coordinating Committee (SNCC, pronounced "snick") to perpetuate and expand the direct action campaign. Just as the young radicals were influenced by older civil rights leaders, their actions affected established civil rights groups. The Congress of Racial Equality (CORE), a small northern interracial group that had brought nonviolent resistance to the civil rights effort in the 1940s, sent representatives to the conference that gave birth to SNCC and advised the young activists on the tactics of direct action. CORE was itself invigorated by the success of the students and, in the year following the sit-ins, grew steadily and expanded its activities into the South. Martin Luther King's philosophy and tactics of nonviolent resistance, developed during the Montgomery bus boycott, had inspired the students, and King himself had participated in the sit-ins. At the same time, the students reaffirmed the potential of direct action for King and his colleagues in the Southern Christian Leadership Conference (SLC), prompting them to place greater emphasis on civil disobedience.

When John F. Kennedy came to the White House in January 1961, black leaders were becoming increasingly bold and impatient. Despite his youthful vigor and personal dislike for segregation, the new president spoke the language of gradualism and moved cautiously on civil rights. Blacks had played a crucial role in his razor thin victory in 1960 and would be taken care of. But they would have to settle for more federal appointments (Thurgood Marshall, for example, was appointed to the U.S. Court of Appeals for the Second Circuit in 1961), vigorous enforcement of the voting rights laws, and an economic policy that promised higher wages to all working-class Americans. Kennedy refused to ask Congress for comprehensive civil rights legislation. It had no chance of passing, he believed, and, besides, it carried too high a price tag. A bold civil rights initiative on Capitol Hill would cost support among southern whites, who would be crucial to a 1964 reelection bid, and alienate southern Democrats in Congress, whose backing on other issues was crucial.

The administration also resisted federal intervention in the South to protect civil rights activists. Attorney General Robert Kennedy resolutely maintained that the federal system gave the states responsibility for general law enforcement; the federal government had neither the constitutional authority nor the personnel to take responsibility for maintaining law and order. He pointed out that the Supreme Court's venerable state action interpretation of the Fourteenth Amendment denied the government authority to prosecute private individuals who used violence and intimidation to deny blacks equal rights and due process. The attorney general also pleaded that the federal government did not possess a police force capable of preserving the peace. Both the United States Marshals Service and the Federal Bureau of Investigation had far too few officers to take responsibility for general law enforcement in the South. Moreover, he maintained that the creation of a national police force was a threat to liberty because it could afford a ruthless president the means to suppress dissent.

Although these objections had some merit, they also "accord[ed] nicely with the political needs of the Kennedy brothers," according to historian Michal Belknap.[19] The state action restriction made successful prosecution of anti-civil rights violence problematical, but the Supreme Court might be convinced to reverse itself, as it had in *Brown*. While there were too few federal officers to police the South, there were enough of them to handle selected cases, and a small number of prosecutions might deter future violence. Federal intervention was neither impossible nor a potential threat to liberty. It was, however, calculated to raise the hackles of white southerners and therefore politically risky.

The administration's response to the freedom rides of 1961 illustrate its reluctance to intervene in the South. In December 1960, the Supreme Court ruled that the Interstate Commerce Act forbade discrimination in bus terminals serving interstate carriers.[20] The following May, CORE and SNCC activists left Washington, D.C. for a bus trip into the Deep South to test compliance with the Court's decision. On May 14, in Anniston and Birmingham and on May 20, in Montgomery, three separate groups of freedom riders were attacked and beaten by mobs of Alabama whites wielding chains, pipes, and baseball bats. Although local police refused to protect the protesters, Robert Kennedy resisted calls for federal intervention, choosing to work behind the scenes to defuse the crisis. He pressed the Interstate Commerce Commission to issue regulations compelling obedience to the Court's decision. (In November, the commission barred interstate carriers from using segregated terminals, forcing most southern terminals to capitulate.) He also prodded state officials to preserve order, repeatedly urging Governor John Patterson of Alabama to protect the riders and sending aides to Montgomery to confer with Patterson and to monitor the situation.

The Justice Department intervened only when state officials proved beyond all doubt that they would not act. On the evening of May 21— after a week of pleading and cajoling—the attorney general finally gave up on state officials when Montgomery police refused to respond as a mob threatened to overrun a church where Martin Luther King, Jr. spoke at a ceremony honoring the freedom riders. Fearing bloodshed, department officials deployed 100 U.S. marshals to hold the angry crowd at bay. Yet this limited intervention was the exception. As the freedom riders moved into Mississippi, the attorney general, fearing a repetition of events in Alabama, negotiated a deal with state officials. The state agreed to guarantee the safety of the riders on the condition that the Justice Department would not interfere with local prosecution of persons who violated state segregation laws. The riders were protected from Mississippi mobs, but by the end of the summer more than 300 of them were in Mississippi jails. During the ensuing months, when mobs threatened freedom riders in three other cities, the attorney general urged state officials to preserve order but rejected calls for federal intervention.

While unsympathetic to direct action, the Kennedys were not oblivious to the demands of blacks. They believed that equality could be achieved gradually and with a minimum of confrontation if barriers to black voting were destroyed. Like Reconstruction-era Republicans, they contended that once blacks possessed the ballot, state officials would become responsive to their demands for justice. Thus the rights of blacks could be protected without major alterations in the federal system and without the need for politically embarrassing federal confrontations with state officials. In the bargain, most new black voters would join the Democratic party, helping reverse the steady erosion of Democratic strength that had occurred during the post-World War II years.

During late 1961 and 1962, administration officials urged civil rights activists to refocus their efforts from direct action to voter registration. Justice Department officials participated in a series of meetings that led to the creation of the Voter Education Project, a two-and-one-half year campaign to register southern blacks which was financed by $870,000 from northern foundations. SCLC, CORE, and NAACP all readily agreed to participate. SNCC leaders were suspicious of being coopted by the administration but ultimately agreed to go along. The voter registration campaign, they believed, could help raise the consciousness of rural southern blacks and encourage them to challenge white supremacy.

As the campaign began, the Justice Department itself devoted greater attention to disfranchisement. Especially in the rural black belt, whites had developed a variety of techniques to keep blacks politically inactive. Although the literacy rate among blacks had increased dramatically, local officials manipulated literacy tests to deny literate blacks the right to vote. Often going beyond the letter of state law, they asked blacks difficult questions about the Constitution and state and local government— questions they never put to whites. In addition, officials developed complex voter registration forms and refused to register blacks (but not whites) who made even slight errors in completing them. Registration boards also foiled blacks' efforts to register by meeting infrequently and irregularly and by not publicizing the hours they were open for business. Officials were only part of the problem. In small towns and rural areas blacks who attempted to register might be fired, turned off the land they farmed, denied credit by local merchants, or worse. In this climate, many blacks did not attempt to register. In 1962, only one-fourth of voting age southern blacks were registered; in Mississippi the figure stood at five percent and in Alabama, thirteen percent.

Intent on rooting out these practices, Robert Kennedy dramatically increased the size of the Civil Rights Division staff and directed it to begin wholesale prosecution of voting rights cases. The primary weapons in the campaign were the provisions of the Civil Rights Act of 1957 permitting the Justice Department to seek injunctions against attempting to prevent citizens from registering or voting. Government lawyers won injunctions barring officials from refusing to register blacks who made minor mistakes on their applications and from imposing more stringent literacy tests on blacks than on whites. They also challenged private intimidation of blacks by securing injunctions against economic coercion directed at blacks who challenged discriminatory registration practices or who were active in voter registration drives.

The campaign's results were mixed. In tandem with the Voter Education Project, Justice Department litigation helped increase the proportion of southern black adults who were registered from twenty-six to forty percent between 1962 and 1964. Nevertheless, department officials had to proceed county by county, conducting in-depth investigations to establish proof of discrimination or economic coercion. The process was time-consuming and limited the number of localities in which cases could be initiated. Furthermore, the injunctions department lawyers won ordered persons to stop a certain type of discriminatory or coercive behavior. Local whites were generally resourceful enough to devise other means to hinder black registration, forcing department lawyers to conduct further investigations and return to court. By the end of 1964, only seven percent of the black adults residing in the 46 counties in which the government had initiated suits were registered, and black registration was below ten percent in 100 southern counties.

The administration's hope that voter registration would cool off tensions produced by the sit-ins and the freedom rides, was soon disappointed. SNCC took its voter registration campaign into black belt counties in Georgia and Mississippi, where whites viewed black political empowerment as a dire threat. Predictably, whites launched a campaign of terror designed to drive out SNCC workers and to intimidate local blacks. Although state officials failed to punish the perpetrators of this violence, the Justice Department refused to make arrests or initiate prosecutions, clinging to its position that responsibility for law enforcement lay primarily with state officials. Only in October 1962, when Mississippi officials and an armed mob prevented enforcement of a court order admitting James Meredith to the University of Mississippi, did the administration act forcefully to curb racist violence. As Eisenhower had done in the Little Rock crisis, Kennedy dispatched U.S. marshals and troops to the campus to break resistance to federal authority and to enable Meredith to enroll.

Events in Birmingham during the spring of 1963, however, finally forced President Kennedy to abandon his cautious approach to civil rights. During the winter of 1962–1963, Martin Luther King, Jr. and his closest advisors devised a bold plan for massive demonstrations in Birmingham, the toughest, most segregated city in the South. King knew that he would meet bitter resistance from the police commissioner, Eugene "Bull" Connor, a hard-line segregationist with a short fuse. Connor, who had earned his spurs during the 1930s in a brutal campaign to keep the unions out of Birmingham's steel mills, ruled the city with an iron fist and could be counted on to respond with violence. Consequently, the city offered King an opportunity to focus the nation's attention on the brutality of segregation, to precipitate a crisis that would force the administration off dead-center, and to win a stunning victory that would reinvigorate a sagging civil rights movement. Wyatt Tee Walker, the SCLC staff member who drafted the Birmingham plan, called it "Project C"—for confrontation.

The Birmingham campaign began in early April with a boycott of downtown merchants, sit-ins at segregated lunch counters, and marches on city hall. Connor responded by arresting protesters and obtaining an injunction against further demonstrations, but the protest continued and grew larger after King himself was arrested on April 12. During the remainder of the month, white leaders refused to negotiate, demonstrations and arrests continued, and police brutality increased. Having won the attention of the administration and the national media, King turned up the pressure. During the first week in May, he brought thousands of black children into the demonstrations, filling the city's jail and pushing Connor over the edge. The police commissioner responded to the "children's crusade" by unleashing club swinging patrolmen, snarling police dogs, and high pressure water hoses on peaceful demonstrators and bystanders, cracking their heads, breaking their bones, tearing their flesh, and bruising their bodies.

King's strategy worked. As pictures of police brutality appeared on the front pages of newspapers and on TV screens in living rooms across the nation, civil rights again took centerstage, and northern support for national action mounted. The president sent Justice Department mediators to Birmingham to arrange a settlement and pressured the city's business elite to compromise. Negotiations began promptly and were successfully concluded on May 10, when King announced that whites had agreed to desegregate lunch counters, drinking fountains, rest rooms, and department store fitting rooms and had pledged to implement a nondiscriminatory hiring program in the city's industries. The victory over Bull Connor emboldened blacks across the South, touching off more than 800 boycotts and demonstrations in 200 southern towns and cities during the summer of 1963. Birmingham kindled a new assertiveness among blacks, leading them to reject tokenism and to demand fundamental change—and to demand it without delay.

Birmingham also forced John Kennedy to make civil rights a top priority—something that no president since Ulysses Grant had done. He realized that blacks were no longer willing to wait patiently and feared that unless sweeping changes were initiated, racial confrontation would tear the nation apart. Indeed, while King continued to espouse nonviolence, there were indications that blacks were growing tired of turning the other cheek. On May 11, in response to a wave of racist bombings, Birmingham blacks took to the streets, pelting police with rocks and bottles and burning several white-owned businesses located in the ghetto. Elsewhere black writer James Baldwin wrote of *The Fire Next Time*, and Malcom X, the militant black nationalist who appeared on television more than any other black leader in 1963, insisted that "the day of nonviolent resistance is over."[21] Faced with a growing racial crisis and sensing greater support for action, Kennedy went on national television on June 11 to announce that he was sending sweeping civil rights legislation to Congress. He appealed to principle, arguing that the nation confronted a moral issue "as old as the scriptures and . . . as clear as the American Constitution." But he also warned that the issue could no longer be avoided. "The events in Birmingham and elsewhere," he suggested, meant that legislation was essential "if we are to move this problem from the streets to the courts."[22]

Having committed himself, the president moved quickly. He submitted legislation strengthening the voting rights laws, authorizing the attorney general to file school desegregation suits, empowering the president to end federal financial assistance to discriminatory state and local programs, and banning discrimination in places of public accommodation such as motels, restaurants, theaters, retail stores, and gas stations. Kennedy could count on support from many labor leaders, the major national Jewish organizations, and liberal groups such as Americans for Democratic Action as well as the votes of northern Democrats, but he needed support from Republican leaders to off set opposition by southern Democrats and to overcome the inevitable Senate filibuster. The president worked hard to line up Republican support, and when liberal Democrats jeopardized his efforts by attempting to broaden the bill, he intervened, convincing liberals to keep amendments to a minimum and preserving bipartisan support. When an assassin's bullet felled Kennedy in November 1963, his successor, Lyndon Johnson, made the civil rights bill his top legislative priority. Strengthening the bipartisan alliance Kennedy had forged, President Johnson secured congressional approval for the bill in June 1964.

The Civil Rights Act of 1964 translated most of the objectives of the early civil rights movement into law, harnessing the principle of equal rights to the engine of federal power. At the heart of the bill lay the goal of banishing segregation from American life, thereby realizing the principle announced ten years earlier in *Brown*. Titles III and IV authorized the attorney general to institute lawsuits challenging discrimination in public schools and other facilities "owned, operated, or managed by or on behalf of any State or subdivision thereof," thus removing from private individuals the entire burden of desegregation. Title VI used the power of the purse to attack discrimination. It directed federal agencies to adopt regulations banning discrimination in all programs receiving federal funds and to cut the flow of federal dollars if they failed to comply. With many state and local governments becoming increasingly dependent on federal largesse, especially to finance public education, this offered a potent weapon against discrimination.

The law also set its sights on discrimination in privately owned and operated businesses that served the public. Relying on an expanded commerce power that was the legacy of the New Deal, Title II prohibited discrimination on account of race, color, religion, or national origin by restaurants, hotels, motels, gas stations, theaters, stadiums, concert halls, or other places of entertainment that "affected" interstate commerce. Although victims of discrimination might institute lawsuits and recover monetary damages, the act's sponsors realized that private citizens might be reluctant to sue. Consequently, they authorized the attorney general to initiate suits against businesses that violated the act.

Finally, the law attacked employment discrimination, a target of black leaders and congressional liberals since the 1930s. Title VII prohibited discrimination on account of race, color, religion, national origin, or sex by employers and labor unions with more than twenty-five employees or members and by employment agencies. Liberals pressed for establishment of an administrative agency to investigate complaints of employment discrimination and to issue cease-and-desist orders against violators. This afforded a far more effective remedy, they argued, than going to court. In order to maintain Republican support, however, the bill's sponsors were forced to accept watered down enforcement provisions. They established a five-member Equal Employment Opportunity Commission (EEOC) and authorized it to investigate complaints of employment discrimination. When it found evidence of discrimination, the commission was to persuade the employer or union to end its discriminatory practices. If conciliation failed, the victim of discrimination could go to court or the commission could ask the attorney general to initiate a lawsuit.

With the Civil Rights Act on the books, President Johnson turned to the problem of disfranchisement. As the administration consulted civil rights leaders and prepared new legislation, events in Selma, Alabama lent greater urgency to the issue. Despite several years of voter registration efforts and Justice Department lawsuits, only two percent of the black adults in Dallas County were registered. In January and February 1965, SNCC and SCLC staged massive demonstrations at the county courthouse in Selma to focus attention to the problem. Local officials responded by arresting more than 3,000 protesters. On March 7, as 500 protesters defied a state court injunction and began a march from Selma to the state capitol in Montgomery, some sixty miles away, state police and a mounted posse led by the sheriff moved against them. As the panic-stricken demonstrators fled, they were trampled by horsemen, shocked with electric cattle prods, and beaten with clubs and chains. That evening the television networks interrupted programs—ABC was airing *Judgment at Nuremberg*—to show the attack, and the next morning Selma was page-one news throughout the country. Lyndon Johnson seized the moment, promptly submitting a sweeping voting rights bill to Congress and making a nationally televised speech to demand speedy passage. Lawmakers quickly fell into line, completing action on the bill in less than five months.

Cutting through state registration requirements and procedures that purported to be racially neutral, the Voting Rights Act of 1965 established formulas to identify and effective means to end discrimination. The act set its sights on the literacy test, historically the most notorious disfranchising devise. In any state or county where fewer than fifty percent of the adults were registered to vote, it automatically suspended the operation of any "test or devise" that was a prerequisite for voting. Congress also provided a remedy for other types of discrimination. In counties in which there was substantial evidence of racial discrimination—as indicated by complaints filed by twenty residents or a voting discrimination suit instituted by the attorney general—federal examiners would be appointed to register voters. Moreover, lawmakers attempted to prevent southern officials from developing new techniques of discrimination. States and localities covered by the act would be required to obtain clearance from the attorney general of a three-judge district court in Washington, D.C. before implementing any new voting requirements or procedures.

After years of temporizing, the president and Congress had finally taken the lead in civil rights, drawing on the deep reservoirs of federal power to promote equality. The Supreme Court quickly gave its blessing. In two 1964 cases, *Heart of Atlanta Motel* v. *United States* and *Katzenbach* v. *McClung,* the Court considered the Civil Rights Act's ban on discrimination by motels and restaurants. Drawing on a long line of cases that gave Congress broad authority to regulate businesses affecting interstate commerce, the Court unanimously upheld the statute. The *McClung* case emphasized the breadth of Congress's authority. The business involved, Ollie's Barbeque, was a small Birmingham restaurant that served a local clientele. The Court noted that Ollie's came within the scope of the law because it was open to interstate customers and because part of the food it sold had moved in interstate commerce. Moreover, it ruled that Congress had "a rational basis" for believing that such businesses affected interstate commerce and for subjecting them to regulation. They not only purchased food and other goods from interstate suppliers, but their discriminatory policies made interstate travel by blacks difficult.[23]

Concurring opinions by Justices William Douglas and Arthur Goldberg offered a more direct way of upholding the act. Congress's authority to enforce the equal protection clause, they maintained, authorized it to ban discrimination in businesses open to the public. Their analysis abandoned the hoary principle, established in the *Civil Rights Cases* of 1883, that the amendment authorized Congress to ban discriminatory action by states but not by private individuals or businesses. Although the majority rejected this approach, its willingness to accept a prohibition against discrimination by private businesses enacted under the commerce power gave Congress the authority to reach most private discrimination and suggested the demise of the old distinction between state and private action that had long crippled effective civil rights legislation.

Two years later, in *South Carolina* v. *Katzenbach* (1966), the Court gave its blessing to the Voting Rights Act. Chief Justice Warren emphasized that in enforcing the Fifteenth Amendment, Congress was free to choose the means best suited to eliminate racial discrimination in voting. Surveying the provisions adopted by Congress—suspension of literacy tests, appointment of federal examiners, and judicial supervision of changes in voting procedures—he concluded that they were clearly designed to meet problems that Congress had encountered in its long struggle to overcome state and local officials' ingenious and persistant efforts to deny blacks the right to vote. Consequently, while the act represented an unprecedented exercise of federal power, it was clearly within Congress's authority to adopt legislation necessary and proper to enforce the Fifteenth Amendment.[24]

The Court not only sustained the Voting Rights Act but went where Congress had feared to tread, striking down the poll tax. This device was a far less serious obstacle to black voting than discriminatory administration of literacy tests; by 1960, all but four states—Virginia, Alabama, Mississippi, and Texas—had repealed it. Nevertheless, in those states it deterred the very poor from voting and had a disproportionate effect on blacks. Anti-poll tax legislation had long received strong support on Capitol Hill, and in 1962 Congress had passed the Twenty-fourth Amendment (which was ratified two years later) banning the poll tax as a requirement for voting in *federal* elections. Although liberals made a strong effort to extend the prohibition to state elections in the Voting Rights Act, doubts about the constitutionality of a poll tax repealer torpedoed their effort. Opponents argued that, unlike literacy tests, which were administered in a discriminatory fashion, the poll tax was applied to whites and blacks alike and therefore did not violate the Fifteenth Amendment. One year later, however, the Supreme Court gave opponents of the poll tax the outright victory that had eluded them for decades. In *Harper* v. *Virginia Board of Elections* (1966), the Court ruled the tax unconstitutional, resting its decision on the Fourteenth rather than the Fifteenth Amendment. Writing for the majority, Justice Douglas asserted that the poll tax discriminated against the poor and thus violated the amendment's guarantee of equal protection.[25]

The Court also expanded the government's authority to punish anti-civil rights violence. By early 1965, growing northern outrage over violence against civil rights workers convinced the Justice Department to initiate prosecutions in several highly publicized cases of racist violence. Because the federal system gave states primary responsibility for criminal justice, crimes such as assault and murder were state, not federal, offenses. There were, however, federal statutes that punished persons who deprived others of their civil rights, and it was these which federal prosecutors employed. Principally, Justice Department officials relied on Title 18, section 241 of the *United States Code,* which punished persons who conspired to use force or intimidation to prevent anyone from exercising rights secured by the Constitution or laws of the United States.

Although the law appeared adequate to the task, many questioned whether it could be used to prosecute perpetrators of racist violence. First, many lawyers and scholars doubted whether the rights protected by section 241 included Fourteenth Amendment rights of equal protection and due process. In 1951, the Court had divided 4–4 on the question, with Justice Frankfurter maintaining that rights mentioned in section 241 were limited to those created by the Constitution (such as the right to vote in *federal* elections), not rights that government was prohibited from violating (such as the Fourteenth Amendment rights of equal protection and due process and the rights mentioned in the Bill of Rights). Otherwise, Frankfurter believed, the federal government would have carte blanche to usurp law enforcement activities that properly belonged to the states. Although Frankfurter's opinion did not represent a majority and was not binding, it cast a shadow over the government's authority to prosecute perpetrators of racist violence on grounds that they denied their victims equal protection or due process.[26] In addition, many observers believed that the state action rule precluded prosecution of private citizens under section 241. Given the long line of Supreme Court rulings holding that the Fourteenth Amendment authorized Congress to provide remedies against state, but not private, denials of equal protection and due process, it was doubtful whether section 241 could be employed against private citizens, even if it were interpreted to protect Fourteenth Amendment rights. Although the Court had whittled away at the state action limitation on the Fourteenth Amendment, it had not abandoned it, as *Heart of Atlanta Motel* and *McClung* had suggested.

Two 1966 rulings swept these doubts aside. In *United States* v. *Price,* which involved the prosecution of eighteen whites implicated in the cold-blooded murder of three civil rights workers in Neshoba County, Mississippi, the Court ruled that Fourteenth Amendment rights were protected by section 241. Justice Abe Fortas pointed out that section 241 had its origins in Reconstruction legislation (the 1870 Enforcement Act) designed to enforce the guarantees of the Fourteenth and Fifteenth Amendments. "In this context," he concluded, "it is hardly conceivable that Congress intended [it] . . . to apply only to a narrow and relatively unimportant category of rights." Unquestionably, its "purpose and effect" was "to reach assaults upon rights under the entire Constitution . . . not merely under part of it."[27]

In a companion case, *United States* v. *Guest,* the Supreme Court considered whether Congress could punish private as well as state interference with Fourteenth Amendment rights. Although Justice Potter Stewart's opinion for the Court ducked the issue, concurring opinions by Justices William Brennan and Tom Clark (which were joined by six justices) were much bolder. Challenging the limitations imposed on Congress in the *Civil Rights Cases* (1883), Justice Brennan insisted that Congress enjoyed broad power to enforce the amendment's guarantees. "Section 5 [of the Fourteenth Amendment] authorizes Congress to make laws that it concludes are reasonably necessary to protect a right created by . . . that Amendment,"he wrote, "and Congress is thus fully empowered to determine that punishment of private conspiracies interfering with the exercise of such a right is necessary to its full protection." In short, Brennan concluded, Congress is authorized "to exercise its discretion in fashioning remedies to achieve civil and political equality for all citizens."[28]

The *Price* and *Guest* cases did not bury the state action rule. They suggested that Congress's authority to enforce the amendment (expressly conferred in section 5) gave it broad discretion to strike at state and private action. Yet the justices did not claim such authority for themselves. When the Court enforced the equal protection clause (rather than congressional legislation enforcing it), it would still require the presence of state action in order to prohibit discrimination. Nevertheless, *Guest* and *Price* gave the government the authority necessary to prosecute anti-civil rights violence. In 1966 and 1967 government lawyers used the newly reinvigorated section 241 to win convictions in several of the most outrageous instances of violence against blacks and civil rights workers. More important, the decisions unshackled Congress from the state action theory, offering it greater authority to protect individual rights. Law-makers promptly took advantage of the Court's largesse. In Title I of the Civil Rights Act of 1968 they established a much clearer definition of federally protected civil rights than did the maddeningly vague section 241. Additionally, they gave the attorney general broad authority to prosecute anyone who used force or intimidation to interfere with these rights.

Consolidation, Expansion, and Opposition, 1965–1969

After a decade of frustration, civil rights advocates had scored major victories, dramatically expanding federal civil rights authority and establishing effective remedies against discrimination. With Lyndon Johnson in the White House, the government moved swiftly and surely, using the new legislation to destroy Jim Crow. Faced with the threat of lawsuit, most public facilities and private businesses covered by the public accommodations provisions of the Civil Rights Act of 1964 voluntarily opened their doors to blacks. Those that refused faced Justice Department lawyers who were determined to compel obedience. When it received complaints of discrimination, the department warned offenders that their practices were illegal and, if the warnings failed, took them to court. By 1968 the attorney general reported that there had been "widespread voluntary compliance" with the public accommodations section of the 1964 act and that most of the complaints that the department received involved "small eating establishments in the more rural areas." By the end of the decade, most white southerners grudgingly accepted what a few years earlier they had viewed as anathema—blacks and whites eating in the same restaurants, attending the same theaters and ball parks, and staying in the same motels.[29]

The problem of school segregation proved tougher to resolve, but by the end of the decade the executive and judicial branches, working together, had transformed the face of southern education. In 1964, a decade after *Brown,* only two percent of the black children living in the states of the former Confederacy attended school with whites. Officials in HEW promptly invoked their authority under the Civil Rights Act to compel desegregation. In December 1964 they informed southern school officials that they must submit desegregation plans to remain eligible for federal funds, and four months later, issued guidelines for schools to follow in drafting plans. Almost ninety-five percent of southern school districts responded, with most adopting so-called freedom of choice plans. While ostensibly these plans offered students the opportunity to attend the school of their choice, they were designed to minimize integration. Whites never chose to send their children to black schools, and many blacks, fearing reprisals by employers and merchants, kept their children in all-black schools. White officials did their best to deter blacks from entering white schools as well. Frequently they required black parents and children to appear in person to apply for transfers to white schools, informed black parents that buses serving the white school did not run through the colored section of town, warned black children that they would not be permitted to join the band, school clubs, or athletic teams, and turned away black applicants on the grounds that the white schools were too crowded.

Although these plans offered little freedom of choice, they did produce some integration in most southern districts. Moreover, HEW soon indicated that freedom of choice plans, by themselves, were not enough. In March 1966 it issued new guidelines stipulating that districts would be judged on their actual progress toward desegregation and establishing goals and timetables to speed-up the process. Clearly, HEW would not settle for token integration and would continue to keep the heat on southern districts.

The federal courts reinforced HEW policy, signaling to school officials that even if they chose to forego federal money (which amounted to almost ten percent of their funding by 1966) they would not escape genuine integration. In December 1966, Judge John Minor Wisdom of the U.S. Court of Appeals for the Fifth Circuit, shocked southern school officials with his landmark opinion in *United States* v. *Jefferson County Board of Education.* Wisdom not only endorsed the HEW guidelines and directed all judges in the fifth circuit to follow them in writing decrees in school desegregation suits. He also announced that compliance with the guidelines was the first step on the road to full integration. The Louisiana native acknowledged that the Constitution prohibited discrimination and did not mandate integration. He held, however, that where segregation had been imposed by law, officials had a responsibility to take positive action to undo the results of their unconstitutional behavior. And that meant integration. *"[T]he only adequate redress for a previously overt system-wide policy of segregation directed at Negroes as a collective entity,"* he asserted, *"is a system-wide policy of integration."* Although Wisdom did not disallow freedom of choice plans, he emphasized that district judges should accept them only if they led to actual integration:

> What the decree contemplates, then, is continuing judicial evaluation of compliance by measuring the performance—not merely the promised performance—of school boards in carrying out their constitutional obligation "to disestablish dual, racially segregated school systems and *to achieve substantial integration in such systems"* [emphasis added]. . . . If school officials in any district should find that their district still has segregated facultes or schools *or only token integration* [emphasis added], their affirmative duty to take corrective action requires them to try an alternative to a freedom of choice plan, such as a geographic attendance plan . . . or some other acceptable substitute. . . . [30]

Wisdom's opinion—which was endorsed by the twelve judges of the United States Court of Appeals for the Fifth Circuit sitting *en banc*—was highly significant. Written as a directive to judges throughout the circuit, it would guide the process of school desegregation in most of the Deep South. Consequently, the decision signaled that compliance with HEW's demands was unavoidable and that schools would be pushed relentlessly to integrate. Wisdom's *Jefferson* opinion also indicated a major shift in the federal courts' approach to civil rights law. Rejecting the notion that the Fourteenth Amendment merely required states to cease discriminating, it announced a result-oriented interpretation of the equal protection clause. In those places in which segregation had been imposed by law and public policy, officials had a legal obligation to take affirmative action to achieve integration. *Jefferson* also signaled a shift to color-consciousness. Although Wisdom acknowledged that the objective of the equal protection clause was colorblind public policy, he suggested that the courts must take color into account (e.g., measuring the degree of racial balance in schools) if they were to root out the effects of past discrimination and achieve genuine equality.

Less than two years later, in *Green v. County School Board* (1968) the United States Supreme Court endorsed Wisdom's approach. The case involved a challenge to a freedom of choice plan in a largely rural Virginia county whose population was equally divided between whites and blacks. The county operated two schools, one, on the east side, which had been the white school, and the other, on the west side, which had been the black school. Although there was little residential segregation in the county and the freedom of choice plan permitted children to choose either school, no whites had elected to attend the black school and only fifteen percent of the blacks had entered the formerly all-white school. The Court held that the county's desegregation efforts were inadequate. *Brown II*, Justice Brennan pointed out, required school officials in states and localities where segregation had been established by law "to effectuate a transition to a racially nondiscriminatory school system." This meant that they were "clearly charged with the affirmative duty to take whatever steps might be necessary to convert to a unitary system in which racial discrimination would be eliminated root and branch." With eighty-five percent of its black children still in one-race schools, Brennan concluded, the county clearly had failed to meet that requirement. "The burden on a school board today," he asserted, "is to come forward with a plan that promises realistically to work, and promises realistically to work *now*." The message was clear. Formerly segregated school districts had the obligation to integrate promptly, and the Court would look carefully at the racial balance in the schools to determine whether they had met their obligation.[31]

Confronting HEW guidelines that annually grew more stringent, an increasing number of Justice Department lawsuits, and courts that demanded results, southern school districts capitulated. In 1968, eighteen percent of southern black pupils were attending white majority schools; two years later the figure stood at thirty-nine percent, and in 1972, it had risen to forty-six percent, making southern schools the most integrated in the nation. (In 1972 only twenty-eight percent of black pupils in the North and West were enrolled in white majority schools.) Desegregation gave black children access to better schools and resulted in improvements in educational performance by southern black children. That was not the only benefit, however. "As long as schools were segregated by law, southern blacks lived in a society whose public authority defined them as inferior and where, for them, democratic principles were a mockery," notes historian Allen Matusow. "Insistence on unitary school systems meant that for blacks and whites there was now one law, one standard of democracy, and one community."[32]

The Johnson administration also moved forcefully against voting discrimination. Under the Voting Rights Act, literacy tests were suspended in six states—Virginia, South Carolina, Georgia, Alabama, Mississippi, and Louisiana—and in parts of North Carolina. While this eliminated the most potent disfranchising device, many registration officials continued to employ dilatory tactics to prevent blacks from registering. In order to overcome this resistance, the Justice Department dispatched federal registrars to fifty-eight counties between 1965 and 1968. Civil rights activists pressed for appointment of more registrars, pointing out that they had been sent to only a third of the counties in which fewer than half of the adult blacks were registered. Nevertheless, the presence of federal registrars not only ended disfranchisement in the counties in which they operated, but convinced officials in neighboring counties to register blacks in order to avoid federal intervention.

The results of the campaign were impressive. Between 1964 and 1969, black registration in the Deep South almost doubled, increasing from thirty-six to sixty-five percent of black adults in the region. In Mississippi, where only seven percent of adult blacks had been registered in 1964, the figure stood at sixty-seven percent in 1969. Moreover, black voting quickly produced significant results. By 1968, in the five states in which federal registrars had been employed (South Carolina, Georgia, Alabama, Mississippi, and Louisiana), more than 120 blacks had won elective office. Granted, most of these served in county and municipal government, but their success marked a dramatic departure in a region in which blacks had not been permitted to vote, much less hold office, for more than seventy years. Nevertheless, blacks were minorities in every southern state, and most whites continued to follow the color line in politics. Consequently, black candidates could reasonably expect success only if they ran in black-majority or near-black-majority districts. And this meant that they had little chance of victory in state-wide contests or in most local elections.

Black voting, however, was not in vain. Even in districts with black minorities, they frequently held the balance of power and could defeat openly racist office seekers. Consequently, white politicians soon learned that appeals to racism were likely to backfire and largely abandoned the scurrilous race-baiting that had been a staple of southern politics. This opened the way for a new generation of moderate white politicians such as Jimmy Carter, Reubin Askew, Ernest Hollings, and Dale Bumpers who emerged in the 1970s, and ultimately convinced even the formerly staunch segregationist George Wallace to court black voters. Furthermore, most white elected officials, aware of the growing power of blacks, became more responsive to them. Dr. John Cashin, the head of Alabama's all-black National Democratic party, noted that black voting had an especially salutary effect on law enforcement. ''It's no longer standard operating procedure for whites to kill blacks at will,'' he explained in 1973. ''And it's all because of politics.''[33] Although southern blacks had a long way to go if they were to exercise effective political power, the Voting Rights Act radically altered southern politics and government.

The late 1960s witnessed the demise of disfranchisement and Jim Crow, bringing to a successful conclusion a campaign by three generations of black activists. As important as this victory was, however, it highlighted how much remained to be done. Because of discrimination by employers and labor unions, low levels of educational achievement (the product of poverty and separate and unequal schools), and despair, far too many blacks were trapped in menial, poorly paying jobs or were chronically unemployed. Mired in poverty, with little hope of improving their lot, they attached little importance to the right to vote or to be served in restaurants they could not afford in the first place. Poverty, combined with the practices of banks, realtors, and city governments, guaranteed that urban blacks remained in the nation's decaying inner cities. There they lived in substandard housing owned by landlords who often extracted exorbitant rents from a captive market. Furthermore, residential segregation meant that black children attended segregated schools. In 1962, for example, two-thirds of the black students in Gary, Indiana were enrolled in schools which were at least ninety-nine percent black. Predictably, these schools were more crowded, enjoyed less modern facilites, and provided environments that were less conducive to learning than predominantly white schools.

These problems were by no means exclusively southern. Indeed, they were most acute in northern cities such as New York, Gary, Cleveland, Boston, Los Angeles, Detroit, and Chicago. Consequently, as the 1960s progressed, civil rights leaders devoted increasing attention to the North. During the first half of the decade CORE and black community organizations picketed segregated housing projects and businesses guilty of employment discrimination, boycotted segregated schools, and staged rent strikes to force landlords to bring their buildings up to standards mandated by city codes. In 1966, with black protest already percolating in northern cities, Martin Luther King, Jr. focused the nation's attention on the racial problems of the North by going to Chicago, where he led a massive campaign against housing discrimination. There, King's marchers were greeted by mobs of virulently racist whites—some waving Confederate flags and wearing Nazi helmets—who were determined to keep blacks in the ghetto. These white mobs were backed by Mayor Richard Daley, head of the most powerful political machine in the nation. King left Chicago after nine months with little to show for his efforts, merely confirming what those who had been in the trenches already knew: the problems that existed in the North would be even more difficult to solve than those the movement had encountered in Birmingham and Selma.

Deadly race riots erupted almost like clockwork during the long, hot summers of the mid and late-1960s, shifting public attention to the northern ghettos. Beginning in Harlem in 1964 and Watts the following summer, riots swept 43 cities in 1966 and 164 urban areas in 1967. Frustrated by the contradiction between the promise of the civil rights movement and the hopelessness of their own situation, urban blacks unleashed the rage that had accumulated during three centuries of oppression. They struck at the most visible symbols of white domination: white policemen and white-owned ghetto businesses. And they struck hard. In Watts rioting lasted for four days and left 34 dead, more than 1,000 injured, and almost 1,000 buildings damaged or destroyed. Three years later, in Detroit, the toll was even worse: 43 persons died, well over 1,000 were injured, and 1,300 buildings were burned.

Although the causes of nothern blacks' dissatisfaction—poverty, employment discrimination, and segregated schools and housing—were obvious, solutions proved elusive. The Civil Rights Act of 1964 had included a nationwide ban on discrimination by employers and labor unions with at least twenty-five employees or members and created the EEOC to supervise implementation. Although the 41,000 complaints brought between 1965 and 1969 suggest broad awareness of the law's provisions, the commission's small staff proved inadequate to the task at hand. By 1969, it had determined that 24,000 of the complaints had merit, but had completed investigations in only 18,000 of these, leaving a backlog of 6,000 cases. After the staff completed its investigation, cases went to the five-member commission, which determined whether there was reasonable cause to believe that a violation had occurred and then drafted its decision. A critical bottleneck developed at this point. By

1969, the commission had written decisions in only 4,800 cases (finding for the complainants in 2,500) and was taking an average of between eighteen and twenty months to dispose of each case. This not only delayed relief for complainants, but meant that many cases had become moot by the time decisions were announced.

The EEOC's chief problem, however, was lack of enforcement authority. If it found reasonable cause that discrimination had occurred, it could attempt to resolve the case through negotiation. If that failed, the commission had two options. It could advise the complainant that he or she could sue or, if the case revealed a widespread pattern of discrimination, request the Justice Department to initiate litigation. With the threat of sanctions remote, the staff had little success in arranging voluntary settlements with employers. By 1969, it had attempted to settle 3,360 cases by negotiation, but had succeeded in only 683 cases affecting 14,000 persons. Moreover, the agency's small staff could not effectively monitor these agreements, and employers and unions sometimes reneged. Thus with limited staff and authority, the commissioners made little headway against discrimination.

The other major federal employment discrimination program accomplished even less. In September 1965, President Johnson issued Executive Order 11246, prohibiting job discrimination by firms which supplied goods or services to the federal government or which held federal construction contracts. The order authorized the secretary of labor to establish regulations outlining fair employment practices and to terminate contracts with those who failed to comply. Beacuse companies holding government contracts employed an estimated one-third of the workforce, vigorous enforcement promised substantial results. After issuing the order, however, the administration—increasingly preoccupied with the Vietnam War and reluctant to ruffle the feathers of conservative politicians, businessmen, and labor leaders whose support for that venture was crucial—quickly forgot it. The Office of Federal Contract Compliance (OFCC), created by the Labor Department to oversee enforcement, was poorly staffed and lethargic. It failed to draft clear guidelines for government agencies to follow in dealing with contractors and imposed no sanctions on contractors until May 1968.

Although the attack on job discrimination was weak, it achieved some modest gains. EEOC won redress for several thousand victims of discrimination and began to attack systemic discrimination. Aware that tests that measured general education created barriers for many blacks (who for decades had endured Jim Crow schools), the commission began a campaign against the use of employment tests that measured knowledge or skills not relevant to the job the applicant was seeking. The commission's effort would bear fruit in the 1970s, curbing a common source of discrimination. While the Justice Department initiated few job discrimination suits, it won several major victories in the lower federal courts, invalidating seniority systems that perpetrated the effects of earlier discrimination and discriminatory practices common among unions in the construction industry. Moreover, the civil rights movement and, especially, the publicity surrounding the Civil Rights Act and the activities of the EEOC, helped alter public opinion. A 1968 poll, conducted in fifteen cities, for example, indicated that only twenty-three percent of those interviewed opposed enforcement of equal employment laws.

Although labor shortages and rapid economic growth played an important role, changes in public opinion and the presence of legal sanctions against discrimination helped black workers score steady gains during the 1960s and early 1970s. The percentage of blacks employed as managers, professionals, and skilled workers almost doubled between 1958 and 1973, while the proportion engaged in service work and farm and nonfarm labor declined by one-third. Black women experienced especially dramatic changes during these years; the proportion working as domestic servants decreased from thirty-three to fifteen percent, while the proportion employed in clerical, sales, and professional jobs increased from nineteen to forty percent. Black workers also saw sharp, although still inadequate, gains in income. In 1959, black men, on average, earned only fifty-three percent as much as white men; by 1971, they earned sixty-six percent as much as whites. During the same period, the income of black women also increased, moving from sixty-six percent to ninety percent of the earnings of white women.

Although these gains were impressive, they should not be exaggerated. Blacks who moved up the ladder to become managers, professionals, and skilled workers, generally made it to the lowest rungs of those occupations. Thus in the professions blacks were concentrated in teaching and social work rather than in the more highly remunerative fields of law and medicine. For many blacks who were trapped in the ghettos and who lacked the education, skills, socialization, and hope necessary to take advantage of a more favorable job market, little changed. They still worked at menial jobs, suffered high rates of unemployment, and often left the job market altogether. The result was broken families, drug addiction, and crime, problems scarcely amenable to resolution by laws guaranteeing equality of opportunity.

Like poverty, nothern school segregation proved an elusive target. In northern cities, residential segregation bred highly segregated neighborhood schools. Observers labeled the outcome de facto segregation to distinguish it from the South's legally imposed, or de jure segregation. School officials themselves, however, often played a subtle but important role in its genesis and perpetuation, developing student transfer policies, drawing school attendance zones, locating new schools, and assigning faculty with an eye toward keeping black and white children separate. The federal courts generally refused to challenge de facto segregation, ruling that the Fourteenth Amendment did not require integration but merely prohibited public officials from segregating students on the basis of race. Even when the federal courts began to require southern schools to integrate, little changed in the North. Federal judges pointed out that southern schools were obligated to integrate in order to correct wrongs that resulted from de jure segregation, but that this obligation did not extend to northern schools, where segregation resulted from residential patterns rather than state law. Although some courts did order desegregation when plaintiffs proved that school officials had adopted policies that were intended to encourage segregation, this requirement placed a heavy burden on plaintiffs and made northern school suits difficult to win. Moreover, until 1973 the Supreme Court remained silent, offering no encouragement to opponents of de facto segregation.

Because residential segregation contributed to school segregation and trapped blacks in economically depressed inner city neighborhoods, federal fair housing legislation became a high priority for civil rights leaders. In 1966, as Martin Luther King's Chicago campaign focused attention on the consequences of housing discrimination, President Johnson recommended passage of a fair housing law. Liberals eagerly supported the bill, but it encountered rough sailing as many northern legislators joined southerners in opposition. As long as discrimination had been as open, obvious, brutal—and remote—as that practiced in the South, northerners had supported legislation to eradicate it. Housing discrimination in the North, however, was another matter. As King's reception in Chicago suggested, many northern whites, who had fled their old neighborhoods when blacks had entered or who feared that integration would lower the value of their property, bitterly opposed open housing legislation. Consequently, Congress stalled for two years before passing a weak bill in 1968.

The new legislation applied to more than eighty percent of the nation's housing stock. When it became fully operational in December 1969, the law banned discrimination on account of race, religion, or national origin in the sale or rental of most apartments and homes. The only dwellings excepted were single-family homes sold or rented without the assistance of a realtor and small apartment buildings with resident owners. The law also prohibited discriminatory lending practices by banks and savings and loan associations. Unfortunately, its enforcement provisions were as weak as its coverage was broad. Instead of creating an enforcement agency with authority to issue cease-and-desist orders against violators, the act empowered the Department of Housing and Urban Development to investigate complaints and to negotiate voluntary agreements with those found guilty of discrimination. If this conciliatory approach failed, the attorney general was authorized to bring lawsuits in cases that revealed a broad pattern of discrimination. Otherwise, individual victims of discrimination would have to initiate their own lawsuits—an expensive and time-consuming process that could drag on for years. Not surprisingly, the fair housing law did little to alleviate the problem of housing discrimination. Because it failed to afford timely redress, victims of discrimination largely disregarded it, filing fewer than 1,500 complaints during the first two years it was in effect.

At the same time that Congress passed the fair housing act, the Supreme Court addressed itself to the housing issue in its landmark decision in *Jones* v. *Alfred H. Mayer Co.* (1968). The case involved a suit brought by a black couple against a St. Louis real estate developer under Title 42, section 1982 of the *United States Code*. Originally enacted as part of the Civil Rights Act of 1866, section 1982 provided that all citizens were entitled to the same right "as is enjoyed by white citizens . . . to inherit, purchase, lease, sell, hold, or convey real and personal property." The Court rejected Mayer's contention that the statute had been aimed at the black codes and did not apply to private action. Justice Potter Stewart held that Congress, acting under the Thirteenth Amendment (which contained no state action limitation) had intended to erase all badges of servitude, whether they were imposed by state law or by private action. Moreover, he concluded that Congress had been fully justified in prohibiting discrimination in the sale of real estate. "At the very least, the freedom that Congress is empowered to secure under the Thirteenth Amendment includes the freedom to buy whatever a white man can buy, the right to live wherever a white man can live," Stewart wrote. "If Congress cannot say that being a free man means at least this much, then the Thirteenth Amendment made a promise the Nation cannot keep."[34]

Although the ruling required victims of housing discrimination to go to court to win redress, it was significant nonetheless. It applied to all housing, even those units that were not covered by the housing act. In addition, *Jones* suggested that the Court would take a broader view of the Reconstruction amendments and federal civil rights laws, offering civil rights lawyers a wider array of weapons against private discrimination. For example, section 1981, also originally enacted as part of the Civil Rights Act of 1866, provided that all persons "shall have the same right . . . to make and enforce contracts . . . as is enjoyed by white persons." Under the *Jones* precedent, persons who were denied employment or admission to a private school on account of race sould seek damages under section 1981, claiming that they had been denied the same rights as white persons to make contracts.[35] Although the Civil Rights Act of 1964 offered remedies against employment discrimination, suits under section 1981 could still prove useful. They could be initiated without first going through the EEOC complaint process, and they offered victims of discrimination monetary damage awards not available under the 1964 act.

While the Court was becoming bolder, politicians were beginning to hedge their bets on civil rights, as the checkered history of the fair housing law suggests. Indeed, by the late 1960s commentators spoke of a "white backlash" that made bold new initiatives risky. As the civil rights movement migrated north, challenging the pervasive job discrimination that benefited white workers and the school and housing segregation that insulated whites from blacks, many northern whites decided that it was time to slow the pace of change. Then, too, many northerners reacted strongly against what they considered bewildering, threatening developments in the black community. They recoiled as young black militants, disillusioned by a lifetime of painful encounters with white racism and despairing of meaningful change within the system, rejected nonviolence and integration and spoke the language of Black Power. Many whites also looked on, first in disbelief and then in anger as urban blacks rioted. Unable or unwilling to understand the rage that had gathered during 300 years of slavery and racism, they increasingly viewed crime control as more important than civil rights. Failing to appreciate the obstacles that many blacks still confronted, they angrily denounced blacks as ingrates who failed to appreciate whites' support for civil rights legislation.

As they soured on civil rights and reacted viscerally against white students who burned draft cards and American flags to protest the Vietnam War, many northerners who had voted for John Kennedy and Lyndon Johnson threw their support to flag-waving conservatives who asserted that individual initiative was the best anti-poverty program and who promised to restore law and order. In the 1966 congressional campaign Republicans picked up forty-seven House seats, while Ronald Reagan, the new darling of the Republican right, won the California gubernatorial election in a landslide. Two years later, the liberals' old nemesis, Richard M. Nixon, captured the White House.

By 1969, as liberals lost control of the presidency, civil rights advocates had cause for alarm. Granted, the 1960s had witnessed unprecedented advances: the destruction of the South's deeply entrenched system of segregation and disfranchisement which for generations had humiliated blacks and kept them powerless; a dramatic expansion of federal power to protect civil rights and to achieve genuine equality; a growing assertiveness and political sophistication among blacks which assured continued pressure for advances in civil rights; and an altered national consciousness which made it difficult for political leaders to ignore civil rights. Nevertheless, difficult, perhaps intractable, problems remained. Yet for many whites these problems were less visible and seemed less pressing than the blatant discrimination and brutality that the civil rights movement had challenged in the South. Moreover, the conservative resurgence suggested that civil rights advocates would encounter growing resistance to new initiatives designed to achieve the long list of objectives that remained unfulfilled.

7

The Elusive Quest for Equality, 1969–1990

The city of Boston was in turmoil as the public schools prepared to open in the fall of 1974. The previous June, Federal District Judge W. Arthur Garrity had ruled that the city's schools were unconstitutionally segregated. As a remedy for the violation of black children's constitutional rights, Garrity had established a desegregation plan that relied heavily on busing. Black children would be transported from predominantly black neighborhoods to schools in white areas, while whites would be bused to ghetto schools. On the average, students would spend thirty minutes per day in transit. Although few whites cheered the ruling, opposition was most intense in the tightly-knit Irish working class neighborhoods of Charlestown and South Boston. There, residents harbored a century-old antipathy to blacks, were devoted to their community schools, and adamantly opposed sending their children to ghetto schools. Whipsawed by the economic stagnation and high inflation of the early 1970s, they bitterly resented what they perceived as the government's special concern for minorities. Moreover, they denounced the inequity of busing, charging that the wealthy could avoid integration by moving to the suburbs or by sending their children to private schools, options that were not available to the working class residents of Charlestown and South Boston. "Someone's got to explain it to me," demanded one white parent. "I'll listen to anybody, but someone's got to tell me how this Garrity guy, this big deal judge gets all this power to move people around, right the hell out of their neighborhood, while everybody else in the world comes out of it free and equal."[1]

White resentment, which had built over the summer, exploded on September 9, 1974, three days before classes were to begin, as 8,000 white parents staged an antibusing rally outside the John F. Kennedy Federal Building in Boston. Hoping to stem the antibusing tide and to prevent disruptive behavior when classes began, Senator Edward M. Kennedy made a surprise appearance at the rally. But Kennedy's presence only inflamed the crowd. A strong advocate of civil rights, the senator had helped defeat antibusing legislation in Congress, convincing the demonstrators that he had betrayed their trust. As he approached the microphone, the crowd responded with boos and catcalls: "Impeach him. Get rid of the bum! . . . Why don't you put your one-legged son on a bus! Yeah, let your daughter get bused, so she can get raped!"[2] Drowned out by the crowd, Kennedy left the microphone and started across the plaza to the Federal Building. His antagonists began lobbing tomatoes and eggs at him, and several ran after him, shouting insults. An angry woman with a small American flag in her hair struck Kennedy on the shoulder, while another heckler landed an elbow in his ribs. Finally, the senator reached the Federal Building and hurried inside, his assailants held at bay by security guards. Seething with anger, the crowd pounded at the windows, sending a huge pane of glass shattering across the lobby.

The attack on Senator Kennedy was the prelude to a turbulent autumn. To no one's surprise, South Boston was the scene of much of the trouble. When classes began on September 12, buses transporting black students from the Roxbury ghetto to South Boston High School passed graffitti reading, "Niggers Go Home" and "This is Klan Country." And when the buses arrived at school, they were met by mobs of rock and bottle-throwing whites. Although police moved in before anyone was injured seriously, tensions remained high. On October 2, a melee between black and white students left eleven persons injured, prompting city officials to assign 300 police officers to patrol the school's corridors. The police restored a semblance of order, but resentment continued to smolder. On December 11, a white mob, incensed by the stabbing of a white boy, laid seige to South Boston High, menacing 135 black students for four hours until police could spirit the blacks out of the building. Officials promptly closed the school, reopening it one month later under the watchful eyes of an expanded force of 500 city and state police.

Although most Boston schools desegregated peacefully and violence gradually subsided in the antibusing hotbeds of South Boston and Charlestown, the city's battle over busing suggested the future of civil rights. Lobbying, litigation, and fund-raising techniques perfected during the long struggle for equality, as well as landmark legislation and court decisions won during the 1960's, gave black leaders the weapons to attack the more subtle forms of discrimination that survived the death of Jim Crow. Combined with the growing political strength and effectiveness of blacks at the grass roots, they enabled civil rights leaders to win surprising victories in the less hospitable climate of the 1970s and 1980s. Thus, as in Boston, civil rights lawyers prodded federal courts to attack school segregation in northern cities, something that they had studiously avoided during the previous decade. The consensus on civil rights that had emerged in the mid-1960s, however, did not survive the decade, as events in Boston made painfully clear. New remedies designed to attack the deeply rooted effects of discrimination encountered growing resistance, and victories won during the Indian Summer of the civil rights movement in the 1970s proved difficult to protect as the nation approached the Constitution's bicentennial.

School Segregation: Advance and Retreat

The 1960s, which had begun with the youthful optimism of the sit-ins, ended with civil rights advocates in disarray and on the defensive. Although the NAACP and the NAACP Legal Defense Fund methodically continued their campaign of lobbying and litigation, other civil rights groups fared less well. By 1968, CORE and SNCC, which had served as the movement's shock troops, were reeling from internecine conflict and dwindling membership. The assassination of Martin Luther King, Jr. in April 1968 deprived the movement of its most charismatic leader and most eloquent and effective spokesperson. Moreover, Richard Nixon's victory in the 1968 presidential election was cause for alarm. During the campaign, Nixon had successfully wooed white southern politicians and voters, promising them relief from federal demands for school desegregation. Although liberals remained a force to be reckoned with on Capitol Hill, the new president controlled the federal agencies responsible for enforcing the civil rights laws. Given his campaign commitments, civil rights leaders feared that Nixon would abandon the vigorous enforcement effort begun during the Johnson administration.

Such fears proved well founded. During the summer of 1969, with several hundred southern school districts still holding out against integra-

tion, the administration signaled its intention to slow down the desegregation process. In July, officials at HEW announced that they were
aware of the difficulties desegregation posed and would not hold school
districts to deadlines established by the department's previous guidelines. Six weeks later, the Fifth Circuit Court of Appeals heard *Alexander
v. Holmes County Board of Education,* a suit against thirty-three Mississippi counties that continued to operate segregated schools fifteen years
after *Brown.* In a dramatic reversal, Justice Department lawyers appeared
on behalf of the state of Mississippi, urging the court to delay desegregation. President Nixon also lashed out against busing. In March 1970, he
denounced recent court decisions that "raised widespread fears that the
nation might face a massive disruption of public education: that wholesale compulsory busing may be ordered and the neighborhood school
virtually doomed."[3] Shortly after Nixon's statement, the Justice Department intervened in the Charlotte, North Carolina case, challenging a
court-ordered desegregation plan that used a variety of techniques,
including busing, to desegregate the city's schools.

Even more alarming to black leaders than the administration's retreat
on school desegregation, was its effort to reshape the Supreme Court.
During the 1968 campaign, Nixon had criticized the Court, charging that
liberal judges had interpreted the Constitution too broadly and had placed
undue restrictions on elected officials. Although his remarks were aimed
primarily at the landmark decisions of the 1960s which expanded the
rights of the criminally accused, his pledge to appoint conservative
judges who adhered to a philosophy of strict construction and self-
restraint alarmed civil rights advocates. During the 1960s, an activist
Court had read the guarantees of the Thirteenth, Fourteenth, and Fifteenth Amendments broadly, sweeping away precedents that had long
prevented effective national protection of civil rights and imposing
restrictions on state and local government, schools, and private businesses in order to guarantee substantive equality. Civil rights proponents
feared that Nixon's appointees would take a narrow view of the Reconstruction amendments and civil rights statutes, denying blacks effective
remedies against such deeply rooted problems as urban school segregation and employment discrimination.

Concern grew as four justices retired during Nixon's first term, giving
him a historic opportunity to reshape the high court. In 1969, Chief
Justice Earl Warren, the guiding force behind the Court's civil rights
revolution, left the bench. To replace him, Nixon chose Warren Burger,

who had earned a reputation as a proponent of stirct construction and judicial self-restraint during his ten years on the prestigious Court of Appeals for the District of Columbia. Even before Nixon had selected Burger, another seat on the Court became vacant when Justice Abe Fortas, a staunch supporter of civil rights, resigned under threat of impeachment for alleged financial improprieties. Prodded by the Black Congressional Caucus, the NAACP, and other civil rights organizations, the Senate killed the nominations of two conservative southerners, Clement Haynesworth and G. Harold Carswell. The president then nominated Harry Blackmun, a conservative federal appeals court judge from Minnesota, and the Senate, exhausted by the bruising battle over Fortas's successor, quickly gave its assent. When Justices Hugo Black and John Harlan retired in 1971, Nixon moved the Court further to the right. He replaced the legendary Black with Lewis Powell, a distinguished Virginia attorney of decidedly conservative views. To fill Harlan's seat, he appointed William Rehnquist, a trenchant and outspoken critic of the Warren Court's activism.

The Burger Court quickly disappointed the president. In October 1969, shortly after Burger became chief justice, the Court considered the administration's effort to slow the pace of southern school desegregation. In August, the Fifth Circuit Court of Appeals had decided the *Alexander* case, accepting a Justice Department request to delay desegregation in thirty-three Mississippi counties. When the NAACP Legal Defense Fund, which represented the plaintiffs, appealed, a unanimous Supreme Court promptly issued a terse one-paragraph opinion, reversing the lower court and prohibiting further delay. "Under explicit holdings of this Court the obligation of every school district is to terminate dual school systems at once," the court emphasized, "and to operate now and hereafter only unitary schools."[4]

Several weeks later, the Court made it clear that "now" meant immediately. In implementing *Alexander*, the fifth circuit judges ordered that desegregation take place in two steps. Faculty, transportation, and student activities were to be desegregated by February 1, 1970. Owing to the difficulty of assigning students to new schools during the middle of the year, however, the court ruled that they could remain in their old, segregated schools until the following September. When the fifth circuit court applied this formula to another group of school cases, plaintiffs in one of these, *Carter* v. *West Feliciana Parish School Board*, appealed. The high court promptly reversed the appeals court, ordering full desegregation of facilities and students no later than February 1, 1970. *Alexander* and *Carter* ended the South's hopes of avoiding desegregation and undermined the administration's last-ditch effort to reward its southern supporters with yet another reprieve from *Brown*. During 1970 and 1971, the federal courts compelled hold-out districts to desegregate, and when classes resumed in the fall of 1972, southern schools were the most integrated in the nation with forty-six percent of the black students attending white majority schools.

Although *Alexander* and *Carter* finished off segregation in the public schools of the rural South, a majority of the nation's blacks lived in cities, where schools remained highly segregated. Urban desegregation posed special problems. In rural areas, where there was little residential segregation, assignment of students to the schools nearest their homes produced integration. In towns and small cities, which encompassed small areas, school attendance zones could easily be drawn to achieve integration. But large cities often sprawled over several hundred square miles and had highly segregated residential patterns. Indeed, the movement of whites to the suburbs in the decades after World War II had intensified racial isolation in the nation's metropolitan areas. Consequently, no matter how school attendance zones were drawn, most neighborhood schools would remain highly segregated. Meaningful desegregation was possible only if children were bused to schools outside their neighborhoods. Without busing, segregated schools would remain a part of the urban landscape, perpetuating racial polarization and denying ghetto children the very real educational advantages of attending integrated schools.

Yet busing was a potentially explosive policy, as events in Boston subsequently demonstrated. The school bus had long been an accepted part of American life, used by rural school districts to carry children to far-off consolidated schools and by urban districts to relieve pressure on overcrowded schools and to transport children to schools with special programs. By 1970, forty percent of the nation's students were bused to school, and North Carolina proudly called itself "the schoolbusingest state in the Union." Yet busing to achieve desegregation was another matter, and most white parents bristled at the mention of transporting children out of their neighborhoods in order to promote integration. Although racism fueled much of the opposition, there was more to the antibusing movement than racism. Many parents who had purchased homes in affluent neighborhoods known for high quality schools were outraged that their children would not be permitted to attend those schools. Others resisted busing because they believed that neighborhood schools gave children and parents a closer identification with their schools, made it easier for parents to be involved in their childrens' schools, and allowed children greater access to extracurricular activities that took place after school. Moreover, many white parents feared for their children's safety in tough inner-city schools.

The Supreme Court first confronted the busing dilemma in 1971, when it decided *Swann* v. *Charlotte-Mecklenburg Board of Education.* The case had begun in 1964, when blacks in Charlotte, North Carolina went to court to compel school desegregation. As the case dragged on, school officials stepped up the token desegregation they had begun in the late 1950s. Nevertheless, when District Judge James B. McMillan took charge of the case in 1968, sixty percent of the city's black students attended schools that were at least ninety-nine percent black. Encouraged by the Supreme Court's ruling in *Green* v. *County School Board* (1968), Julius Le Vonne Chambers, the young black attorney who represented Charlotte blacks, pressed Judge McMillan to end tokenism and order meaningful desegregation. In 1969, the judge responded with a sweeping new desegregation decree. He ruled that the persistence of segregation in Charlotte schools meant that the school board had not met the constitutional obligation established by the *Green* case to "take whatever steps might be necessary" to eliminate the effects of past discrimination.[5] Because blacks were concentrated in the northwest quarter of the city, McMillan concluded that even the most careful redrawing of school attendance zones would leave the schools segregated. Therefore, he adopted a plan that required 13,000 of the district's 84,000 students to be bused and that produced schools ranging from nine to thirty-eight percent black.

As local whites launched a massive antibusing campaign, the Charlotte school board, assisted by an *amicus curiae* brief filed by the Justice Department, appealed Judge McMillan's ruling, ultimately bringing the highly charged busing issue before the Supreme Court. With two Nixon appointees (Burger and Blackmun) now on the bench, most observers predicted that the *Swann* case would splinter the Court, ending its unanimity on school desegregation. And some even suggested that the new appointees might forge an antibusing majority. Although the justices were divided in their early discussions of *Swann,* the force of precedent and tradition led them to uphold the district court's decision. A ruling against busing meant that the wrongs of the past would remain un-remedied and segregation would persist in urban America. The *Green* precedent, with its demand for affirmative action to root out the effects of past discrimination, and the weight of the Court's role as the champion of civil rights made such an outcome unacceptable to most of the justices. With a solid majority supporting the lower court, the Nixon appointees probably did not wish to enter a dissent that would make them appear to be puppets of the president. In the end the pundits were confounded as a unanimous Court endorsed busing in an opinion written by Chief Justice Burger.

Following the logic of the Court's holding in *Green,* the chief justice ruled that where school officials had been guilty of discrimination, as in Charlotte, they had an obligation to dismantle segregation. If they failed to do so, the federal courts had broad authority to devise remedies that would work, even if they required transportation of students. "Deseg-regation plans cannot be limited to the walk-in school," the chief justice emphasized. He acknowledged that busing "may be administratively awkward, inconvenient . . . and may impose burdens on some." But he asserted that this "cannot be avoided in the interim period when remedial adjustments are being made to eliminate the dual school systems." Although Burger rejected the use of rigid racial quotas to guarantee that all schools in a system have the same racial mix as the system as a whole, he held that the district court had not erred in taking racial balance into account in devising a desegregation plan. "As we said in *Green,* . . . a district court's remedial decree is to be judged by its effectiveness," Burger wrote. "Awareness of the racial composition of the whole school system is likely to be a useful starting point in shaping a remedy to correct past constitutional violations."[6]

Civil rights advocates were pleased that the Court had upheld busing, but one aspect of the opinion troubled them. Burger had emphasized repeatedly that the federal courts could impose desegregation plans only to remedy past discrimination by school officials. While this gave the green light to desegregation in southern cities, where segregation had been established by law, it created an obstacle to desegregation in the North. In the decades before *Brown,* most northern states had not enacted school segregation laws, and many had explicitly banned segregation. Therefore, plaintiffs in northern school desegregation cases had to prove that, in the absence of laws, school officials had acted covertly to create segregated schools. This required time-consuming investigations and protracted trials to show that officials had chosen school sites, drawn school attendance zones, and adopted transfer policies designed to maximize segregation.

Although the Court did not remove this burden, it lightened it somewhat when it decided *Keyes* v. *School District No. 1, Denver, Colo.* in 1973. When the case was tried in federal district court, lawyers from the Legal Defense Fund had shown that in the Park Hill section, where one-third of Denver's blacks lived, school officials had adopted policies that had created segregated schools. In response, the court had ordered a desegregation plan for the schools in Park Hill; however, even though blacks living in other parts of the city attended segregated schools, the judge refused to order a city-wide desegregation plan without proof that schools in other neighborhoods had been intentionally segregated. The implications were clear: plaintiffs would have to demonstrate, school-by-school, that segregation was the result of policies intentionally adopted to achieve that end. This would increase the already considerable time and expense required to litigate northern desegregation cases.

In deciding *Keyes,* the Supreme Court considerably reduced the burden on plaintiffs in northern desegregation cases. Writing for the Court, Justice William Brennan ruled that adoption of a city-wide plan did not require school-by-school proof of intentional segregation. "[W]here plaintiffs prove that the school authorities have carried out a systematic program of segregation affecting a substantial portion of the students, schools, teachers and facilities, . . ." Brennan explained, "it is only common sense to conclude that there exists a predicate for a finding of the existence of a dual school system. . . ."[7] Only if school officials could prove that their policies had neither created nor contributed to segregation in other schools, he concluded, would they be able to avoid imposition of a city-wide desegregation plan. The Court sent the case back to the district court, which subsequently adopted a system-wide busing plan.

In the wake of *Swann* and *Keyes*, NAACP attorneys initiated desegregation suits on behalf of black community groups in cities across the North, and federal courts responded with desegregation orders that relied heavily on busing. Predictably, as busing spread northward, white opposition mounted and became a powerful force on Capitol Hill. In 1972, legislation drastically restricting the federal courts' authority to order busing gained broad support in Congress, and only a filibuster by Senate liberals prevented passage. Two years later, similar legislation was defeated by one vote in the upper house. In the face of these defeats, antibusing sentiment became more powerful, and congressional opponents of busing redoubled their efforts. Although ultimately they were unable to end the federal courts' authority to order busing, in early 1976 the antibusing forces enacted legislation stripping HEW of authority to cut off federal aid to school districts that refused to adopt busing plans to achieve integration. As a result, the agency lost its authority to invoke the power of the purse—which had been crucial in desegregating schools in the rural South—to achieve integration in the nation's cities.

As antibusing pressure grew in Congress, the Supreme Court itself imposed a significant restriction on the tools available to remedy segregation. In 1971, a federal district court ruled that the Detroit school board had engaged in a wide range of activities consciously designed to promote school segregation. Because blacks constituted sixty-five percent of the city's school-age population, however, any desegregation plan that was limited to the city itself would leave many schools between seventy-five and ninety percent black. Moreover, it would accelerate "white flight" to the suburbs, undermining even the minimal desegregation achieved. In order to devise an effective remedy that would uproot the effects of past discrimination, the court joined the Detroit school district with fifty-three surrounding suburban districts and ordered that black children be bused to the suburbs and white suburban children be transported to schools in the city.

When the Detroit case, *Milliken* v. *Bradley*, reached the Supreme Court in 1973, the future of urban school desegregation hung in the balance. Like Detroit, most large American cities had growing black majorities in their schools, guaranteeing that a desegregation plan limited to the city itself would leave black children in predominantly black schools and hasten the migration of whites to the suburbs. In these circumstances metropolitan plans were essential because they permitted meaningful integration while reducing the incentives for white flight.

In June 1974, with Justice Potter Stewart joining the four Nixon appointees to form a 5–4 majority, the Court reversed the district court, dealing a crippling blow to metropolitan desegregation. The federal courts could not arbitrarily interfere with local school district lines, Chief Justice Burger wrote for the majority, asserting that "[n]o single tradition in public education is more deeply rooted than local control over the operation of schools."[8] Only if the state had drawn school district boundaries with intent to establish segregated schools or if the suburban districts themselves had adopted policies that contributed to segregation would the district court have been justified in ordering cross-district busing. Burger concluded, however, that while there was abundant evidence that Detroit school officials were guilty of practices that contributed to segregation within the city, the record suggested that boundaries between the Detroit school district and the suburban districts had not been drawn with segregative intent and that the policies of the suburban districts had not contributed to segregation within the city. Consequently, he concluded that the district court lacked authority to order cross-district busing.

The four dissenters blasted the chief justice's analysis. Pointing out that school districts were merely administrative subdivisions of the state, Justice Byron White charged that the majority had unjustifiably transformed school district lines into artificial barriers that blocked effective desegregation. "I cannot understand, . . ." White wrote, "why a federal court may not order an appropriate inter-district remedy, if this is necessary or more effective to accomplish this constitutionally mandated task [i.e., desegregation]."[9] Justice Thurgood Marshall, who during his long career with the NAACP had relentlessly pressed the Court to strike down segregation, warned that the majority had taken "a giant step backwards." Marshall argued that the Court had consistently held that where officials of the state or any of its political subdivisions were guilty of discrimination (as in Detroit), the state had a duty to eliminate the consequences of their action. Since that could only be done in Detroit through cross-district busing, the district court's desegregation plan was fully justified. Not only was the majority's legal analysis misguided, Marshall concluded, but the consequences of its ruling would be disastrous. "In the short run," he predicted, "it may seem to be the easier course to allow our great metropolitan areas to be divided up each into two cities—one white, the other black—but it is a course, I predict, our people will ultimately regret."[10]

The ensuing years demonstrated that Marshall's claim was not hyperbolic. In cities with metropolitan-wide school districts (such as Charlotte) *Milliken* did not pose a barrier to desegregation. In cities such as Louisville, Kentucky, or Wilmington, Delaware, where civil rights attorneys could show that school district boundaries had been drawn with segregative intent or that the policies of suburban districts contributed to segregation in the city, federal courts remained free to impose metropolitan desegregation plans. Nevertheless, *Milliken* meant that in most of the nation's large cities—New York, Chicago, Atlanta, Philadelphia, Kansas City, among others—the courts' hands were tied. When they ordered city-wide plans—as they did in Detroit—they ended up spreading a few white students among predominantly black schools. They could—as they did in Kansas City and Chicago—devise plans that compensated for past discrimination by enhancing the quality of inner-city schools. This, however, seemed more like a reversion to the separate but equal doctrine than a fulfillment of *Green*'s promise of rooting out segregation. By devising plans that called for establishing schools with special curricula (so-called magnet schools), judges could attract white as well as black students to selected inner-city schools, thereby creating pockets of integration in a sea of predominantly black schools. In the absence of cross-district busing, however, the federal courts lacked the tools to desegregate most cities. Consequently, the rapid progress toward school integration that had occurred during the late 1960s and early 1970s came to a halt; by the late 1980s, schools in most of the nation's large cities, where a majority of blacks lived, were more segregated than they had been in 1968.

Employment Discrimination and the Affirmative Action Controversy

Like school desegregation, elimination of employment discrimination was a goal that had eluded civil rights advocates in the 1960s and remained at the forefront of the civil rights agenda in the 1970s. Deeply rooted discrimination in the North as well as the South had relegated most blacks to unskilled, menial, and low-paying jobs and had produced an extremely high rate of poverty among blacks. Discrimination, poverty, and inferior schools undermined young blacks' incentive and ability to finish high school, thereby locking them into low-paying, dead-end jobs. Title VII of the Civil Rights Act of 1964 had attempted to deal with the economic problems of blacks, prohibiting discrimination by private employers and creating the EEOC to monitor compliance. The civil rights act and changing attitudes generated by the civil rights movement had eliminated much of the most blatant (''no colored need apply'') discrimination and had contributed to significant gains in employment and earnings for blacks during the late 1960s and early 1970s. Yet discrimination did not disappear; it became more subtle, harder to detect, and more difficult to prove. Even more troubling, those who had been denied education, job training, and employment experience by past discrimination continued to find the promise of economic opportunity and a better life elusive.

Employment discrimination was not only a problem for black men; it was also sorely felt by women of both races. The 1960s and 1970s saw increasing numbers of women in the workforce as families adapted to changing social patterns and increased expectations of material comfort. Higher divorce rates left many women and the family members they had to support dependent on their ability to earn decent pay and benefits. Increasing numbers of college-educated women aspired to careers that would make them life-long, full-time members of the workforce. Moreover, the consumer culture that blossomed during this period added to the economic pressures on both married and single women. As material expectations rose, women in the workforce increasingly regarded themselves as primary breadwinners rather than dilettantes working for pin money. As more women came to regard jobs and careers as integral parts of their lives, they chafed under employment practices established by men which excluded them from competition for good jobs and occupational advancement. Under the influence of a burgeoning women's liberation movement, they realized striking parallels between their position and that of blacks: they were ghettoized in poorly paid, dead-end jobs and were for the most part excluded from positions that offered security, advancement, fringe benefits, and fair compensation. And like blacks, they demanded vigorous action against employment discrimination.

The 1970s proved a less propitious time than the 1960s to tackle these difficult problems. Not only had the conservative political tide deprived civil rights leaders and feminists of allies in the White House, but the economic climate militated against further efforts to redress the effects of past discrimination. The dynamic economic growth of the 1960s slowed during the 1970s, and sharply rising inflation alarmed most Americans, convincing them that it was harder to make ends meet and to maintain their standard of living. (In fact, real income and purchasing power grew during the decade.) Afraid that the pie was no longer growing, many whites felt threatened by programs that promised a bigger piece to blacks, and many men were equally resentful of gains made by women. Consequently, like busing, the issue of employment discrimination became highly charged and hotly debated.

Nevertheless, the combined efforts of civil rights and women's groups produced important gains against employment discrimination in a conservative decade. In 1972, a wide array of civil rights and women's groups prodded Congress to pass the Equal Employment Opportunity Act, broadening the coverage of Title VII and increasing EEOC's power. The law extended Title VII's coverage to state and local government and to employers and unions with fifteen or more employees or members (originally the number had stood at twenty-five). It also conferred greater enforcement power on the EEOC. Whereas Title VII originally had denied the agency authority to issue cease-and-desist orders or to sue parties who were guilty of discrimination, the 1972 law strengthened the EEOC's hand, giving it authority to take to court employers or unions that refused to abandon discriminatory practices.

Congress also substantially enlarged the budget and staff of the EEOC. During the late 1960s the agency had been woefully underfunded and had insufficient personnel to investigate the avalanche of complaints it had received or to follow up on settlements that it had negotiated with employers. Between 1970 and 1981, its budget increased by a factor of ten, growing from $13 million to more than $140 million and enabling it to expand both the size of its staff and the range of its activities. Indeed, by 1977, EEOC's Office of General Counsel employed more than 300 attorneys to litigate discrimination cases that could not be resolved through negotiation.

Despite these changes, problems continued to plague the agency during the early 1970s. Although resources grew, so did the number of complaints, increasing from around 15,000 in 1970 to 75,000 in 1981. Although such a dramatic increase would have posed a difficult challenge under the best of circumstances, ineffective leadership compounded the problem. Because President Nixon and his successor, Gerald Ford, did not assign a high priority to the federal effort against discrimination, there was a rapid turnover among the commissioners and the commission's upper level management. As a result, the agency drifted. The backlog of cases mushroomed, the time required to resolve complaints grew to two years, and settlements with employers were not adequately monitored to assure compliance. This began to change in 1977, when President Jimmy Carter appointed Eleanor Holmes Norton, a Yale Law School graduate and former head of the New York City Commission on Human Rights, to chair EEOC. Under Norton's vigorous leadership, the commission slashed its backlog, investigated new cases more expeditiously, increased the number of employment discrimination suits it filed, and became a formidable force with which employers and unions had to reckon.

Until EEOC hit its stride, private attorneys shouldered most of the responsibility for enforcing Title VII's guarantees. Beginning in 1965, the Legal Defense Fund devoted a substantial portion of its resources to employment discrimination cases. With a staff of only 20 full-time lawyers assisted by 200 cooperating attorneys (privately employed lawyers who volunteer their services), the Legal Defense Fund lacked the vast resources of EEOC. Nevertheless, as it had done thirty years earlier in its campaign against school segregation, the organization developed an imaginative program of litigation, focusing its resources on cases that promised to establish important legal precedents. In addition to the Legal Defense Fund, other civil rights groups—the Lawyers' Constitutional Defense Committee, the Employment Rights Project of the Columbia Law School, the Lawyers' Committee for Civil Rights Under Law—and many private attorneys also took employment discrimination cases. Indeed, after 1976, when Congress authorized the federal courts to award attorneys' fees to victorious parties in civil rights suits, private enforcement activity grew even faster.

The private enforcement effort chalked up significant victories in the federal courts which dramatically expanded the scope of Title VII. The most important of these came in 1971, when the Supreme Court issued its landmark decision in *Griggs* v. *Duke Power*. Prior to 1965, when attorneys from the Legal Defense Fund initiated the suit, black employees at the company's Dan River plant had been assigned exclusively to the Labor Department, where the highest wage was lower than the lowest wage paid to employees in other departments. In 1965, when the company opened jobs in other departments to blacks, it required that all applicants have a high school diploma or pass an aptitude test. Although the new policy established criteria that applied to whites and blacks alike and was not openly discriminatory, it nevertheless adversely affected blacks. Only twelve percent of North Carolina's black males, compared with thirty-four percent of the state's white males, had graduated from high school. And given their heritage of separate and unequal education, black applicants failed the aptitude test at a far higher rate than whites, (ninety-four to forty-two percent). Moreover, the requirements appeared unrelated to the unskilled jobs the black employees sought; at the time the case was filed, whites who had won promotions out of the Labor Department before the new requirements took effect and who did not have high school diplomas "continued to perform satisfactorily and achieve promotions" in other departments.[11] Claiming that the company's policy was discriminatory and unrelated to job performance, a group of black employees who had been denied transfers from the Labor Department because they failed the aptitude test sued, charging the company with violating Title VII.

Writing for a unanimous Court, Chief Justice Burger again surprised courtwatchers with a bold opinion declaring the company's policy illegal. Burger held that Congress's objective in passing the law had been "to achieve equality of employment opportunities and remove barriers that have operated in the past to favor an identifiable group of white employees over other employees." Consequently, employment policies that had a discriminatory effect were suspect under Title VII, even if adopted without intent to discriminate. The chief justice added that employment criteria that had an adverse impact on blacks could be justified only if employers could prove that they were job related. "The touchstone is business necessity," he wrote. "If an employment practice which operates to exclude Negroes cannot be shown to be related to job performance, the practice is prohibited."[12] Since neither a high school diploma nor a passing score on the aptitude test was related to actual performance of the unskilled jobs the Duke employees had sought, Burger concluded, the company's policies violated Title VII, even though they were nondiscriminatory in appearance. The Griggs case was an important victory because it lightened the burden on plaintiffs in employment discrimination cases. Once they could demonstrate that employment practices had an adverse impact on blacks and women, the burden of proof shifted to employers. They had to prove that there was a genuine relationship between the hiring criteria they had established and applicants' ability to perform the job they sought.

Five years later, in Washington v. Davis (1976), the Court seemed to retreat from the implications of Griggs. The majority admitted that in enacting Title VII, Congress had used its broad legislative authority to proscribe racially neutral policies that had a discriminatory effect on minorities; however, it held that this standard did not apply to challenges to discrimination brought under the Fourteenth Amendment's equal protection clause. (The plaintiffs in Washington v. Davis charged that the allegedly discriminatory hiring practices of the Washington, D.C., Police Department violated the equal protection clause. They relied on that provision rather than Title VII because at the time they filed suit Title

VII did not apply to government.) In suits brought under the amendment, the majority ruled, plaintiffs must prove discriminatory intent (although it admitted that the discriminatory effects of a policy could be used as evidence of discriminatory intent). More important, the majority suggested that, even in Title VII cases, it would reduce the burden of proof on employers once plaintiffs proved that their policies had a discriminatory effect. Rather than proving scientifically that employment requirements were related to job performance, employers need only establish a reasonable relationship between the two.[13] Nevertheless, the *Griggs* test, while somewhat weakened, remained "alive and reasonably well"[14] and continued to offer minorities a potent weapon to challenge employment discrimination.

By the early 1970s, affirmative action programs also offered a potentially effective, if highly controversial and frequently misunderstood, remedy for discrimination in the workplace. In 1965, President Johnson had issued Executive Order 11246, prohibiting discrimination by firms doing business with the federal government and requiring them to take "affirmative action" to remedy the effects of past discrimination. The Labor Department, which was given responsibility for enforcement, established the Office of Federal Contract Compliance (OFCC) to monitor federal contractors and to terminate contracts with violators. Between May 1968 and December 1971, OFCC issued a series of orders that clarified employers' obligations. Employers were to determine the percentage of minorities and women in their workforce and compare this with the percentage of these groups in the labor pool. (A company making boilers, for example, would compare the percentage of blacks and women among its welders with the ratio of black/female to white/male welders in the local or regional labor market.) If the firm was "deficient in the utilization of minority groups and women," it was to establish "goals and timetables" for redressing this imbalance.[15]

The OFCC guidelines had a limited impact on government contractors. Affirmative action plans might make employers aware of standards to which they should aspire and might even encourage them to work to increase the number of women and blacks on their payrolls; however, there was little pressure to achieve the goals or to stick to the timetables. OFCC's only means of enforcing compliance was to terminate contracts with businesses that failed to make a good faith effort to carry out their plans, and it rarely used this authority. Employers could go through the motions of creating goals while making little or no effort to achieve them, knowing full well that their chances of losing federal contracts were nil.

Although OFCC proved to be a paper tiger, its affirmative action guidelines were not without effect. EEOC soon took the position that all employers, not just federal contractors, should adopt affirmative action programs. In 1974, for example, the commission warned employers that "equal employment opportunity usually requires positive *affirmative action* beyond establishment of neutral 'nondiscriminatory' and 'merit-hiring' practices."[16] A number of factors gave weight to the EEOC's call for affirmative action: the commission's newly-won authority to sue employers it deemed guilty of discrimination; the dramatic growth of employment discrimination suits (from 340 in 1970 to 5,480 nine years later); the federal courts' deference to EEOC guidelines; and plaintiffs' success in employment cases. Consequently, firms became increasingly sensitive to the threat of litigation, and many adopted and even implemented affirmative action programs as a hedge against lawsuits.

Affirmative action also won endorsement from the federal courts. When employment cases revealed intentional, invidious, illegal discrimination, federal judges imposed mandatory, court-supervised programs to remedy the effects of the discrimination. In 1969, for example, the Court of Appeals for the Fifth Circuit found the Asbestos Workers' Union—which controlled access to employment by referring workers to particular jobs—guilty of systematic discrimination against blacks. As a remedy, it ordered union officials to alternate between blacks and whites in assigning workers to jobs. Similarly, when a federal court found the Minneapolis Fire Department guilty of discriminatory hiring practices, it ordered department officials to hire at least one black for every three whites hired until there were twenty minority firefighters.

Like busing, affirmative action generated passionate arguments that reverberated throughout the 1970s and the 1980s. Critics charged that it amounted to "reverse discrimination," giving special preferences to blacks and women, thereby discriminating against white men. They also argued that by assigning rights on the basis of race, affirmative action violated the principle of colorblind citizenship established by the Fourteenth Amendment and threatened the most important accomplishment of the civil rights movement. Critics cited the words of the great contemporary constitutionalist Alexander Bickel to support their position: "The lesson of the great decisions of the Supreme Court and the lesson of contemporary history have been the same for at least a generation: discrimination on the basis of race is illegal, immoral, unconstitutional, inherently wrong, and destructive of a democratic society."[17] This was true, the critics argued, whether the discrimination was against blacks or in their favor.

Defenders of affirmative action responded that rules that were formally equal often served to perpetuate discrimination and inequality. Although it generally took more subtle forms, they asserted, discrimination against blacks and women continued to be a reality. White men generally controlled hiring decisions in business, government, and education. Even when not consciously prejudiced, they frequently felt most comfortable with applicants who were like themselves, believed that they would "fit in" better than blacks and women, and thus subtly slanted hiring decisions in favor of white males. According to its defenders, affirmative action would serve as a check against subtle forms of discrimination that were still all too prevalent.

Proponents of affirmative action also argued that while a colorblind society was a laudable goal, it was essential to take color into account in the present in order to remedy the continuing effects of past discrimination. Otherwise, the nation's promise of equality would again be a hollow one, much like *Plessy*'s promise of separate but equal. Generations of white men, they pointed out, had benefited from a de facto affirmative action program that had reserved the choicest jobs for white men and relegated blacks mainly to low-paying and menial positions. Moreover, they argued that the legacy of segregation, unequal education, and poverty made it difficult for blacks to overcome the historic advantages enjoyed by whites and threatened to leave them stuck at the bottom of the economic ladder. "To break this cycle requires, as a matter of common sense, special treatment for the victims of past discrimination . . . ," explained J. Skelly Wright of the U.S. Court of Appeals for the District of Columbia. "Such special treatment may appear unnatural—even unfair in the short run—but the only alternative is to allow the effects of our history of discrimination to plague our civic life in perpetuity."[18] The temporary special protection afforded by affirmative action, Judge Wright and others concluded, was designed to achieve meaningful equality and therefore was fully in keeping with the spirit of the Fourteenth Amendment and the civil rights movement.

Opponents countered that affirmative action penalized persons who themselves were not guilty of discrimination in order to rectify wrongs committed by previous generations. By giving special consideration to blacks, they argued, affirmative action programs created a situation in which equally qualified or even better qualified white males were passed over for jobs and promotions. Consequently, they would be made to suffer, not because of wrongful behavior on their part, but because of their race. Concomitantly, individual black applicants would benefit, not because they themselves had been the victims of discriminatory acts, but because members of their race had been subject to discrimination. Furthermore, critics pointed out that for many lower-class whites who came from disadvantaged backgrounds, affirmative action would be one more obstacle to overcome. Indeed, middle-class blacks would reap the benefits of affirmative action programs, even though they were not disadvantaged, while whites would be penalized, regardless of their background.

To claim that special treatment for blacks inflicted wrongs on innocent whites, proponents of affirmative action responded, was only half the story. Even if blatant, systematic discrimination against blacks had ended, they argued, its effects continued to burden young blacks who had never known the harshness of Jim Crow. High rates of poverty, unemployment, illiteracy, and broken homes in the black community were the legacy of centuries of discrimination. As a result, young blacks all too frequently lacked the supportive home environment that was crucial to success in school; grew up without role models to encourage success; found schools frustrating places that were irrelevant to them and dropped out; and lived in urban ghettos where high unemployment made it difficult to obtain essential work experience. Refusing blacks special assistance would only condemn them to compete in a game whose rules were stacked against them and perpetuate injustice in the name of policies that were formally neutral but actually gave decided advantages to whites. While defenders of affirmative action admitted that there were disadvantaged whites, they pointed out that, as a group, blacks labored under a heritage of discrimination that was far more severe than that whites had ever known. In fact, it was so severe and so pervasive that policymakers were justified in giving special treatment to blacks as a group.

Questions of justice aside, opponents charged that affirmative action subverted the principle of reward according to merit and thus threatened to bury American society in mediocrity. Although they admitted that most affirmative action programs did not establish formal quotas, critics contended that they put almost irresistable pressure on employers to hire blacks and women regardless of their qualifications. They argued that this made race rather than merit the crucial factor in hiring decisions. At a time when American firms were coming under increasingly sharp competition from abroad, the critics argued, the nation could ill afford to promote mediocrity.

Defenders of affirmative action strenuously denied these charges. Pointing to the *Griggs* case, they argued that employers frequently established arbitrary qualifications which were irrelevant to job performance but which effectively screened out blacks and women. Proponents charged that the critics had created a largely imagined golden age, before the onset of affirmative action, when employment decisions were made solely on the basis of merit. They pointed out that employment decisions frequently had been based on race and gender (excluding blacks and women from consideration regardless of their qualifications) or on family influence and personal connections rather than merit. Plenty of mediocre and incompetent white men had found their way into jobs without raising the hue and cry that greeted affirmative action. By encouraging the hiring and promotion of blacks and women, proponents argued, affirmative action would help break down the "old boy" networks that had long worked in favor of white males.

As the debate became sharper and more feverish, both sides looked to the Supreme Court for a resolution. In 1977 the justices signaled their willingness to tackle the issue when they agreed to hear *Regents of the University of California* v. *Bakke*. The *Bakke* case dealt not with employment but with medical school admissions. While blacks made up eleven percent of the nation's population in 1970, they claimed only two percent of its doctors. As a result, many black communities suffered from a shortage of physicians, and black children were deprived of professional role models. Although the medical school at the University of California at Davis had been established in 1968 and had no history of discrimination, it instituted a voluntary affirmative action plan designed to increase the enrollment of minorities. The school set aside 16 of the 100 seats in its entering class for minorities and admitted some minority students who had lower college grades and test scores than many whites who were denied admission. Allen Bakke, an aerospace engineer and Marine Corps veteran in his early thirties, was one such white applicant. After twice being rejected while minority applicants with lower grades and test scores won admission, Bakke brought suit in the California courts, charging that the medical school's policy constituted racial discrimination that was prohibited by the Fourteen Amendment and the

Civil Rights Act of 1964. When the California Supreme Court agreed with Bakke, the university appealed, bringing the case and the troubling questions raised by affirmative action before the Supreme Court.

Like the rest of the country, the Court was badly divided over the Davis program, especially its use of quotas as a tool of affirmative action. Four justices—Warren Burger, William Rehnquist, Potter Stewart, and John Paul Stevens (a Ford appointee who had joined the Court in 1975)—concluded that the University had denied Bakke admission on account of his race in violation of the Civil Rights Act of 1964. Four of their colleagues—William Brennan, Thurgood Marshall, Harry Blackmun, and Byron White—disagreed, arguing that the civil rights act and the equal protection clause had been adopted to root out America's racial caste system. To read them to prohibit programs designed to overcome the effects of past discrimination, they charged, was to transform them into barriers to genuine equality. "In order to get beyond racism, we must first take account of race," Justice Blackmun explained. "And in order to treat some persons equally, we must treat them differently. We cannot—we dare not—let the Equal Protection Clause perpetuate racial supremacy."[19]

Justice Lewis Powell, the conservative Virginian, cast the decisive vote and wrote the opinion of the Court. Powell went beyond his conservative colleagues to argue that the Davis admissions program violated the Constitution's equal protection clause as well as the civil rights act. By setting aside sixteen seats for minorities, it created a special privilege for minorities, thereby denying whites equal rights on the basis of race. "The guarantee of equal protection cannot mean one thing when it is applied to one individual and something else when applied to a person of another color," he wrote. "If both are not accorded the same protection, then it is not equal."[20] Powell admitted that courts might impose quotas in cases in which an employer or school had been found guilty of discrimination, but noted that this was not relevant to the *Bakke* case, where there was no proof that the medical school had discriminated. Although Powell took a hard line against the use of quotas to compensate for past discrimination in the absence of a showing of a specific constitutional violation, he broke ranks with the other conservative justices by holding that less rigid affirmative action programs were acceptable. Schools had a legitimate educational interest in obtaining diversity in their student bodies, Powell noted, and were free to take race into account in the selection process in order to achieve that diversity.

Indeed, he praised Harvard College, which openly admitted that in the interests of diversity, race (as well as geographic origin and socio-economic background) played a role in its admissions decisions.

Powell's effort to take the middle course produced a curious decision. That part of his decision striking down quotas in the absence of proof of discrimination had the backing of the four opponents of affirmative action, who believed that the medical school was forbidden to take race into account in considering applications; however, his assertion that schools could use race as one criterion, prevailed because of the support of the four proponents of affirmative action. If by the slimmest of margins and the most circuitous of routes, the Court had given its blessing to flexible affirmative action programs.

Subsequently, the Court underscored its cautious, qualified acceptance of affirmative action. In *United Steel Workers* v. *Weber* (1979), it considered a voluntary affirmative action program adopted by Kaiser Aluminum and the steel workers' union to redress the almost complete absence of blacks in skilled jobs at the company's plants. The company established a program to train unskilled employees for higher paying craft positions and specified that half of the openings in the program would be reserved for blacks until the percentage of black craft workers approximated the percentage of blacks in the local labor force. In a 5–2 decision (Justices Powell and Stevens did not participate), the Court upheld the Kaiser program against charges that it violated Title VII's ban on racial discrimination in employment. Writing for the Court, Justice Brennan emphasized that the Kaiser program did not involve state action (and thus did not violate the Fourteenth Amendment) and that it was temporary. He also denied that the program violated Title VII which, he claimed, had been adopted to remedy deeply rooted economic discrimination against blacks. "It would be ironic indeed if a law triggered by a Nation's concern over centuries of racial injustice," Brennan explained, ". . . constituted the first legislative prohibition of all voluntary, private, race conscious efforts to abolish traditional patterns of racial segregation and hierarchy."[21]

One year later, in *Fullilove* v. *Klutznik* (1980), the Court gave its blessing to a controversial congressionally mandated affirmative action program established in 1977 to redress discrimination that had stifled the growth of minority businesses. Congress stipulated that ten percent of all money expended on state and local public works projects undertaken with federal funds must go to firms owned by minorities. In a 6–3 decision, with the opinion written by Chief Justice Burger, the Court sustained the legislation. While the federal courts could provide remedies only for specific acts of discrimination, Congress's power was far broader, Burger argued. Congress enjoyed express authority to enforce the equal protection clause, he explained, and if it believed that equality necessitated a sweeping program to remedy past discrimination, it could act. "It is not a constitutional defect in this program that it may disappoint the expectations of nonminority firms," Burger explained. "When effectuating a limited and properly tailored remedy to cure the effects of prior discrimination, such 'a sharing of the burden' by innocent parties is not impermissible."[22]

Although civil rights advocates built on the successes of the 1960s and won surprising victories against employment discrimination in the 1970s and early 1980s, many wondered whether they were winning the battles but losing the war. To be sure, affirmative action helped open avenues of opportunity to blacks in business, labor, education, government, and the professions. Many observers pointed to the existence of a growing black middle class as proof that blacks were slowly but surely moving into the mainstream of American life. Black students were graduating in greater numbers than ever before from America's most prestigious undergraduate and professional schools. After graduation they were being recruited by businesses, universities, law firms, and government. Indeed, in 1978, the black sociologist William Julius Wilson published a prize-winning study proclaiming *The Declining Significance of Race.*

Yet Wilson and many others who applauded the growth of the black middle class were not sanguine about the future. Paradoxically, while some blacks were reaping the fruits of the civil rights movement and entering the middle class, unemployment and poverty among blacks actually grew during the late 1970s and early 1980s. The nation's inner cities contained a growing black underclass beset by joblessness, poverty, single-parent families, low levels of educational achievement, crime, drugs, and despair. Yet affirmative action, which helped open opportunities for those who had the basic qualifications for employment, could do little for those who had no work experience or skills and little education. Moreover, the changing structure of the economy locked these people—Wilson called them "the truly disadvantaged"—into poverty.[23] The drift of businesses to the suburbs put many jobs beyond their reach. More important, the decline of the automobile, steel, and other basic industries during the 1970s and 1980s denied unskilled and semiskilled blacks access to jobs that paid well and offered hope of economic mobility. New jobs opened primarily in the service industries, where those without skills could expect to earn low wages and live close to or even below the poverty level.

Voting Rights and Black Political Power

As they attempted to expand the meaning of equal employment opportunity, black leaders also worked to preserve and extend their newly won political rights. Although the Voting Rights Act of 1965 had opened the polls to southern blacks, black voters continued to confront barriers to effective use of the ballot. Given the prevalence of racial bloc voting, black candidates could usually hope to win elections only in districts with a majority or near-majority of black voters. White politicians sought to minimize the number of black officials—and thereby reduce the effect of black voting—by establishing multiseat electoral districts and at-large elections. For purposes of illustration, consider a hypothetical city with a five-member city council and a black population of forty percent. If the city were divided into five wards, each electing one councilmember, blacks would be likely to have majorities in two wards and elect two black councilmembers. Yet if members were elected at-large, with voters throughout the city casting ballots for all five seats, the white majority could preserve a lily-white council.

There was sharp debate over whether the Voting Rights Act prohibited such electoral changes. In states and counties with a history of discrimination, the act required preclearance of any change in "voting qualification or prerequisite to voting, or standard, practice, or procedure with respect to voting" by the Justice Department or a district court in Washington, D.C. The change would be permitted only if the attorney general or the court were satisfied that it had neither a discriminatory purpose nor effect. Civil rights advocates contended that laws establishing at-large elections and other electoral changes that diluted the black vote were not only subject to preclearance but were illegal because of their discriminatory effect. Conservatives disagreed, arguing that the Voting Rights Act prohibited laws and regulations designed to prevent individuals from registering and voting, but that it did not apply to all changes in the electoral process. In fact, they charged civil rights advocates with attempting to transform a measure that had been adopted to protect the right to vote into a guarantee of proportional representation for blacks. Like affirmative action, they contended, this gave blacks a privilege that no other group possessed.

The Supreme Court quickly swept aside arguments for a narrow interpretation of the law. In *Allen* v. *State Board of Elections* (1969), a suit brought by the Legal Defense Fund, the Court held that a law replacing single-member districts with multiseat districts and at-large elections was subject to preclearance and should not be allowed to take effect if it diluted black votes. According to the Court, the Voting Rights Act gave "a broad interpretation to the right to vote, recognizing that voting includes 'all action necessary to make a vote effective.'" Procedures diluting the votes of blacks would "nullify their ability to elect the candidate of their choice just as would prohibiting some of them from voting" and therefore came within the act's purview.[24] Four years later, in *Georgia* v. *United States* (1973), the Court ruled that Georgia's plan for reapportioning seats in the state legislature was covered by the preclearance requirement and suggested that it could be rejected if it made it more difficult for blacks to elect candidates of their choice.

Under the terms of the Voting Rights Act, the preclearance requirement was to remain in effect for only five years. Fearful that expiration would encourage adoption of new laws designed to minimize black political power, in 1969 members of the Black Congressional Caucus, Clarence Mitchell (the NAACP's veteran lobbyist), and representatives of the Leadership Conference on Civil Rights (which represented a number of civil rights organizations) began to press for its renewal. The Nixon administration, adhering firmly to its southern strategy, skillfully opposed extension, arguing that it imposed on the South a humiliating requirement that did not apply to the rest of the nation. Nevertheless, in 1970, Democratic leaders in Congress, with crucial support from northern Republicans, extended the preclearance requirement for five years. (It was extended for seven years in 1975 and twenty-five years in 1982.) Moreover, black leaders rallied congressional liberals to press a reluctant Justice Department to adopt tougher procedures for screening electoral changes. In May 1971, the department announced guidelines that placed the burden of proof on state and local officials; if they could not prove that proposed changes were nondiscriminatory, the department would not permit them to take effect. Vigorously enforced by career lawyers in the

Civil Rights Division, the guidelines proved an effective tool against new laws aimed at diluting black voting strength.

The rigorous preclearance process, however, applied only to new laws, not to measures in force before 1965. During the 1970s blacks began to challenge pre-1965 laws establishing at-large elections and multiseat districts, many of which had been enacted around the turn of the century as part of the disfranchisement campaign. Initially, the Supreme Court proved receptive to claims that these laws were discriminatory and therefore violated the Voting Rights Act and the Fourteenth and Fifteenth Amendments. In *White* v. *Regester* (1973), the Court established a flexible standard for establishing unconstitutional discrimination. According to Justice White, who wrote the opinion for a 5–4 majority, whether an electoral scheme was discriminatory depended on "an intensely local appraisal" by the district court of its *"design and impact* [emphasis added] . . . in light of past and present reality, political and otherwise."[25] Therefore while the discriminatory effect of an established electoral practice did not by itself establish proof of discrimination, it went a long way toward doing so. With the burden on plaintiffs lightened, civil rights lawyers enjoyed considerable success in challenging established electoral practices which reduced blacks' chances of electing candidates of their choice.

In 1980, however, the Court dealt civil rights advocates a severe blow in *City of Mobile* v. *Bolden,* increasing the burden of proof on those challenging existing voting laws. In order to establish discrimination, the Court held, plaintiffs must prove that the electoral practice they challenged had been adopted and maintained with actual intent to discriminate against blacks. "[R]acially discriminatory motivation," wrote Justice Stewart, "is a necessary ingredient of a Fifteenth Amendment violation."[26] The new standard was not impossible to overcome; indeed, when the *Mobile* case was retried in the district court under the new intent standard, the plaintiffs succeeded in proving that the city's at-large elections had been adopted with the intent of diluting the black vote and thus violated the Fifteenth Amendment. Nevertheless, establishing proof of conscious discriminatory intent was time-consuming and expensive, making cases more difficult to win. After the Supreme Court remanded the *Mobile* case to the district court, for example, it took the plaintiffs nearly two years to establish proof of discriminatory intent.

The Reagan Administration and Civil Rights in the 1980s

For civil rights advocates, the Court's decision in the *Mobile* case, while a serious setback, provided less cause for alarm than Ronald Reagan's landslide victory in the 1980 presidential election. A leader of the Republican right since the mid-1960s, Reagan had long been at odds with black leaders. As a prominent supporter of Barry Goldwater's unsuccessful bid for the presidency in 1964, he had vigorously defended the candidate's vote in the Senate against the Civil Rights Act. And in his own successful campaign for the California governorship two years later, Reagan had skillfully exploited the white backlash generated by the Watts riot. During the 1970s he became reconciled to the Civil Rights Act but continued his running battle with black leaders, fervently denouncing busing and affirmative action. Nor were civil rights leaders concerned only with Reagan's pedigree. Conservative southern whites, members of the religious right, and northern Democrats who had left their party because of its support for civil rights, were important groups within the Reagan coalition and would exert pressure on his administration to roll back the civil rights gains of the 1970s. Appointments to crucial civil rights enforcement positions suggested that the new president was prepared to accede to their demands. Reagan named William Bradford Reynolds, a sharp critic of "reverse discrimination" and color-conscious remedies for past discrimination, assistant attorney general for civil rights. For chair of the Civil Rights Commission, he appointed Clarence Pendleton, a conservative black who decried affirmative action as "a bankrupt public policy."[27]

The administration's role in *Bob Jones University* v. *United States* soon demonstrated that civil rights leaders' fears were well founded. The school, a nonprofit fundamentalist institution with unabashedly racist policies, challenged its loss of tax-exempt status under an Internal Revenue Service (IRS) policy that denied exemptions to institutions that practiced discrimination. In January 1982, shortly after the Supreme Court agreed to hear the case, the administration bent to pressure from Senator Trent Lott, the Mississippi Republican, and announced that it would file a brief on behalf of the university. Ultimately, Reagan's decision backfired. A torrent of protest led administration officials to scramble for cover. Denying their de facto support for discrimination, they claimed to have challenged the IRS policy only because it had been adopted without authorization by Congress. Then in a rapid about-face, they announced support for legislation giving express statutory authority to the very same IRS policy they were challenging in court. When the Court announced its decision in 1983, an 8–1 majority curtly rejected the administration's position. Although it did no damage to the civil rights cause, the *Bob Jones* fiasco revealed the administration's agenda. "The consequence was akin to an unmasking," noted Joel Selig, a former attorney in the Civil Rights Division, "the administration had aligned itself as a willing partner of unalloyed racism."[28]

As the controversy over the *Bob Jones* case erupted, the administration was locked in battle with civil rights leaders over voting rights. In 1981, black leaders pressed Congress to extend the preclearance provisions of the Voting Rights Act, which were to expire the following year. They also urged adoption of a law voiding existing electoral laws and regulations that had a discriminatory effect, thereby eliminating the burdensome intent test established by the *Mobile* case. A bill incorporating their demands sailed through the House of Representatives, winning approval by a 389–24 margin in early October. Although administration leaders decided that opposition to extension of the act was not politically feasible, they nevertheless launched a campaign to preserve the intent test as the bill moved to the Senate. Ignoring the discriminatory impact of practices that diluted black votes and unsympathetic to the difficulty of proving intent, they charged that the effect standard amounted to political affirmative action. In mid-December, President Reagan claimed that abandoning the intent standard "could lead to the type of thing in which [discriminatory] effect could be judged if there was some disproportion in the number of [minority] public officials who were elected at any government level. . . ." The result, he warned, would be that "all of society had to have an actual quota system."[29]

Administration officials kept up the attack during the first three months of 1982. In February, William Bradford Reynolds denounced "race conscious remedies which require preferential treatment for minorities" in a speech to the Delaware Bar Association. And in late March, Attorney General William French Smith lambasted "the abhorrent notion that blacks can only be represented by blacks and whites can only be represented by whites" in an attack on the House bill that appeared on the Op-Ed page of the *New York Times*.[30] Nevertheless, the administration offensive failed miserably, and Senate Republican leaders agreed to a compromise bill that satisfied Democrats and civil rights advocates. The compromise extended the preclearance provision for twenty-five years and swept aside the Court's ruling in the *Mobile* case. It banned existing electoral laws and practices which, given "the totality of the circumstances" (including minorities' success in winning office), afforded minorities "less opportunity than other members of the electorate . . . to elect representatives of their choice."[31] In June the compromise passed the Senate by a 86–8 margin and won quick acceptance from the House. As he signed the bill at a White House ceremony attended by more than 300 guests, President Reagan made the best of a bad situation. Forgetting his opposition, he cited the law as evidence of "our unbending commitment to voting rights."[32]

Despite the president's disingenous words, the Justice Department continued to demonstrate opposition to the effect standard it had so vigorously opposed. For one-and-a-half years after the new law was adopted, department lawyers ignored it, failing to challenge electoral practices that had discriminatory effects. Although subsequently the department did initiate some vote dilution cases, it remained quite sluggish in carrying out its responsibility to enforce the effect standard. Despite its substantial resources, private groups brought ten times more lawsuits challenging discriminatory electoral practices than did the Justice Department during the Reagan years. Moreover, in 1985 when the Supreme Court agreed to hear *Thornburg* v. *Gingles*, a case that involved interpretation of the 1982 law, the department filed an *amicus curiae* brief calling for a narrow reading of the effect standard. Although the Court rejected the department's argument, the case demonstrated the administration's continued opposition to effective remedies for plaintiffs in vote dilution cases.[33]

Nor were Justice Department officials especially vigilant in executing their preclearance responsibility. In 1981, for example, in the course of redrawing the state's congressional districts, Louisiana legislators deftly divided the New Orleans black community between two congressional districts, thereby splitting a large concentration of black voters between two districts with white majorities and avoiding creation of a district with a black majority. A Republican who had served in the Nixon Justice Department characterized the plan as "a blatant intentional racial gerrymander,"[34] and career attorneys in the Civil Rights Division urged their boss to reject it. Nevertheless, Assistant Attorney General Reynolds overrode these objections and approved the plan; only a lawsuit brought by black voters prevented the scheme from taking effect. Nor was this a momentary lapse. During the Reagan administration, the rate of approval of electoral changes submitted for preclearance was significantly higher than it had been during the previous fifteen years.

The Reagan Justice Department also clashed with civil rights advocates over appropriate remedies for employment discrimination. Department officials denounced affirmative action plans and even opposed court orders establishing hiring and promotion goals for employers who had been found guilty of discrimination. The Fourteenth Amendment and Title VII of the Civil Rights Act of 1964, they argued, banned all forms of race and sex discrimination, including discrimination against white men. In addition, they maintained that when employers were found guilty of discrimination against blacks or women, judges could only order them to end their discriminatory practices and to hire or promote individuals who had proven that they had been wrongfully denied jobs or promotions. Critics pointed out that by limiting remedies to individuals who proved discrimination—an extremely expensive and time-consuming process— the administration's approach would freeze into place the effects of past discrimination and guarantee that redressing the effects of past discrimination proceeded at a glacial pace. Nevertheless, officials in the Justice Department remained adamant that "public policy must be racially neutral" and that "counting by race is a form of racism."[35]

Committed to reversing precedents favorable to affirmative action established in the 1970s, the Justice Department took the offensive, regularly going to court on behalf of white males who challenged affirmative action. In 1983 it intervened in *Firefighters* v. *Stotts*, seeking to overturn a federal district court decision setting aside the seniority rights of white firefighters. The district court had concluded that because blacks had been excluded from the force by discrimination until recently, layoffs based on seniority would perpetuate the effects of past discrimination. Consequently, it had ordered the department to adopt a layoff plan that would not reduce the proportion of blacks on the force, even if that meant laying off whites who had more seniority than blacks who kept their jobs. In 1984 the Supreme Court reversed the lower court. A slender majority of five justices, speaking through Justice White, ruled that under Title VII federal courts could set aside seniority systems only if they had been adopted and maintained with discriminatory intent.[36]

Although the *Stotts* ruling was quite limited, Justice Department officials were buoyed by language in Justice White's opinion suggesting that Title VII denied the courts authority to establish goals and quotas. They pounced on White's cryptic remark, using it to challenge consent decrees establishing hiring and promotion goals in more than fifty fire and police departments. (A consent decree is a voluntary agreement between the parties to a lawsuit which is accepted by the judge and promulgated in a court order settling the case.) Moreover, during the next two years the department filed *amicus curiae* briefs in several important affirmative action cases, hoping for a clear-cut ruling against goals and quotas.

During 1986 and 1987, however, the Court dealt the Reagan administration a series of sharp reverses. In *Wygant* v. *Jackson Board of Education* (1986), the Court struck down a layoff plan—voluntarily adopted by a teacher's union and a school board—which compromised the seniority rights of white teachers. Nevertheless, Justice Powell's decision for the majority rejected the administration's contention that race-conscious remedies were never acceptable. "We have recognized," Powell explained, "that in order to remedy the effects of prior discrimination, it may be necessary to take race into account. As part of this nation's dedication to eradicating racial discrimination, innocent persons may be called upon to bear some of the burden of the remedy." He carefully distinguished between preferential treatment for minorities in carrying out layoffs and other forms of affirmative action, noting that hiring goals "simply do not impose the kind of burden that layoffs impose."[37]

As Powell's comments suggested, a majority was willing to accept race-conscious remedies that were narrowly drawn. In *Local 28 of the Sheet Metal Workers' International Association* v. *Equal Employment Opportunity Commission* (1986) and *United States* v. *Paradise* (1987), the Court approved lower court decisions establishing hiring and promotion quotas to remedy the effects of intentional discrimination by an employer and a union. Both opinions were written by Justice Brennan and were heavily qualified, limiting the use of court-imposed quotas to cases of egregious discrimination and emphasizing that they were temporary remedies and did not require employers to hire unqualified candidates. Nevertheless, the cases dealt a blow to the Justice Department's contention that goals and quotas were impermissible and that judicial remedies could benefit only persons who proved that they had suffered actual discrimination. "The plain language of Title VII," noted Justice

Powell, in his concurring opinion in *Local 28,* "does not clearly support a view that all remedies must be limited to benefitting victims."[38]

The Court also accepted voluntary affirmative action plans, refusing to retreat from its 1979 ruling in the *Weber* case. In *Local Number 93, International Association of Firefighters* v. *City of Cleveland* (1986), the Court turned back the Justice Department's challenge to consent decrees establishing hiring and promotion goals. Justice Brennan's majority opinion held that consent decrees were voluntary agreements rather than orders imposed by a court. "Therefore," Brennan concluded, "there is no reason to think that voluntary race conscious affirmative action such as was held permissible in *Weber* is rendered impermissible by Title VII simply because it is incorporated into a consent decree."[39] One year later, in *Johnson* v. *Transportation Agency* (1987), the Court rejected a challenge to a local government's voluntary affirmative action program. The case had been initiated by a white man who had been passed over for promotion in favor of a woman who had received a passing but slightly lower score (73 as opposed to 75) on her interview. Justice Brennan, who again wrote for the majority, pointed out that the plan did not reserve any positions for women and minorities but merely used race and gender as two factors among many in hiring and promotion decisions. "Such a plan is fully consistent with Title VII," Brennan concluded, "for it embodies the contribution that voluntary employer action can make in eliminating the vestiges of discrimination in the workplace."[40]

These decisions were sharp setbacks for the Reagan administration, demonstrating that it had not convinced the Court to jettison race-conscious remedies. During his first seven years in office, Reagan had filled two vacancies on the Court. In 1981, he had named Sandra Day O'Connor to fill the seat vacated by Potter Stewart, and when Chief Justice Warren Burger had resigned in 1986, he had elevated Justice William Rehnquist to the chief justiceship and appointed Antonin Scalia to the position vacated by Rehnquist. The Reagan appointments did not shift the balance of power on civil rights, however. Four justices— Brennan, Marshall, Blackmun, and Stevens—accepted the constitutionality of color-conscious remedies, and a fifth—Justice Powell— consistently supported affirmative action programs that were narrowly drawn and did not place severe burdens on white men. That left only four justices—Rehnquist, O'Connor, Scalia, and White (who had become increasingly conservative on civil rights)—who were hostile to affirma tive action. Moreover, Justice O'Connor, while highly skeptical of affirmative action, did not reject color-conscious remedies out of hand and occasionally defected from the conservative bloc.

By the end of the decade, however, there were indications that the administration's persistence might pay off. In 1987 Justice Powell, who had frequently provided the swing vote in affirmative action decisions, announced his retirement. Aware that Powell's replacement would dramatically affect the court's position on civil rights, the president nominated Robert Bork, an outspoken critic of affirmative action and judicial activism, to fill the vacancy. A wide array of civil rights and women's organizations launched a well-coordinated offensive against the nominee and convinced the Senate to block Bork's nomination. (Southern Democrats, fearful of alienating black constituents who were adamantly opposed to the nomination, played a crucial role in the outcome, attesting to the impact of the Voting Rights Act on southern politics.) Although Reagan's second nominee, Douglas Ginsburg, withdrew his name from consideration when reports surfaced that he had smoked marijuana while a member of the Harvard Law School faculty (an embarrassing revelation for an administration that was admonishing the nation's youth to "Just say no to drugs"), the third time proved to be the charm. In early 1988, the Senate, weary from the bruising battle over Bork, confirmed Anthony Kennedy, a quiet and cautious conservative who had served on the U.S. Court of Appeals for the Ninth Circuit.

Although little was known of Kennedy's views on civil rights when he joined the court, his voting during his first term (1988–1989) suggested that Reagan had forged a new conservative majority. In three major civil rights cases, the freshman justice joined Rehnquist, Scalia, White, and O'Connor in decisions that represented major setbacks for civil rights advocates. In *Martin* v. *Wilks*, the new five-justice majority struck a severe blow at voluntary affirmative action agreements that were embodied in consent decrees. Even though white workers who were affected by the decree in question had declined to enter the case at the outset and had had their objections considered by the judge, the majority ruled that they might institute a new lawsuit challenging the terms of the decree. The implications of the ruling were significant. It meant that consent decrees would not protect employers from further litigation, one of the chief attractions of such settlements. The result, many predicted, would be protracted litigation which would increase the time and expense required to challenge employment discrimination. Indeed, the case under consideration by the Court—which originated in a lawsuit by black firefighters and the Birmingham, Alabama chapter of the NAACP against the city's fire department—had been in the courts for fifteen years. And the Supreme Court's ruling guaranteed that it would remain there several more years.[41]

The same 5–4 majority also badly weakened one of the principal weapons against job discrimination. Since 1976 the Court had held that Title 42, section 1981 of the *United States Code* (all persons "shall have the same right . . . to make and enforce contracts . . . as is enjoyed by white persons") applied to private contracts. As a result, black plaintiffs increasingly had relied on section 1981 in employment discrimination suits. In its 1989 decision in the highly publicized case of *Patterson* v. *McLean Credit Union*, the conservative majority agreed that section 1981 was applicable to private contracts; however, it read the provision narrowly, holding that although it prevented discrimination in hiring, it did not offer a remedy against racially motivated harassment on the job. In an opinion reminiscent of the narrow formalism that had enabled the Court to accept the separate but equal doctrine in 1896, Justice Kennedy explained that section 1981 "extends only to the formation of a contract, but not to problems that may arise later from the conditions of continuing employment."[42] Granted, a victim of on-the-job discrimination had a remedy under Title VII, as the majority pointed out; however, because section 1981 offered victims of job discrimination more extensive remedies than did Title VII (including punitive damages), the Court's disclaimers were unpersuasive.

The new conservative majority dealt its severest blow to civil rights advocates in *Ward's Cove Packing Company* v. *Atonio*. Since 1971, when it had decided the *Griggs* case, the Court had maintained that plaintiffs in job discrimination suits need not prove intentional discrimination. Instead, when they established that employment practices had a discriminatory effect, the employer assumed the burden of proving that its policies were justified by business necessity. In *Ward's Cove*, however, the Court pulled back from the *Griggs* rule, holding that the burden of proof remained on the plaintiffs to prove that employment practices were not necessary. Although the dispute was over a technical, seemingly insignificant point, the Court's ruling would make it substantially more difficult for minorities and women to prove job discrimination.

A fourth case decided at the 1988–1989 term called into question the constitutionality of voluntary affirmative action programs. In *Richmond*

v. *Croson*, Justice Stevens joined the conservative bloc in a 6–3 decision striking down a Richmond, Virginia, ordinance requiring businesses holding municipal construction contracts to subcontract at least thirty percent of the dollar value of their jobs to minority-owned firms. In the opinion of the Court, Justice O'Connor noted that government programs giving preferences on the basis of race were inherently suspect. They were not permissible to redress general societal discrimination that historically had denied blacks opportunity for economic advancement and had contributed to the paucity of black entrepreneurs. Rather, such programs were justified only as remedies for actual discrimination against the parties that would benefit from them. In the present case, O'Connor explained, there was no evidence of systematic discrimination against minority-owned construction firms and therefore no justification for the city's policy. She was careful to distinguish Richmond's policy from a strikingly similar congressional program that the Court had sustained in *Fullilove* v. *Klutznik* (1980). Unlike states and cities, she explained, Congress had express authority to enforce the guarantees of the Fourteenth Amendment's equal protection clause. It might use this broad discretionary authority to adopt measures designed to redress the effects of societal discrimination if it believed that they were necessary to achieve equality. Although this concession offered some consolation to civil rights advocates, the decision suggested that voluntary affirmative action programs established by state and local government (and perhaps by private businesses) were in trouble. Indeed, in the year following *Croson*, lower courts struck down programs establishing set-asides for minority-owned businesses in six cities and one state.

The 1989 decisions suggested to many that the Reagan position on civil rights had finally triumphed. "The decisions left no doubt," according to *New York Times* legal reporter Linda Greenhouse, "that Ronald Reagan, out of office five months, finally succeeded in a goal that had appeared to elude him for much of his eight years in the White House: to shift the Supreme Court's direction on civil rights."[43] From the bench, Justice Harry Blackmun, the Nixon appointee who had become a staunch civil rights advocate, lamented the direction of the Court. "One wonders whether the majority still believes that race discrimination—or more accurately, race discrimination against nonwhites—is a problem in our society," he mused, "or even remembers that it ever was."[44]

As the 1980s came to an end, black leaders shared Blackmun's gloomy assessment. Recalling that a century earlier the nation had reneged on its promise of equality, they were increasingly pessimistic about the future of civil rights. During the previous two decades they had moved against the tide, skillfully building on the historic gains of the 1960s to expand guarantees for civil rights. In the process, they had prodded the courts and Congress to adopt controversial measures designed to breathe life into formal guarantees of equality. Nevertheless, as the decade came to an end, race remained the most divisive, the most explosive, and the most intractable problem confronting the nation. America's cities and schools remained highly segregated, and, despite a concerted campaign for equal employment opportunity, the legal victories of the 1970s and 1980s offered too little to the growing black underclass that remained trapped in poverty. Yet in the conservative atmosphere of post-Reagan Washington, the bold new initiatives that were necessary to deal with these problems were unlikely to receive serious consideration. Indeed, the Supreme Court's 1988–1989 term suggested that civil rights leaders would be hard-pressed to protect the hard-won gains of the 1970s and 1980s, much less push the nation to carry forward the struggle for equality.

Despite the gloomy outlook, however, the civil rights wars were not over. A coalition of civil rights and women's groups called on Congress to patch up the damage done by the Court's recent decisions, and in early 1990, Senator Edward Kennedy and Representative Augustus Hawkins introduced new civil rights legislation. The bill reversed several of the Court's most damaging 1989 rulings. It required employers to demonstrate that personnel policies that had a discriminatory effect on the hiring and promotion of women and minorities had "a substantial and demonstrable relationship to effective job performance" (reversing *Ward's Cove*); stipulated that section 1981 prohibited discriminatory treatment on the job as well as discrimination in hiring (reversing *Patterson*); and barred challenges to consent decrees by third parties who had bypassed the opportunity to make a timely objection (reversing *Martin*). The Kennedy–Hawkins bill also strengthened Title VII of the Civil Rights Act of 1964 by authorizing persons who suffered employment discrimination on account of race, sex, religion, or national origin to sue for monetary damages (rather than merely for reinstatement in their jobs and back pay, as Title VII currently provided). This offered significantly sharper sanctions against discrimination and extended to women remedies that racial minorities had enjoyed since the mid-1970s under judicial interpretations of section 1981. By midsummer the bill's chances looked good. Although President George Bush voiced objections, he clearly wished to avoid a veto that would weaken his surprising popularity among black voters. Moreover, there was broad bipartisan support for the bill on Capitol Hill, and some observers predicted that supporters had enough votes to override a veto.[45]

As the new civil rights bill made its way through the legislative process, civil rights advocates scored two surprising victories in the Supreme Court. In both cases, Justice White provided the crucial vote, breaking ranks with the Reagan appointees (with whom he had voted on civil rights cases during the 1988–1989 term) and giving the liberal bloc narrow 5–4 victories. In *Missouri* v. *Jenkins,* the Court authorized a federal district judge to order local officials to raise taxes in order to pay for an extensive magnet school program that he had ordered as a remedy for unconstitutional segregation. The opinion, which was written by Justice White, significantly strengthened the hand of federal courts in school segregation cases. The Court also upheld controversial affirmative action policies adopted by the Federal Communications Commission and Congress to increase the number of minority-owned radio and television stations. In *Metro Broadcasting* v. *Federal Communications Commission,* the justices ruled that the policies were designed to promote diversity in broadcasting and to redress the historic exclusion of minority firms from the broadcast industry. Consequently, they came within Congress's broad discretionary authority to regulate interstate commerce, to promote the general welfare, and to enforce the guarantees of the equal protection clause. The Court thus refused to extend its ruling in *Croson* (1989) to congressionally mandated affirmative action programs. By doing so, it preserved the principle established in *Fullilove* v. *Klutznik* (1980) and prevented further erosion of affirmative action.[46]

As the nation entered the 1990s, the future of civil rights remained unclear. Although buoyed by the victories in *Jenkins* and *Metro Broadcasting,* few civil rights leaders believed that they signalled an end to the Court's conservative posture on civil rights. And with a conservative Republican in the White House, they realized that any new appointment would move the Court farther to the right. Nevertheless, the broad support for new civil rights legislation in Congress suggested that whatever happened in the Supreme Court, civil rights leaders continued to influence national policy. Although predictions are hazardous, one thing seems certain. Just as race was a pivotal issue at the Constitution's inception and had played a crucial role in constitutional development during the ensuing two centuries, it would remain a fault line of controversy and debate during the nation's third century under the Constitution.

NOTES

Chapter 1

1. The phrase comes from Gary B. Nash, *Forging Freedom: The Formation of Philadelphia's Black Community, 1720–1840* (Cambridge, Mass., 1989), p. 134.

2. "To the President, Senate, and House of Representatives," 23 January 1797, ed. Herbert Aptheker, *A Documentary History of the Negro People in the United States,* 3 vols. (New York, 1951–74), 1:43.

3. Smith quoted in Donald L. Robinson, *Slavery in the Structure of American Politics, 1765–1820* (New York, 1971), p. 289.

4. First Continental Congress, Declaration and Resolves, 17 October 1774; Second Continental Congress, Declaration of the Causes and Necessities of Taking up Arms, 6 July 1775, ed. Richard Hofstadter, *Great Issues in American History,* 3 vols. (New York, 1958), 2:30, 52.

5. John Phillip Reid, *The Concept of Liberty in the Age of the American Revolution* (Chicago, 1988), p. 49.

6. Quoted in Winthrop D. Jordan, *White Over Black: American Attitudes Toward the Negro, 1550–1812* (Chapel Hill, N.C., 1968), p. 293.

7. Ibid., p. 413.

8. U.S., *Constitution,* Article I, sec. 2.

9. Max Farrand, ed., *The Records of the Federal Convention of 1787,* rev. ed. in 4 vols. (New Haven, Conn., 1966), 1:593.

10. Ibid., 2:143.

11. Ibid., p. 222.

12. U.S., *Constitution,* Article I, sec. 9.

13. Farrand, *Records,* 2:364.

14. Ibid., p. 443.

15. U.S., *Constitution,* Article IV, sec. 2.

16. Farrand, *Records,* 2:417.

17. Don E. Fehrenbacher, *The Dred Scott Case: Its Significance in American Law and Politics* (New York, 1978), p. 86.

18. Paul Finkelman, *"Prigg* v. *Pennsylvania* and Northern State Courts: Anti-Slavery Uses of a Pro-Slavery Decision," *Civil War History* 25 (March 1979): 5–35.

19. *Barron* v. *Baltimore,* 7 Peters 243 (1833).

20. *Livingston* v. *Van Ingen,* 9 Johnson's Reports 507 (NY, 1812), p. 577.

21. *Corfield* v. *Coryell,* 6 Fed. Cases 546 (No. 3230) (C.C.E.D. Pa. 1823), pp. 551–52. For a good treatment of judicial interpretation of the privileges and immunities clause, see James H. Kettner, *The Development of American Citizenship, 1608–1870* (Chapel Hill, N.C., 1978), pp. 255–61.

22. Quoted in William M. Wiecek, *The Sources of Antislavery Constitutionalism in America, 1760–1848* (Ithaca, N.Y., 1977), pp. 123–24.

23. Ibid., p. 123.

24. Wirt did not expressly say that blacks who had full citizenship rights in the state in which they resided were United States citizens. He did say, however, that it was clear that "no person is included in the description of citizen of the United States who has not the full rights of a citizen in the State of his residence." Because few states allowed blacks to vote (and the number shrank over time), most free blacks did not possess full citizenship rights in their home state and would not be considered national citizens under Wirt's criterion. *Official Opinions of the Attorneys General of the United States,* 10 vols. (Washington, D.C., 1852), 1:507.

25. Quoted in Kenneth M. Stampp, *The Peculiar Institution: Slavery in the Antebellum South* (New York, 1956), p. 197.

26. Ibid., p. 198.

27. Ibid., p. 208.

28. Ibid., p. 219.

29. Quoted in Ira Berlin, *Slaves Without Masters: The Free Negro in the Antebellum South* (New York, 1974), p. 89.

30. Quoted in Theodore Brantner Wilson, *The Black Codes of the South* (University, Ala., 1965), p. 35.

31. Ibid., p. 27.

32. Ibid., p. 35.

Chapter 2

1. Philip S. Foner and George E. Walker, eds., *Proceedings of the Black State Conventions, 1840–1865,* 2 vols. (Philadelphia, 1979), 1:259–60.

2. Ibid., p. 261.

3. Ibid., pp. 262–63.

4. [William Lloyd Garrison], "Henry Clay's Colonization Address," *The Genius of Universal Emancipation*, 12 February 1830; Romans 13:9; Elizur Wright, Jr., *The Sin of Slavery and Its Remedy* (New York, 1836), reprinted in John L. Thomas, ed., *Slavery Attacked* (Englewood Cliffs, N.J., 1965), p. 11.

5. Garrison quoted in Louis Filler, *The Crusade Against Slavery, 1830–1860* (New York, 1960), p. 216.

6. Philip S. Foner, ed., *The Life and Writings of Frederick Douglass*, 4 vols. (New York, 1950), 2:415, 420, 423.

7. William Goodell quoted in William M. Wiecek, *The Sources of Antislavery Constitutionalism in America, 1760–1848* (Ithaca, N.Y., 1978), p. 265.

8. Foner and Walker, *Black State Conventions*, 1:11, 192.

9. *Colored American*, 9 May 1840; Hosea Easton, *A Treatise on the Intellectual Character and Civil and Political Condition of the Colored People of the United States* (Boston, 1837), p. 47.

10. Foner and Walker, *Black State Conventions*, 1:21.

11. Ibid., p. 22; Kirk H. Porter and Donald Bruce Johnson, *National Party Platforms, 1840–1956* (Urbana, Ill., 1956), pp. 7–8.

12. Tiffany quoted in Jacobus ten Broek, *Equal Under Law*, rev. ed. (New York, 1965), p. 110.

13. Quotes are from Sumner's brief in Leonard Levy and Douglas Jones, ed., *Jim Crow in Boston: The Origin of the Separate but Equal Doctrine* (New York, 1974), pp. 181, 210.

14. *Frederick Douglass' Newspaper*, 11 May 1855, p. 1.

15. *New York Times*, 27 August 1855, p. 3; 20 December 1856, p. 2.

16. Roy P. Basler, ed., *The Collected Works of Abraham Lincoln*, 9 vols. (New Brunswick, N.J., 1953–55), 3:16.

17. Comity is the courtesy one nation or state pays another by recognizing and giving effect to its laws. This is done as a matter of respect rather than obligation and recognizes that no nation or state is bound to give effect to "foreign" laws which are contrary to its policy.

18. Don E. Fehrenbacher, *The Dred Scott Case: Its Significance in American Law and Politics* (New York, 1978), pp. 333–34.

19. *Dred Scott* v. *Sandford*, 19 Howard 393 (1857), p. 407.

20. Ibid., pp. 451–52.

21. Foner, *Writings of Frederick Douglass*, 2:412–14.

Chapter 3

1. *Coger* v. *The North West Union Packet Co.*, 37 Iowa 145 (1873), pp. 148, 149.

2. Ibid., pp. 153, 155, 156.

3. Ibid., pp. 149, 153–54.

4. Quoted in Harold M. Hyman, *A More Perfect Union: The Impact of the Civil War and Reconstruction on the Constitution* (New York, 1973), p. 543.

5. Roy P. Basler, ed., *The Collected Works of Abraham Lincoln*, 9 vols. (New Brunswick, N.J., 1953–55), 4:263; U.S., Congress, Senate, *Congressional Globe*, 37th Cong., 1st sess., 22 July 1861, pp. 222–23.

6. Philip S. Foner, ed., *The Life and Writings of Frederick Douglass*, 4 vols. (New York, 1952), 3:64–65; resolution of New York convention quoted in Ira Berlin, et al., eds., *Freedom: A Documentary History of Emancipation. Series II. The Black Military Experience* (Cambridge, U.K., 1982), p. 9.

7. LaWanda Cox, *Lincoln and Black Freedom: A Study in Presidential Leadership* (Columbia, S.C., 1981), p. 6.

8. One year earlier, in August 1861, Congress had enacted a more limited Confiscation Act which authorized seizure of property—including slaves—used to support the Confederate war effort.

9. U.S., *Statutes at Large*, 12:592.

10. Richard Hofstadter, *The American Political Tradition and the Men who Made It* (New York, 1948), p. 131.

11. Hyman, *A More Perfect Union*, pp. 124–40 and passim.

12. Schenck quoted in Herman Belz, *A New Birth of Freedom: The Republican Party and Freedmen's Rights, 1861 to 1866* (Westport, Conn., 1976), p. 108.

13. George Rawick, ed., *The American Slave: A Composite Autobiography*, 39 vols. (Westport, Conn. 1972–79), vol. 2, pt. 1, p. 328; Supplement, ser. 2, 6:1945, 1947; Leon Litwack, *Been in the Storm So Long: The Aftermath of Slavery* (New York, 1979), p. 224.

14. Lt. A. Dyer, "Report of Refugees, Freedmen, and Abandoned Lands for the Month Ending June 30, 1866," Records of the Freedmen's Bureau, Assistant Commissioner for Arkansas, Reports, Record Group 105, National Archives, Washington, D.C.

15. Eric Foner, *Free Soil, Free Labor, Free Men: The Ideology of the Republican Party Before the Civil War* (New York, 1970).

16. U.S., *Congressional Globe*, 39th Cong., 1st sess., pt. 1, January 19, 1866, p. 320 (remarks of Lyman Trumbull).

17. The text of the Freedmen's Bureau bill is reprinted in Edward McPherson, ed., *The Political History of the United States . . . During the Period of Reconstruction . . .* (Washington, 1875), pp. 72–74.

18. U.S., *Statutes at Large*, 14:27–30.

19. Colfax to Ames, 10 April 1866, Mary Clemmer Ames Papers, Rutherford B. Hayes Library, Fremont, Ohio; U.S., *Congressional Globe*, 39th Cong., 1st sess., pt. 2, 2 March 1866, p. 1154 (remarks of Charles Eldridge).

20. Michael Les Benedict, *A Compromise of Principle: Congressional Republicans and Reconstruction, 1863–1869* (New York, 1974) and "Preserving the Constitution: The Conservative Basis of Radical Reconstruction," *Journal of American History* 61 (June 1974): 65–90.

21. U.S., *Congressional Globe,* 39th Cong., 1st sess., pt. 2, 10 May 1866, p. 2542 (remarks of John A. Bingham).

22. Capt. H. Sweeney to General J. W. Sprague, 5 January 1867, Freedmen's Bureau Records, Assistant Commissioner for Arkansas, Letters Received.

23. G. Franklin, et al. to General Daniel Sickles, 8 August 1866, Records of the Freedmen's Bureau, Assistant Commissioner for South Carolina, Letters Received.

24. Lt. George Cook to Capt. R. S. Lacey, 31 October 1866, Records of the Freedmen's Bureau, Assistant Commissioner for Virginia, Reports.

25. Maj. Fred Thibant to General Absalom Baird, 6 November 1866, Records of the Freedmen's Bureau, Office of the Commissioner, Letters Received.

26. James Bailey to Robert K. Scott, 26 February 1870, Governor's Papers, South Carolina Archives.

27. Lawrence Smith to E. B. Seabrook, 17 December 1869; Joseph Sanders to Johnson Hagood, 17 May 1877, Legislative Records, Penal System File, South Carolina Archives.

28. Benjamin Perry quoted in Eric Foner, *Reconstruction: America's Unfinished Revolution, 1863–1877* (New York, 1988), p. 294; *Daily Arkansas Gazette,* 8 February 1868 quoted in Allen Trelease, *White Terror: The Ku Klux Klan Conspiracy and Southern Reconstruction* (New York, 1971), p. xxxvi; *Montgomery* (Alabama) *Daily Advertiser,* 7 January 1868 and *Natchez* (Mississippi) *Democrat,* 15 January 1875 quoted in Michael Les Benedict, "The Problem of Constitutionalism and Constitutional Liberty in the Reconstruction South," ed. Kermit L. Hall and James W. Ely, Jr., *An Uncertain Tradition: Constitutionalism and the History of the South* (Athens, Ga., 1989), pp. 238, 240.

Chapter 4

1. *Brenham Daily Banner,* 9 December 1886, p. 1.

2. U.S., Congress, Senate, *Congressional Globe,* 42nd Cong., 1st sess., pt. 1, 3 April 1871, p. 427 (remarks of George McKee).

3. Rainey quoted in Eric Foner, *Reconstruction: America's Unfinished Revolution, 1863–1877* (New York, 1988), p. 456.

4. U.S., *Statutes at Large,* 17:13. The writ of habeas corpus commanded officials to bring persons who were under arrest before a judge for an inquiry into the legality of their arrest and detention. Suspension of habeas corpus would

enable federal officials to make mass arrests without having to prepare formal charges and justify them in court immediately. This would enable them to act quickly, reducing the chance that some suspects would be tipped off and flee before arrests could be made. Suspension did not mean that persons arrested would be tried in military courts.

5. *United States* v. *Hall et al.*, 26 Fed. Cases 79 (No. 15,282) (C.C.S.D., Ala., 1871).

6. U.S., *Congressional Globe*, 43rd Cong., 2nd sess., pt. 2, 4 February 1875, p. 980 (remarks of Ellis Roberts).

7. Quoted in William Gillette, *Retreat from Reconstruction, 1869–1879* (Baton Rouge, La., 1979), p. 199.

8. *Harper's Weekly*, 10 January 1874, p. 27; U.S., *Congressional Globe*, 43rd Cong., 2nd sess., pt. 2, 3 February 1875, p. 944 (remarks of John Lynch); Downing quoted in McPherson, "Abolitionists and the Civil Rights Act of 1875," *Journal of American History* 52 (December 1965): 505; U.S., *Congressional Globe*, 43rd Cong., 1st sess., pt. 4, 29 April 1874, p. 3452 (remarks of Frederick Frelinghuysen).

9. Quoted in Gillette, *Retreat from Reconstruction*, p. 209.

10. Quoted in Vernon Lane Wharton, *The Negro in Mississippi, 1865–1900* (Chapel Hill, N.C., 1947), p. 206.

11. *The Slaughter-House Cases*, 83 U.S. 36 (1873), pp. 78, 129.

12. Ibid., p. 71.

13. *United States* v. *Cruikshank*, 92 U.S. 542 (1876), p. 554.

14. *The Civil Rights Cases*, 109 U.S. 1 (1883), pp. 20–21, 24.

15. Ibid., p. 26.

16. *Strauder* v. *West Virginia*, 100 U.S. 303 (1880), pp. 307–308.

17. *Ex Parte In the Matter of The Commonwealth of Virginia and J. D. Coles*, 100 U.S. 339 (1880), pp. 345, 347; *Neal* v. *Delaware*, 103, U.S. 370 (1880).

18. *Yick Wo* v. *Peter Hopkins*, 118 U.S. 356 (1887), pp. 373–74.

19. *United States* v. *Hiram Reese and Matthew Foushee*, 92 U.S. 214 (1876), p. 218; *United States* v. *Butler*, 25 Fed. Cases 213 (14,700) (C.C.D.S.C., 1877).

20. *Ex Parte: In the Matter of Jasper Yarbrough, et al.*, 110 U.S. 651 (1884), p. 662.

21. Lucius Northrup, the United States attorney in South Carolina, quoted in Robert Goldman, "'A Free Ballot and a Fair Count': The Department of Justice and the Enforcement of Voting Rights in the South, 1877–1893," (Ph.D. diss., Michigan State University, 1976), p. 122.

22. *Ferguson* v. *Gies*, 82 Michigan 358 (1890), pp. 363, 364.

23. J. Morgan Kousser, *The Shaping of Southern Politics: Suffrage Restriction and the Establishment of the One-Party South, 1880–1910* (New Haven, Conn., 1974), p. 62.

24. The term Jim Crow first appeared in the North in the 1830s as the title of a

minstrel song-and-dance show. (Minstrel shows were presented by white performers with blackened faces, and contained a series of sketches that portrayed black life, humor, and music in a patronizing and derogatory fashion.) As early as the 1840s the term was applied to cars set aside for blacks on Massachusetts railroads.

25. *Nashville Clarion* and *Jacksonville Florida Times-Union* quoted in August Meier and Elliot Rudwick, "The Boycott Movement Against Jim Crow Streetcars in the South, 1900–1906," *Journal of American History* 45 (March 1969): 761.

26. *Plessy* v. *Ferguson,* 163 U.S. 537 (1896), pp. 544, 551, 559.

27. *Ratliff* v. *Beale,* 74 Mississippi 247, as quoted in *Williams* v. *Mississippi,* 170 U.S. 213 (1898), p. 222.

28. Ibid.

Chapter 5

1. Wechsler quoted in Richard Kluger, *Simple Justice* (New York, 1975), p. 160.

2. Ibid., p. 159.

3. Ibid., pp. 159–60.

4. Restrictive convenants were special provisions added to real estate deeds that limited the owner's freedom to use or sell the property in some specified manner.

5. Stephan Thernstrom, *The Other Bostonians: Poverty and Progress in the American Metropolis, 1880–1970* (Cambridge, Mass., 1973), p. 197.

6. Villard quoted in Charles Flint Kellogg, *NAACP: A History of the National Association for the Advancement of Colored People, 1890–1920* (Baltimore, 1967), pp. 297–98.

7. Unlike the House of Representatives, the smaller Senate prided itself on being a truly deliberative body, and its rules allowed unlimited debate. In practice, this permitted members to hold the floor indefinitely, enabling a determined minority to bring the business of the Senate to a halt. Once they were recognized by the presiding officer, members bent on obstruction could speak on any topic that came to mind and frequently read from books or newspapers. Moreover, when one filibustering senator became too tired to continue, he could yield the floor to a co-conspirator who could carry on the obstruction. In 1917 the Senate adopted a rule that permitted a majority of two-thirds of senators present to adopt a motion of "cloture," ending debate and requiring a vote on the pending measure. Southern strength in the Senate, however, made obtaining cloture difficult to achieve.

8. *Clyatt* v. *United States*, 197 U.S. 207 (1905); *Bailey* v. *Alabama*, 219 U.S. 219 (1911); *United States* v. *Reynolds*, 235 U.S. 133 (1914).

9. Pete Daniel, *The Shadow of Slavery: Peonage in the South, 1901–1969* (New York, 1972).

10. The phrase means "friend of the court." Groups or individuals who are not parties to a case but who have an interest in its outcome or special expertise on issues raised by it are often allowed to submit briefs on behalf of one of the parties.

11. *Guinn* v. *United States*, 238 U.S. 347 (1915).

12. *Buchanan* v. *Warley*, 245 U.S. 60 (1917), pp. 76, 79, 82.

13. The *Corrigan* case arose in the District of Columbia, technically not a state but an area subject to the jurisdiction of the federal government. Therefore, there was doubt as to whether the Fourteenth Amendment, which barred *states* from denying persons due process of law, was applicable. However, the Fifth Amendment, which applied to the federal government, provided that no person "shall be . . . deprived of life, liberty, or property without due process of law" and was therefore relied on by the NAACP.

14. *Corrigan* v. *Buckley*, 271 U.S. 323 (1926).

15. *Moore* v. *Dempsey*, 261 U.S. 86 (1923).

16. Harvard Sitkoff, *A New Deal for Blacks. The Emergence of Civil Rights as a National Issue: The Depression Decade* (New York, 1978), pp. 66, 69.

17. *Powell* v. *Alabama*, 287 U.S. 45 (1932).

18. *Twining* v. *New Jersey*, 211 U.S. 78 (1908), p. 114.

19. *Brown* v. *Mississippi*, 297 U.S. 278 (1936), p. 286.

20. *Chambers* v. *Florida*, 309 U.S. 227 (1940), p. 238.

21. *Norris* v. *Alabama*, 294 U.S. 587 (1935).

22. *Smith* v. *Texas*, 311 U.S. 128 (1940).

23. *University of Maryland* v. *Murray*, 169 Maryland 478 (1936).

24. *Missouri ex rel Gaines* v. *Canada*, 305 U.S. 337 (1938), pp. 346, 349.

25. *Mills* v. *Board of Education of Ann Arundel County*, 30 F. Supp. 245 (D. Maryland 1939).

26. *Alston* v. *School Board of City of Norfolk*, 112 F.2d 992 (4th Cir. 1940).

27. Schuyler's *Pittsburgh Courier* editorial of 5 October 1940 and War Department order of 5 September 1940 quoted in Sitkoff, *New Deal for Blacks*, pp. 301, 305.

28. White and Randolph quoted in Sitkoff, *New Deal for Blacks*, pp. 324–25.

29. President's Committee on Civil Rights, *To Secure These Rights* (Washington, D.C., 1947), p. 148.

30. *Grovey* v. *Townsend*, 295 U.S. 45 (1935).

31. In 1939 tax considerations prompted the NAACP board of directors to establish the NAACP Legal Defense and Education Fund to manage the organization's increasingly ambitious program of litigation. Because the NAACP en-

gaged in lobbying, it did not enjoy tax exempt status. As a separate entity that did not lobby, however, the LDF qualified as a tax exempt oranization and contributors' donations were tax deductible. During the first twenty years of the LDF's existence the separation was largely nominal. Members of the NAACP's board served as directors of the LDF, and Thurgood Marshall, who became director of the LDF, remained an NAACP employee. Only in 1958 (when this close relationship threatened its tax exempt status) did the LDF become a truly independent organization.

32. *Smith* v. *Allwright*, 321 U.S. 649 (1944), pp. 663, 664.

33. *Shelley* v. *Kraemer*, 334 U.S. 1 (1948), p. 19.

34. *Morgan* v. *Virginia*, 328 U.S. 373 (1946).

35. Clark quoted in Mark Tushnet, *The NAACP's Legal Strategy Against Segregated Education, 1925–1950* (Chapel Hill, N.C. 1987), p. 132; *Sweatt* v. *Painter*, 339 U.S. 629 (1950), p. 634.

36. Tushnet, *The NAACP's Legal Strategy*, p. 132.

37. *Henderson* v. *United States*, 339 U.S. 816 (1950).

Chapter 6

1. David J. Garrow, *Bearing the Cross: Martin Luther King and the Southern Christian Leadership Conference* (New York, 1986), pp. 23–24; Taylor Branch, *Parting the Waters: America in the King Years, 1954–1963* (New York, 1988), pp. 138–42.

2. Branch, *Parting the Waters*, p. 168.

3. *Gayle* v. *Browder*, 352 U.S. 903 (1956).

4. Garrow, *Bearing the Cross*, p. 24.

5. The state cases turned on whether the Fourteenth Amendment's stipulation that no state shall "deny any person . . . equal protection of the laws" outlawed segregation. Since the District of Columbia was not a state, the Fourteenth Amendment did not apply to it. Segregation there had to be challenged as a violation of the Fifth Amendment's prohibition against federal action which denied persons due process of law.

6. Richard Kluger, *Simple Justice* (New York, 1975), p. 679.

7. *Brown* v. *Board of Education of Topeka*, 347 U.S. 483 (1954), pp. 493–95.

8. *Brown* v. *Board of Education of Topeka*, 349 U.S. 294 (1955), pp. 300, 301.

9. Jack W. Peltason, *Fifty-eight Lonely Men: Southern Federal Judges and School Desegregation* (New York, 1961), p. 60.

10. Alabama pupil placement law as quoted in Peltason, *Fifty-eight Lonely Men*, p. 83.

11. Frederick Morrow quoted in Michal R. Belknap, *Federal Law and*

Southern Order: Racial Violence and Constitutional Conflict in the Post-Brown South (Athens, Ga., 1987), pp. 33–34.

12. Davidson quoted in Peltason, *Fifty-eight Lonely Men*, p. 119, 121.

13. Eisenhower quoted in Ibid., p. 49.

14. *Cooper* v. *Aaron,* 358 U.S. 1 (1958), pp. 17, 19–20.

15. *Mayor of Baltimore* v. *Dawson,* 350 U.S. 877 (1955); *Holmes* v. *City of Atlanta,* 350 U.S. 879 (1955); *Gayle* v. *Browder,* 352 U.S. 903 (1956); *New Orleans Park Improvement Association* v. *Detige,* 358 U.S. 54 (1958).

16. *Burton* v. *Wilmington Parking Authority,* 365 U.S. 715 (1961).

17. *NAACP* v. *Alabama,* 357 U.S. 449 (1958); *Bates* v. *Little Rock,* 361 U.S. 516 (1960).

18. Quoted in Harvard Sitkoff, *The Struggle for Black Equality, 1954–1980* (New York, 1981), p. 79.

19. Belknap, *Federal Law and Southern Order,* p. 74.

20. *Boynton* v. *Virginia,* 364 U.S. 454 (1960).

21. Sitkoff, *Struggle for Black Equality,* p. 154.

22. Kennedy quoted in Carl M. Brauer, *John F. Kennedy and the Second Reconstruction* (New York, 1977), p. 260.

23. *Heart of Atlanta Motel* v. *United States,* 379 U.S. 241 (1964); *Katzenbach* v. *McClung,* 379 U.S. 294 (1964).

24. *South Carolina* v. *Katzenbach,* 383 U.S. 301 (1966).

25. *Harper* v. *Virginia Board of Elections,* 383 U.S. 667 (1966).

26. *United States* v. *Williams,* 341 U.S. 70 (1951).

27. *United States* v. *Price,* 383 U.S. 787 (1966), p. 805.

28. *United States* v. *Guest,* 383 U.S. 745 (1966), pp. 782, 784.

29. *Annual Report of the Attorney General of the United States, 1968* (Washington, D.C., 1969), p. 67.

30. *United States* v. *Jefferson County Board of Education,* 372 F.2d 836 (5th Circuit, 1966), p. 869.

31. *Green* v. *County School Board,* 391 U.S. 430 (1968), pp. 435, 437–38, 439.

32. Allen Matusow, *The Unraveling of America: A History of Liberalism in the 1960s* (New York, 1984), p. 194.

33. Cashin quoted in Steven F. Lawson, *Black Ballots: Voting Rights in the South, 1944–1969* (New York, 1976), p. 339.

34. *Jones* v. *Alfred H. Mayer Co.,* 392 U.S. 409 (1968), p. 443.

35. The Supreme Court so ruled in *Runyon* v. *McCrary,* 427 U.S. 160 (1976).

Chapter 7

1. J. Harvie Wilkinson, III, *From Brown to Bakke: The Supreme Court and School Integration, 1954–1978* (New York, 1979), p. 210.

2. J. Anthony Lukas, *Common Ground: A Turbulent Decade in the Lives of Three American Families* (New York, 1985), p. 261.

3. Nixon quoted in Gary Orfield, *Must We Bus? Segregated Schools and National Policy* (Washington, D.C., 1978), p. 244.

4. *Alexander* v. *Holmes County Board of Education,* 396 U.S. 19 (1969), p. 20.

5. *Green* v. *County School Board,* 391 U.S. 430 (1968), p. 437.

6. *Swann* v. *Charlotte-Mecklenburg Board of Education,* 402 U.S. 1 (1971), pp. 25, 28, 30.

7. *Keyes* v. *School District No. 1, Denver, Colo.,* 413 U.S. 189 (1973), p. 201.

8. *Milliken* v. *Bradley,* 418 U.S. 717 (1974), p. 741.

9. Ibid., p. 772.

10. Ibid., pp. 782, 814–15.

11. *Griggs* v. *Duke Power,* 401 U.S. 424 (1971), p. 427.

12. Ibid., pp. 429–30, 431.

13. *Washington* v. *Davis,* 426 U.S. 229 (1976).

14. Paul Brest, "Race Discrimination," ed. Vincent Blasi, *The Burger Court: The Counter-Revolution That Wasn't* (New Haven, Conn., 1983), p. 121.

15. *Federal Register,* 4 December 1971, sec. 60–2.10, p. 23, 153.

16. Equal Employment Opportunity Commission, *Affirmative Action and Equal Employment* (Washington, D.C., 1974), p. 1.

17. Alexander Bickel, *The Morality of Consent* (New York, 1975), p. 133. Bickel's statement was the starting point for one of the most sharply argued challenges to affirmative action, William Van Alstyne, "Rites of Passage: Race, the Supreme Court, and the Constitution," *University of Chicago Law Review* 46 (1979): 775–810.

18. J. Skelly Wright, "Color-Blind Theories and Color-Conscious Remedies," *University of Chicago Law Review* 47 (1980): 213–45.

19. *Regents of the University of California* v. *Bakke,* 438 U.S. 265 (1978), p. 407.

20. Ibid., pp. 289–90.

21. *United Steelworkers of America* v. *Weber,* 443 U.S. 193 (1979), p. 204.

22. *Fullilove* v. *Klutznik,* 448 U.S. 448 (1980), p. 484.

23. William Julius Wilson, *The Truly Disadvantaged: The Inner City, the Underclass, and Public Policy* (Chicago, 1987).

24. *Allen* v. *State Board of Elections,* 393 U.S. 544 (1969), pp. 565–66, 569.

25. *White* v. *Regester*, 412 U.S. 756 (1973), pp. 769–70.

26. *City of Mobile* v. *Bolden*, 446 U.S. 55 (1980), p. 62.

27. Pendleton quoted in "The Rise and Fall of the United States Commission on Civil Rights," *Harvard Civil Rights-Civil Liberties Review* 22 (1987): 484.

28. Joel Selig, "The Reagan Administration Justice Department: What Went Wrong," *University of Illinois Law Review* (1985): 820.

29. Reagan quoted in Steven F. Lawson, *In Pursuit of Power: Southern Blacks and Electoral Politics, 1965–1982* (New York, 1985), p. 288.

30. Ibid., pp. 288–89.

31. *United States Code*, Title 42, sec. 1973.

32. Reagan quoted in Lawson, *Pursuit of Power*, p. 292.

33. *Thornburgh* v. *Gingles*, 478 U.S. 30 (1986).

34. U.S., Senate Committee on the Judiciary, *Hearing on the Nomination of William Bradford Reynolds to be Associate Attorney General of the United States*, 99th Cong., 1st sess., p. 390.

35. The quote is from Edwin M. Meese, III, who replaced William French Smith as attorney general in 1985. *New York Times*, 7 October 1985, p. 20.

36. *Firefighters* v. *Stotts*, 467 U.S. 561 (1984).

37. *Wygant* v. *Jackson Board of Education*, 476 U.S. 267 (1986), pp. 280–81, 282.

38. *Local 28 of the Sheet Metal Workers' International Association* v. *Equal Employment Opportunity Commission*, 478 U.S. 421 (1986), p. 483.

39. *Local Number 93, International Association of Firefighters* v. *City of Cleveland*, 478 U.S. 501 (1986), p. 518.

40. *Johnson* v. *Transportation Agency*, 480 U.S. 616 (1987), p. 642.

41. *Martin* v. *Wilks*, 57 *United States Law Week* 4616 (1989).

42. *Patterson* v. *McLean Credit Union*, 57 *United States Law Week* 4705 (1989), p. 4708.

43. *New York Times*, 18 June 1989, sec. 4, p. 1 (national edition).

44. *Ward's Cove Packing Company* v. *Atonio*, 57 *United States Law Week* 4583 (1989), p. 4593.

45. *New York Times*, 15 May 1990, p. 1; 18 May 1990, p. 10; 28 May 1990, p. 7; Diana R. Gordon, "A Civil Rights Bill for Workers," *The Nation*, 251 (July 9, 1990):44–46.

46. *Missouri* v. *Jenkins*, 58 *United States Law Week* 4880 (1990); *Metro Broadcasting, Inc.* v. *Federal Communications Commission*, 58 *United States Law Week* 5053 (1990).

BIBLIOGRAPHICAL ESSAY

Prodded by the sweeping changes in race relations that have occurred during the past forty years, scholars have produced an impressive body of literature on law and race in American history. I have relied heavily on this scholarship in writing *Promises to Keep;* indeed, without it, undertaking this project would have been unthinkable. What follows is a brief essay on the secondary sources that I have found most useful and that, I believe, will be especially helpful to those who wish to pursue topics and issues treated in this book. For a more extensive bibliography, readers should consult Kermit L. Hall, comp., *A Comprehensive Bibliography of American Constitutional and Legal History*, 5 vols. (1984).

A number of general works serve as useful starting points for the study of law and race in America. Alfred Kelly, Winfred Harbison, and Herman Belz, *The American Constitution: Its Origins and Development*, 6th ed. (1982); Melvin I. Urofsky, *A March of Liberty: A Constitutional History of the United States* (1988); William Wiecek, *Liberty Under Law: The Supreme Court in American Life* (1988); and Kermit L. Hall, *The Magic Mirror: Law in American History* (1989) provide good introductions to American constitutional–legal history. John Hope Franklin and Alfred A. Moss, Jr., *From Slavery to Freedom: A History of Negro Americans*, 6th ed. (1988) and Mary Frances Berry and John Blassingame, *Long Memory: The Black Experience in America* (1982) are excellent surveys of African-American history, while Herbert Aptheker, ed., *A Documentary History of the Negro People in the United States*, 3 vols. (1973) is an indispensible collection of sources. Mary Frances Berry, *Black Resistance/White Law: A History of Constitutional*

Racism in America (1971); Michael Les Benedict, *Civil Rights and Civil Liberties* (1987); and Stanley N. Katz, ''The Strange Birth and Unlikely History of Constitutional Equality,'' *Journal of American History* 75 (1988) are stimulating overviews of civil rights and the law. Richard Bardolph, ed., *The Civil Rights Record: Black Americans and the Law, 1849–1970* (1970) is a useful documentary collection.

From the Revolution to the Civil War

The literature on the debate over slavery in the age of the American Revolution is voluminous. David Brion Davis, *The Problem of Slavery in the Age of Revolution, 1770–1823* (1975); Bernard Bailyn, *The Ideological Origins of the American Revolution* (1967); Winthrop D. Jordan, *White Over Black: American Attitudes Toward the Negro, 1550–1812* (1968); and John Phillip Reid, *The Concept of Liberty in the Age of the American Revolution* (1988) offer brilliant analysis of the tension between liberty and racial subordination during the Revolutionary era. Arthur Zilversmit, *The First Emancipation: The Abolition of Slavery in the North* tells the story of the first antislavery movement, while Robert McColley, *Slavery and Jeffersonian Virginia* (1964) examines the limits of antislavery action in the South. Benjamin Quarles, *The Negro in the American Revolution* (1961); Gary B. Nash, *Forging Freedom: The Formation of Philadelphia's Black Community, 1720–1840* (1988); and Ira Berlin and Reginald Horsman, eds., *Slavery and Freedom in the Age of the American Revolution* (1983) are important studies of African-Americans' quest for freedom during the Revolutionary era.

The role of slavery at the Constitutional Convention has generated considerable scholarship and scholarly controversy. Paul Finkelman, ''Slavery and the Constitutional Convention: Making a Covenant with Death,'' ed. Richard Beeman, Stephen Botein, and Edward C. Carter, II, *Beyond Confederation: Origins of the Constitution and American National Identity* (1987) and William M. Wiecek, *The Sources of Antislavery Constitutionalism in America, 1760–1848* (1977) make the most persuasive case for viewing the Constitution as thoroughly proslavery. Don E. Fehrenbacher, *The Dred Scott Case: Its Significance in American Law and Politics* (1978) and William W. Freehling, ''The Founding Fathers and Slavery,'' *American Historical Review* 77 (1972), disagree, suggesting that, despite concessions to southerners, the framers created a document that was open-ended with respect to slavery and that contained provisions that could be turned against the institution. Other useful treatments of the framers and slavery include Donald L. Robinson, *Slavery in the Structure of American Politics, 1765–1820* (1971); Staughton Lynd, *Class Conflict, Slavery, and the United States Constitution* (1967); Howard A. Ohline, "Republicanism and Slavery: Origins of the Three Fifths Clause of the United States Constitution," *William and Mary Quarterly* 28 (1971); and Calvin Jillson and Thornton Anderson, "Realignments in the Convention of 1787: The Slave Trade Compromise," *Journal of Politics* 39 (1977).

A number of important studies examine the role of slavery in American politics and national policy with respect to slavery from the ratification of the Constitution to the Mexican War. Don E. Fehrenbacher's *The Dred Scott Case*, mentioned earlier, is a masterful treatment of these matters. Other important studies include Robinson's *Slavery in the Structure of American Politics*; Richard H. Brown, "The Missouri Crisis, Slavery, and the Politics of Jacksonianism," *South Atlantic Quarterly* 65 (1966); Glover Moore, *The Missouri Controversy* (1966); William J. Cooper, *The South and the Politics of Slavery, 1828–1856* (1978) and *Liberty and Slavery: Southern Politics to 1860* (1983); Leonard Richards, *The Life and Times of Congressman John Quincy Adams* (1986); William W. Freehling, *Prelude to Civil War: The Nullification Controversy in South Carolina, 1816–1836* (1966); Robert Remini, *Martin Van Buren and the Making of the Democratic Party* (1959); and Robert L. Kelley, *The Cultural Pattern in American Politics: The First Century* (1979).

Slavery and race had a pervasive effect on constitutional development in the antebellum era. Harold M. Hyman and William M. Wiecek, *Equal Justice Under Law: Constitutional Development, 1835–1875* (1982) and Fehrenbacher's *Dred Scott Case* are the best overall treatments. James H. Kettner, *The Development of American Citizenship, 1608–1870* (1978) is an important study that shows how slavery and race affected Americans' understanding of the meaning of citizenship and the rights of citizens. Philip M. Hamer, "Great Britain, the United States, and the Negro Seamen Acts, 1822–1848," *Journal of Southern History* 1 (1935) remains a valuable study of a perennial flash point in the controversy over black citizenship. Paul Finkelman, *An Imperfect Union: Slavery, Federalism, and Comity* (1981) is the definitive study of slavery and interstate relations. On the controversy over fugitive slaves, see Thomas D. Morris, *Free Men All: The Personal Liberty Laws of the North, 1780–*

1861 (1974); Stanley W. Campbell, *The Slave Catchers: Enforcement of the Fugitive Slave Law, 1850–1860* (1968); and Paul Finkelman, *"Prigg v. Pennsylvania* and Northern State Courts: Anti-Slavery Uses of a Pro-Slavery Decision," *Civil War History* 25 (1979). Russell B. Nye, *Fettered Freedoms: Civil Liberties and the Slavery Controversy* (1963) and Clement Eaton, *Freedom of Thought in the Old South* (1940) are important studies of the effect of slavery on the liberty of whites. Robert M. Cover, *Slavery Accused: Antislavery and the Judicial Process* (1975) is a penetrating analysis of the moral dilemma that slavery presented to judges. For the Supreme Court and slavery, see Donald M. Roper, "In Quest of Judicial Objectivity: The Marshall Court and the Legitimation of Slavery," *Stanford Law Review* 21 (1969) and William Wiecek, "Slavery and Abolition Before the United States Supreme Court, 1820–1860," *Journal of American History* 65 (1978).

The legal position of blacks in antebellum America has generated a rich literature. On the law of slavery, Kenneth M. Stampp's *The Peculiar Institution: Slavery in the Antebellum South* (1956) remains the starting point; however, it should be supplemented with Daniel J. Flanigan, "Criminal Procedure and Slave Trials in the Antebellum South," *Journal of Southern History* 40 (1974); Michael S. Hindus, *Prison and Plantation: Crime, Justice, and Authority in Massachusetts and South Carolina, 1767–1878* (1980); and Phillip J. Schwartz, *Twice Condemned: Slaves and the Criminal Laws of Virginia, 1705–1865* (1988). Ira Berlin, *Slaves Without Masters: The Free Negro in the Antebellum South* (1974); Theodore Brantner Wilson, *The Black Codes of the South* (1965); and Leon Litwack, *North of Slavery: The Negro in the Free States, 1790–1860* (1961) examine the anomalous position of free blacks in antebellum America. Litwack's classic study must be supplemented, however, with Paul Finkelman's important essay, "Prelude to the Fourteenth Amendment: Black Legal Rights in the Antebellum North," *Rutgers Law Journal* 17 (1986).

The best study of the development of antislavery constitutionalism is William M. Wiecek, *The Sources of Antislavery Constitutionalism in America, 1760–1848* (1977). Other important works on this topic include Jacobus ten Broek, *The Anti-Slavery Origins of the Fourteenth Amendment* (1951); Howard J. Graham, *Everyman's Constitution: Essays on the Fourteenth Amendment, the "Conspiracy Theory," and American Constitutionalism* (1968); William E. Nelson, "The Impact of the Antislavery Movement Upon Styles of Judicial Reasoning in Nineteenth

Century America,'' *Harvard Law Review* 87 (1974); and Aileen Kraditor, *Means and Ends in American Abolitionism* (1969). Earl M. Maltz, "Fourteenth Amendment Concepts in the Antebellum Era," *American Journal of Legal History* 32 (1988) examines the debate between antislavery and proslavery advocates over the meaning of due process, equal protection, and privileges and immunities.

Scholars have written little on antislavery constitutionalism among antebellum free blacks. Philip S. Foner and George E. Walker, eds., *Proceedings of the Black State Conventions, 1840–1865*, 2 vols. (1979) is an indispensible source, however. It can be supplemented with Benjamin Quarles, *The Black Abolitionists* (1969); R. J. M. Blackett, *Beating Against the Barriers: Biographical Essays in Nineteenth Century Afro-American History* (1986); Vincent Harding, *There is a River: The Black Freedom Struggle in America* (1981); and Jane H. Pease and William H. Pease, *They Who Would be Free: Blacks' Search for Freedom, 1830–1861* (1974).

There is a vast literature on the political and constitutional conflict over slavery during the late 1840s and the 1850s. Arthur Bestor, "State Sovereignty and Slavery: A Reinterpretation of Proslavery Constitutional Doctrine, 1848–1860," *Journal of the Illinois State Historical Society* 54 (1961) delineates proslavery constitutional ideas. Eric Foner, *Free Soil, Free Labor, Free Men: The Ideology of the Republican Party Before the Civil War* (1970) is a classic study of the growth of political antislavery in the North which pays careful attention to matters of constitutionalism and race. Also useful on the North are Richard Sewell, *Ballots for Freedom: Antislavery Politics in the United States, 1837–1860* (1976) and Hans Trefousse, *The Radical Republicans: Lincoln's Vanguard for Racial Justice* (1968). The definitive work on the pivotal *Dred Scott* case is Fehrenbacher's magisterial study, *The Dred Scott Case*.

The Civil War, Reconstruction, and Its Aftermath

The best treatments of the constitutional issues of the Civil War and Reconstruction are Harold M. Hyman, *A More Perfect Union: The Impact of the Civil War and Reconstruction on the Constitution* (1973); Harold M. Hyman and William M. Wiecek, *Equal Justice Under Law: Constitutional Development, 1835–1875* (1982); and Phillip S. Paludan, *A Covenant With Death: The Constitution, Law, and Equality in the Civil*

War Era (1975). Eric Foner's monumental *Reconstruction: America's Unfinished Revolution, 1863–1877* (1988) is the best treatment of the struggle for black freedom during the war and its aftermath.

LaWanda Cox, *Lincoln and Black Freedom: A Study in Presidential Leadership* (1981) offers a subtle analysis of the wartime president's approach to emancipation and the place of blacks in postwar America. For a different perspective, however, see Don E. Fehrenbacher, "Only His Stepchildren: Lincoln and the Negro," *Civil War History* 22 (1974) and George M. Fredrickson, "A Man and Not a Brother: Abraham Lincoln and Racial Equality," *Journal of Southern History* 41 (1975). Other important studies of the evolution of Republican policy with respect to slavery and race during the war years include Herman Belz, *Reconstructing the Union: Theory and Policy During the Civil War* (1969) and *A New Birth of Freedom: The Republican Party and Freedmen's Rights* (1976); Hans L. Trefousse, ed., *Lincoln's Decision for Emancipation* (1975); John Hope Franklin, *The Emancipation Proclamation* (1963); and Mary F. Berry, *Military Necessity and Civil Rights Policy: Black Citizenship and the Constitution* (1977). For the role of abolitionists and blacks in this process, see James M. McPherson, *The Struggle for Equality: Abolitionists and the Negro in the Civil War and Reconstruction* (1964); McPherson, ed., *The Negro's Civil War* (1965); and Ira Berlin, ed., *Freedom: A Documentary History of Emancipation, 1861–1867,* 2 vols. to date (1982, 1985).

Historians have devoted considerable attention to the evolution of Republican civil rights policy during Reconstruction. LaWanda Cox and John H. Cox, *Politics, Principle, and Prejudice: Dilemma of Reconstruction America, 1865–1866* (1963) first established civil rights as the pivotal issue of Reconstruction. Michael Les Benedict, *A Compromise of Principle: Congressional Republicans and Reconstruction, 1863–1869* (1974) and "Preserving the Constitution: The Conservative Basis of Radical Reconstruction," *Journal of American History* 61 (1974) show Republicans' reluctance to abandon a state-centered federal system. Robert J. Kaczorowski, "Revolutionary Constitutionalism in the Era of the Civil War and Reconstruction," *New York University Law Review* 61 (1986) offers a different perspective, arguing that Republican policy makers intended to nationalize protection of individual rights. William E. Nelson, *The Fourteenth Amendment: From Political Principle to Judicial Doctrine* (1988) is essential to understanding that crucial amendment. Other useful studies include Alfred H. Kelly, "The Fourteenth

Amendment Reconsidered: The Segregation Question,'' *Michigan Law Review* 54 (1956); Alexander M. Bickel, "The Original Understanding and the Segregation Decision,'' *Harvard Law Review* 69 (1955); Laurent B. Frantz, "Congressional Power to Enforce the Fourteenth Amendment Against Private Acts," *Yale Law Journal* 73 (1964); and Jonathan Lurie, "The Fourteenth Amendment: Uses and Applications in Selected State Court Civil Liberties Cases," *American Journal of Legal History* 28 (1984).

William Gillette, *The Right to Vote: Politics and the Passage of the Fifteenth Amendment* (1965) views the suffrage amendment as a product of Republican political opportunism, an interpretation challenged by LaWanda Cox and John H. Cox, "Negro Suffrage and Republican Politics: The Problem of Motivation in Reconstruction Historiography," *Journal of Southern History* 33 (1967). Republican civil rights policies during the 1870s have not received adequate attention, but William Gillette, *Retreat from Reconstruction* (1979) and William S. McFeely, *Grant* (1981) make an important beginning.

The effect of Republican civil rights policies at the grass-roots is the subject of a number of studies. Donald G. Nieman, *To Set the Law in Motion: The Freedmen's Bureau and the Legal Rights of Blacks, 1865–1868* (1979) examines the bureau's effort to afford former slaves personal security. Allen Trelease, *White Terror: The Ku Klux Klan Conspiracy and Southern Reconstruction* (1971); Everett Swinney, "Enforcing the Fifteenth Amendment, 1870–1877," *Journal of Southern History* 28 (1962); Robert J. Kaczorowski, *The Politics of Federal Judicial Interpretation: The Federal Courts, the Department of Justice, and Civil Rights, 1866–1876* (1985); and Kermit L. Hall, "Political Power and Constitutional Legitimacy: The South Carolina Ku Klux Klan Trials, 1871–1872," *Emory Law Journal* 33 (1984) explore the federal campaign against political terrorism in the South. For the effect of Reconstruction on southern constitutionalism and law, see Jack B. Scroggs, "Carpetbagger Constitutional Reform in the South Atlantic States, 1867–1868," *Journal of Southern History* 27 (1961); Eric Foner, *Nothing But Freedom* (1983); Thomas Holt, *Black Over White: Negro Political Leadership in South Carolina During Reconstruction* (1977); and Donald G. Nieman, "Black Political Power and Criminal Justice: Washington County, Texas, 1868–1884," *Journal of Southern History* 55 (1989). Michael Les Benedict, "The Problem of Constitutionalism and Constitutional Liberty in the Reconstruction South," ed. Kermit L.

Hall and James W. Ely, Jr., *An Uncertain Tradition: Constitutionalism and the History of the South* (1989) offers an incisive analysis of white southerners' reaction to these changes.

In recent years, historians have developed a more sophisticated understanding of law, politics, and race in the two decades after Reconstruction. Michael Les Benedict's revisionist essay, "Preserving Federalism: The Waite Court and Reconstruction," *Supreme Court Review 1978* (1979) offers an important reconsideration of the Supreme Court's role in the retreat from Reconstruction. See also Kaczorowski's *The Politics of Judicial Interpretation* and Charles Fairman, *Reconstruction and Reunion: 1864–1888,* 2 vols. (1971, 1987). John Hope Franklin, "Enforcement of the Civil Rights Act of 1875," *Prologue* 6 (1974) and Robert Goldman, "'A Free Ballot and Fair Count:' The Department of Justice and Enforcement of Voting Rights in the South, 1877–1893," Ph.D. dissertation, Michigan State University (1976) are important studies of federal civil rights enforcement. J. Morgan Kousser has produced a number of pioneering works demonstrating blacks' continuing effort to use political and legal means to protect their newly won rights: *The Shaping of Southern Politics: Suffrage Restriction and the Establishment of the One-Party South, 1880–1910* (1974); *Dead End: The Development of Nineteenth Century Litigation on Racial Discrimination in Schools* (1986); "Making Separate Equal: Integration of Black and White School Funds in Kentucky," *Journal of Interdisciplinary History* 10 (1980). For northern civil rights legislation, see Valeria W. Weaver, "The Failure of Civil Rights, 1875–1883 and Its Repercussions," *Journal of Negro History* 54 (1969).

The classic work on the development of segregation is C. Vann Woodward, *The Strange Career of Jim Crow,* 3rd ed. (1974). It must be supplemented with Howard N. Rabinowitz, *Race Relations in the Urban South, 1865–1890* (1978) and the sparkling exchange between Rabinowitz and Woodward in the *Journal of American History* 75 (1988). Kousser, *The Shaping of Southern Politics* is the best treatment of the disfranchisement movement. William Cohen, "Negro Involuntary Servitude in the South, 1865–1940: A Preliminary Inventory," *Journal of Southern History* 42 (1976) and Harold D. Woodman, "Post-War Southern Agriculture and the Law," *Agricultural History* 53 (1979) show the worsening legal position of black agricultural laborers. Edward L. Ayers, *Vengeance and Justice: Crime and Punishment in the 19th-Century American South* (1984) is a brilliant study of southern criminal justice and the convict-lease system. On the United States Supreme Court's capitulation to racism in the 1890s, see Charles Lofgren, *The Plessy Case* (1987); J. Morgan Kousser, "Separate but *not* Equal: The Supreme Court's First Decision on Racial Discrimination in Schools," *Journal of Southern History* 46 (1980); and Alexander M. Bickel and Benno C. Schmidt, Jr., *The Judiciary and Responsible Government, 1910–1921* (1984).

The Age of Segregation

The classic account of the impact of segregation and discrimination on blacks in the early decades of the twentieth century is Gunnar Myrdal, *An American Dilemma: The Negro Problem and Modern Democracy*, 2 vols. (1944). For the situation in the South, see Robert Haws, ed., *The Age of Segregation: Race Relations in the South, 1890–1945* (1978); John Dollard, *Caste and Class in a Southern Town* (1937); Pete Daniel, *The Shadow of Slavery: Peonage in the South, 1901–1969* (1972); Arthur Raper, *Preface to Peasantry* (1936) and *The Tragedy of Lynching* (1933). The nature of discrimination in the North is the subject of a large and growing literature. Especially important are Mary White Ovington, *Half a Man: The Status of the Negro in New York* (1911); David A. Gerber, *Black Ohio and the Color Line, 1860–1915* (1976); Kenneth Kusmer, *A Ghetto Takes Shape: Black Cleveland, 1870–1930* (1976); Michael W. Homel, *Down from Equality: Black Chicagoans and the Public Schools, 1920–1941* (1984); Judith Jolley Moharz, *The Separate Problem: Case Studies of Black Education in the North, 1900–1930* (1979); Vincent P. Franklin, *The Education of Black Philadelphia: The Social and Educational History of a Minority Community, 1900–1950* (1979); August Meier and Elliott Rudwick, *Black Detroit and the Rise of the UAW* (1979); and Stephan Thernstrom, *The Other Bostonians: Poverty and Progress in the American Metropolis, 1880–1970* (1973).

There is a large literature on the growth of blacks' challenge to discrimination. August Meier, *Negro Thought in America, 1880–1915* (1963) is a pioneering study that examines the emergence of black protest thought in the early twentieth century. August Meier, Elliott Rudwick, and Francis Broderick, eds., *Black Protest Thought in the Twentieth Century*, 2nd ed. (1971) is a useful documentary collection. On the origins of the National Association for the Advancement of Colored

People (NAACP), see James M. McPherson, *The Abolitionist Legacy: From Reconstruction to the NAACP* (1975); Charles Flint Kellogg, *NAACP: A History of the National Association for the Advancement of Colored People, 1890–1920* (1967); and Mary White Ovington, *The Walls Came Tumbling Down* (1947). Robert L. Zangrando, *The NAACP Crusade Against Lynching, 1909–1950* (1980) is an illuminating analysis of the organization's changing leadership and tactics, as well as its antilynching campaign. Jacqueline D. Hall, *Revolt Against Chivalry: Jessie Daniel Ames and the Women's Campaign Against Lynching* (1979) is a fascinating study of southern whites' opposition to lynching.

For the NAACP's early efforts to use litigation as a tool of social change, see William B. Hixson, Jr., "Moorfield Storey and the Struggle for Equality," *Journal of American History* 55 (1968) and *Moorfield Storey and the Abolitionist Tradition* (1972). Bickel and Schmidt's *The Supreme Court and Responsible Government* offers a brilliant analysis of the Supreme Court's response to Storey and his colleagues. Richard C. Cortner, *A Mob Intent on Death* (1988) is a gripping account of *Moore* v. *Dempsey,* one of the NAACP's most important early courtroom victories.

The 1930s was a pivotal decade in the struggle for equality. Harvard Sitkoff, *A New Deal for Blacks. The Emergence of Civil Rights as a National Issue: The Depression Decade* (1978) is an incisive and highly readable analysis of black protest and federal policy during these years. Dan T. Carter, *Scottsboro: A Tragedy of the American South* (1966) is a brilliant and compelling account of the decade's *cause celebre.* Charles H. Martin, *The Angelo Herndon Case and Southern Justice* (1976) and Richard C. Cortner, *A "Scottsboro" Case in Mississippi: The Supreme Court and Brown v. Mississippi* (1986) are able studies that highlight the Supreme Court's growing responsiveness to blacks. For the origins of the NAACP's campaign against school segregation, see Richard Kluger, *Simple Justice* (1975); Mark Tushnet, *The NAACP's Campaign Against Segregated Education, 1925–1950* (1987); Genna Rae McNeil, "Justiciable Cause: Howard University Law School and the Struggle for Civil Rights," *Howard Law Journal* 22 (1979); McNeil, *Groundwork: Charles Hamilton Houston and the Struggle for Civil Rights* (1983); Randall W. Bland, *Private Pressure on Public Law: The Legal Career of Justice Thurgood Marshall* (1973); and Daniel T. Kelleher, "The Case of Lloyd Lionel Gaines: The Demise of the 'Separate-but-Equal' Doctrine," *Journal of Negro History* 56 (1971).

Richard Dalfiume, "The Forgotten years of the Negro Revolution," *Journal of American History* 55 (1968) and Peter J. Kellogg, "Civil Rights Consciousness in the 1940s," *The Historian* 42 (1979) offer useful analysis of the growing velocity of the campaign for equality during World War II and its aftermath. Donald R. McCoy and Richard T. Ruetten, *Quest and Response: Minority Rights in the Truman Administration* (1973) examines Truman's bold but unsuccessful civil rights initiatives, while Mary L. Dudziak, "Desegregation as a Cold War Imperative," *Stanford Law Review* 41 (1988) explores the relationship between Cold War rhetoric and civil rights. Will Maslow and Joseph B. Robinson, "Civil Rights Legislation and the Fight for Equality, 1862–1952," *University of Chicago Law Review* 20 (1953); Duane Lockard, *Toward Equal Opportunity: A Study of State and Local Anti-Discrimination Laws* (1968); and Milton R. Konvitz, *A Century of Civil Rights* (1961) trace the growth of state civil rights legislation. On the Supreme Court's increasingly bold stand on civil rights, see Tushnet, *The NAACP's Campaign Against Segregated Education;* Darlene Clark Hine, *Black Victory: The Rise and Fall of the White Primary in Texas* (1979); Clement E. Vose, *Caucasians Only: The Supreme Court, the NAACP, and the Restrictive Covenant Cases* (1959); and Catherine A. Barnes, *Journey From Jim Crow: The Desegregation of Southern Transit* (1983).

The Civil Rights Movement and After

There is a large and rapidly growing literature on the civil rights movement of the 1950s and 1960s. Harvard Sitkoff, *The Struggle for Black Equality, 1954–1980* (1981) and Robert Weisbrot, *Freedom Bound: A History of America's Civil Rights Movement* (1989) offer good brief overviews. Charles Eagles, ed., *The Civil Rights Movement in America* (1986) is a valuable collection of perceptive essays. David L. Lewis, *King: A Biography of Martin Luther King, Jr.*, 2nd ed. (1978); David J. Garrow, *Bearing the Cross: Martin Luther King, Jr. and the Southern Christian Leadership Conference* (1986); and Taylor Branch, *Parting the Waters: America in the King Years, 1954–1963* (1988) are superb studies of the great civil rights leader. August Meier and Elliott Rudwick, *C.O.R.E.: A Study in the Civil Rights Movement (1973);* Clayborne Carson, *In Struggle: SNCC and the Black Awakening of the*

1960s (1981); and Adam Fairclough, *To Win the Soul of America: The Southern Christian Leadership Conference and Martin Luther King, Jr.* (1987) examine three of the major civil rights organizations. William H. Chafe, *Civilities and Civil Rights: Greensboro, North Carolina and the Black Struggle for Freedom* (1980); Robert J. Norrell, *Reaping the Whirlwind: The Civil Rights Movement in Tuskegee* (1985); and David Colburn, *Racial Change and Community Crisis in St. Augustine, Florida, 1877–1980* (1985) are important local studies. Allen J. Matusow, *The Unraveling of America: A History of Liberalism in the 1960s* (1984) places the civil rights struggle in the context of national politics.

On the *Brown* case, see Kluger, *Simple Justice;* G. Edward White, *Earl Warren: A Biography* (1984); Dennis Hutchinson, "Unanimity and Desegregation: Decision-Making in the Supreme Court, 1948–1958," *Georgetown Law Journal* 68 (1979); Alfred H. Kelly, "The School Desegregation Case," ed. John Garraty, *Quarrels That Have Shaped the Constitution* (1964); and Morton J. Horowitz, "The Jurisprudence of *Brown* and the Dilemmas of Liberalism," *Harvard Civil Rights–Civil Liberties Review* 14 (1979). Reaction to the decision is ably treated in Numan V. Bartley, *The Rise of Massive Resistance: Race and Politics in the South during the 1950s* (1969); Neil McMillen, *The Citizens Council: Organized Resistance to the Second Reconstruction, 1954–1964* (1971); and David R. Colburn, "Florida's Governors Confront the *Brown* Decision: A Case Study of the Constitutional Politics of School Desegregation, 1954–1970," ed. Kermit L. Hall and James W. Ely, Jr., *An Uncertain Tradition: Constitutionalism and the History of the South* (1989). On the federal courts and the problems of implementation, see J. Harvie Wilkinson, III, *From Brown to Bakke: The Supreme Court and School Integration, 1954–1978* (1979); Jack W. Peltason, *Fifty-eight Lonely Men: Southern Federal Judges and School Desegregation* (1961); Jack Bass, *Unlikely Heroes* (1981); Frank T. Read, *Let Them Be Judged: The Judicial Desegregation of the Deep South* (1978); Tony Freyer, *The Little Rock Crisis: A Constitutional Interpretation* (1984); Tinsley Yarbrough, *Judge Frank Johnson and Human Rights in Alabama* (1981); Mary L. Dudziak, "The Limits of Good Faith: Desegregation in Topeka, Kansas, 1950–1956," *Law and History Review* 5 (1987); Note, "The Federal Courts and the Integration of Southern Schools: Troubled Status of Pupil Placement Acts," *Columbia Law Review* 62 (1962); and Alexander M. Bickel, "The Decade of School Desegregation: Progress and Prospects," *Columbia Law Review* 64 (1964). On early school desegregation litigation in the North, see Paul R. Diamond, "School Desegregation in the North: There is But One Constitution," *Harvard Civil Rights–Civil Liberties Review* 7 (1972). Benjamin Muse, *Ten Years of Prelude: The Story of Integration Since the Supreme Court's 1954 Decision* (1964) and Donald B. King and Charles W. Quick, eds., *Legal Aspects of the Civil Rights Movement* (1965) detail the slow progress of desegregation.

Robert Frederick Burk, *The Eisenhower Administration and Black Civil Rights* (1984) and Carl M. Brauer, *John F. Kennedy and the Second Reconstruction* (1977) offer judicious treatments of presidential policy. Steven F. Lawson, *Black Ballots: Voting Rights in the South, 1944–1969* (1976) is the definitive treatment of the long campaign to end disfranchisement, while Charles V. Hamilton, *The Bench and the Ballot* (1973) provides an incisive analysis of the federal courts and voting rights. Michal R. Belknap, *Federal Law and Southern Order: Racial Violence and Constitutional Conflict in the Post-Brown South* (1987) is a superb study that examines anti-civil rights violence and illuminates the political and legal barriers to effective federal protection of civil rights activists. Gary Orfield, *The Reconstruction of Southern Education* (1969) is a careful study of the Johnson administration, the Civil Rights Act of 1964, and the desegregation of southern education. Herbert Hill, *Black Labor and the Legal System*, 2 vols. (1977) and Robert Belton, "A Comparative Review of Public and Private Enforcement of Title VII of the Civil Rights Act of 1964," *Vanderbilt Law Review* 31 (1978) are indispensible on employment discrimination. G. Sidney Buchanan, "The Quest for Freedom: A Legal History of the Thirteenth Amendment," *Houston Law Review* 12 (1976) examines the Supreme Court's revival of the abolition amendment as an effective civil rights weapon.

The busing controversy, which generated such passionate debate during the 1970s, is the subject of a large literature. For balanced treatments of the problem, see Wilkinson, *From Brown to Bakke* and Gary Orfield, *Must We Bus? Segregated Schools and National Policy* (1978). Useful case studies of urban school desegregation include Bernard Schwartz, *Swann's Way: The School Busing Case and the Supreme Court* (1986); Eleanor P. Wolf, *Trial and Error: The Detroit School Desegregation Case* (1981); Daniel J. Monti, *A Semblance of Justice: St. Louis School Desegregation and Order in Urban America* (1985); George R. Metcalf, *From Little Rock to Boston* (1983); and Paul R. Diamond, *Beyond Busing: Inside the Challenge of Urban Segregation*

(1985). Raymond Wolters, *The Burden of Brown: Thirty Years of School Desegregation* (1984) and Lino Graglia, *Disaster By Decree: The Supreme Court Decisions on Race and the Schools* (1976) are sharply critical of the federal courts' desegregation effort. For school desegregation in the aftermath of *Milliken* v. *Bradley,* see Robert A. Sedler, "The Profound Impact of *Milliken* v. *Bradley,*" *Wayne Law Review* 33 (1987); Nathaniel R. Jones, "The Desegregation of Urban Schools Thirty Years After *Brown,*" *University of Colorado Law Review* 55 (1984); Joseph A. Sullivan, "Equal Protection in the Post-*Milliken* Era: The Future of Interdistrict Remedies in Desegregating Public Schools," *Columbia Human Rights Review* 18 (1986); Michael W. Combs, "The Federal Judiciary and Northern School Desegregation: Judicial Management in Perspective," *Journal of Law and Education* 13 (1984); and William M. Gordon, "School Desegregation: A Look at the 70s and 80s," *Journal of Law and Education* 18 (1989).

On the evolution of remedies for employment discrimination and the emergence of affirmative action, see Paul Burstein, *Discrimination, Jobs, and Politics: The Struggle for Equal Employment Opportunity in the United States Since the New Deal* (1985); George Rutherglen, "Disparate Impact Under Title VII: An Objective Theory of Discrimination," *Virginia Law Review* 73 (1987); Finis Welch, "Affirmative Action and Its Enforcement," *American Economic Review* 71 (1981); James P. Smith and Finis Welch, "Affirmative Action and Labor Markets," *Journal of Labor Economics* 2 (1984); Ray Marshall, Charles B. Knapp, Malcolm H. Liggett, Robert W. Glover, *Employment Discrimination: The Impact of Legal and Administrative Remedies* (1976); Leonard J. Hausman, Orley Ashenfelter, Bayard Rustin, Richard F. Schubert, Donald Slaiman, eds., *Equal Rights and Industrial Relations* (1977). Timothy J. O'Neill, *Bakke and the Politics of Equality* (1985) is an important assessment of that pivotal case. For positive appraisals of affirmative action, see Joe R. Feagin and Nijole V. Benokraitis, *Affirmative Action and Equal Opportunity: Action, Inaction, Reaction* (1978); J. Skelly Wright, "Color-Blind Theories and Color-Conscious Remedies," *University of Chicago Law Review* 47 (1980); Ronald Dworkin, *Taking Rights Seriously* (1977); Timothy J. O'Neill, "The Language of Equality in a Constitutional Order," *American Political Science Review* 75 (1981); and Boris I. Bitker, *The Case for Black Reparations* (1973). William Van Alstyne, "Rites of Passage: Race, the Supreme Court, and the Constitution," *University of Chicago Law Review* 46 (1979); Terry

Eastland and William J. Bennet, *Counting By Race: Equality From the Founding Fathers to Bakke and Weber* (1979); and Nathan Glazer, *Affirmative Discrimination* (1975) are sharply critical of affirmative action.

Steven F. Lawson, *In Pursuit of Power: Southern Blacks and Electoral Politics, 1965–1982* (1985) is an exhaustively researched, well-balanced account of recent battles over voting rights. Chandler Davidson, ed., *Minority Vote Dilution* (1984) is an important collection of essays. For a sharply critical view of federal voting rights law, see Abigail Thernstrom, *Whose Vote Counts? Affirmative Action and Minority Voting Rights* (1987).

The Reagan administration's civil rights policies generated considerable controversy. For critical appraisals of administration policy, see James Nathan Miller, "Ronald Reagan and the Techniques of Deception," *The Atlantic Monthly* 253 (1984); Lani Guinier, "Keeping the Faith: Black Voters in the Post-Reagan Era," *Harvard Civil Rights–Civil Liberties Review* 24 (1989); and Joel L. Selig, "The Reagan Administration and Civil Rights: What Went Wrong?," *University of Illinois Law Review* (1985). For a defense of Reagan policies, see William Bradford Reynolds, "Individualism vs. Group Rights: The Legacy of *Brown*," *Yale Law Journal* 93 (1984) and "The Reagan Administration and Civil Rights: Winning the War Against Discrimination," *University of Illinois Law Review* (1986). On the Bork nomination and Reagan's effort to remake the Supreme Court, see Robert Bork, *The Tempting of America: The Political Seduction of the Law* (1989) and Michael Pertschuk and Wendy Schaetzel, *The People Rising: The Campaign Against the Bork Nomination* (1989).

For assessments of the changes wrought by the civil rights revolution, see Michael Namorato, ed., *Have We Overcome? Race Relations Since Brown* (1979); Sar A. Levitan, William B. Johnston, and Robert Taggart, *Still A Dream: The Changing Status of Blacks Since 1960* (1975); William Julius Wilson, *The Declining Significance of Race* (1978); Elliot Zashin, "The Progress of Black Americans in Civil Rights: The Past Two Decades Assessed," *Daedalus* (1978); and Reynolds Farley, "Trends in Racial Inequalities: Have the Gains of the 1960s Disappeared in the 1970s?," *American Sociological Review* 42 (1977). For disturbing assessments of how far we have to go to achieve equality, see William Julius Wilson, *The Truly Disadvantaged: The Inner City, the Under-*

class, and Public Policy (1987); Alphonso Pinkney, *The Myth of Black Progress* (1984); Fred R. Harris and Roger W. Wilkins, eds., *Quiet Riots: Race and Poverty in the United States* (1988); and Derrick Bell, *And We Are Not Saved: The Elusive Quest for Racial Justice* (1987).

Table of Cases

257

Index